Providing Quality in the
Public Sector

Public Policy and Management

Series Editor: Professor R.A.W. Rhodes, Department of Politics, University of Newcastle.

The effectiveness of public policies is a matter of public concern and the efficiency with which policies are put into practice is a continuing problem for governments of all political persuasions. This series contributes to these debates by publishing informed, in-depth and contemporary analyses of public administration, public policy and public management.

The intention is to go beyond the usual textbook approach to the analysis of public policy and management and to encourage authors to move debate about their issue forward. In this sense, each book describes current thinking and research and explores future policy directions. Accessibility is a key feature and, as a result, the series will appeal to academics and their students as well as to the informed practitioner.

Current titles:

Providing Quality in the Public Sector

A Practical Approach to Improving Public Services

Lucy Gaster and Amanda Squires
with John Crawley, Michael Greenwood,
Tessa Harding, Carol Hayden and Pat Scrutton

Open University Press
Maidenhead · Philadelphia

Open University Press
McGraw-Hill Education
McGraw-Hill House
Shoppenhangers Road
Maidenhead
Berkshire
England
SL6 2QL

email: enquiries@openup.co.uk
world wide web: www.openup.co.uk

and
325 Chestnut Street
Philadelphia, PA 19106, USA

First Published 2003

A catalogue record of this book is available from the British Library

ISBN   0 335 20955 6 (pb)   0 335 20956 4 (hb)

Library of Congress Cataloging-in-Publication Data
Providing quality in the public sector : a practical approach to improving public services / Lucy Gaster and Amanda Squires ; with John Crawley . . . [*et al.*].
    p.   cm. – (Public policy and management)
    Includes bibliographical references and index.
    ISBN 0-335-20956-4 – ISBN 0-335-20955-6 (pbk.)
    1. Public administration–Great Britain.   2. Municipal services–Great Britain–Management.   I. Gaster, Lucy, 1940–   II. Series.

JN425 .P75 2003
352.3′57′0941–dc21   2002074962

Typeset by Graphicraft Limited, Hong Kong
Printed in Great Britain by Biddles Limited, www.biddles.co.uk

To our dear families, old and young, who have seen us through in one way or another.

Contents

Figures, tables and annexes

x Figures, tables and annexes

About the authors

John Crawley has been Chief Executive, fch Housing and Care (formerly Friendship Housing and Care) since 1984. John has worked in the voluntary housing movement for over 25 years, in England and Scotland. Long-serving member of national housing bodies, including the National Housing Federation, Board member of several Midlands housing and regeneration forums and, since 2000, a non-executive director of Birmingham Health Authority. Chairman of a new primary care trust in Sandwell, West Midlands since April 2002. He has wide experience across the housing, social care and health sectors and this cross-sector interest informs his approach to the debate about quality in public services.

Dr Lucy Gaster retired in autumn 2000 from the Institute of Local Government Studies, University of Birmingham (now Honorary Senior Research Fellow). She joined the School for Advanced Urban Studies, University of Bristol in 1990 after several years as a local government officer and (before that) as a 'community activist' in London. She specialized in all aspects of the relationship between local government (especially the 'front line') and the public, researching, teaching, speaking and publishing on public service quality, decentralization and local working, public participation and the role of councillors.

Michael Greenwood has been Chief Executive of Tameside Council since 1990. Before that he was Chief Executive and County Treasurer of Powys County Council. Since the early 1990s, he has become very interested in the means of delivering improvement by local authorities. In this regard, he has found the management philosophy of Dr Edwards Deming very useful as a framework to help the improvement and transformation of public services and as an antidote to arbitrary change.

Tessa Harding is Head of Policy at Help the Aged, member of the Better Government for Older People steering group and adviser to the Joseph Rowntree Foundation's Older People's programme. She convened the Older People's Reference Group, which advised on the development of the Department of Health's National Service Framework for Older People. She previously worked at the National Institute for Social Work, the National Council for Voluntary Organizations and for three local authorities. Recent publications include *Our Future Health – Older People's Priorities for Health and Care* (HOPe/Help the Aged 2000); and the concluding chapter in *Age Discrimination in Public Policy* (Help the Aged 2002).

Carol Hayden currently works as a Policy Advisor at the Audit Commission. She previously held posts in local authority management and public sector research. Her experience includes establishing 'area coordination' in Coventry to tackle social exclusion through a partnership approach, and leading the Better Government for Older People evaluation while employed at Warwick University.

Pat Scrutton has been Project Manager of Better Government for Older People in South Lanarkshire since 1998. While raising a family she was active in the voluntary sector. Since returning to paid employment in 1989, her posts as Divisional Coordinator, Consumer Involvement Officer and Planning Officer, as well as her current post, have all involved both community development and partnership working.

Dr Amanda Squires is a Clinical Governance Review Manager at the Commission for Health Improvement. She is a Fellow in the Department of Health and Human Sciences, University of Essex. She trained as a Chartered Physiotherapist working in south London in the highly interdisciplinary/multi-agency area of rehabilitation of older people. Her clinical and academic work has focused on satisfying the needs of all stakeholders and particularly facilitating those of older service users. Her PhD was entitled *Stakeholder Quality in Healthcare: Synthesising Expectations for Mutual Satisfaction* (City University, London 2002) and recent publications include the third edition of *Rehabilitation of the Older Person: A Handbook for the Interdisciplinary Team* (Nelson Thornes 2002).

Preface and acknowledgements

Although we would reject any claim that – unlike many books written about 'quality' – this is a 'missionary' book, we do unashamedly declare that we – and all our contributors – have a missionary zeal to make public services better. We have been infected with this for many years, as service users, practitioners and academics, and both of us have written about it in the past.

Now we have come together to try to present a rounded and comprehensive picture of what 'quality' could be like and, in our practical examples, what it *is* like. From our own experience of teaching and working with students and practitioners, we think that this mixture of theory and practice could help to disentangle the threads and make the idea *and* the practice of 'quality' less daunting and more mainstream. However, we certainly do not claim to have the 'answers' and this is no handbook or 'how to do it' manual.

We are extremely anxious that ideas about quality are not subsumed within vague talk of 'modernization'. Of course it is helpful to have a government that says it is committed to the public services, but it does not say what it means by 'quality'. We see our book as quite separate from, and independent of, discussion about who should be delivering public services and how many resources should be devoted to them. For us, like everyone connected with public services, these issues are of course important. But it is only if real efforts are made from within, to improve the overall quality of services in the long term, that we think any real differences for the public will become visible and tangible. There – we *are* missionaries!

For us, the crucial actors are front-line staff and the users and citizens who, if the climate is right, can and must be actively involved. And leadership, as every quality manual stresses, is vital, while the political direction and context set the scene for what kind of 'quality' we should be aiming for. This stakeholder approach underpins the book, making quality not an absolute, but a negotiated concept, where different groups express their needs, and contribute their ideas and their expertise. Above all, in the widest sense of the term, quality must be 'citizen-centred'.

Perhaps it is because we are all climbing up the chronological ladder that we are particularly concerned about how public services are designed and delivered for older people, and what input older people can have into this. This has provided a linking theme for the book, although not all the chapters explicitly address it. Evidence of ageism and age discrimination against older people lends force to the idea that this group of citizens needs urgent attention.

We should like to thank all the contributors to this book – John Crawley, Michael Greenwood, Tessa Harding, Carol Hayden and Pat Scrutton – who all lead incredibly busy lives but gave up time and used their expertise to write five of the chapters. This makes the book 'grounded' in a way that we hope will appeal to our readers.

We should also like to acknowledge the following people and organizations:

- Chapters 6 and 7: Staff at the Cabinet Office and Audit Commission who gave interviews and read through and commented on the draft chapters.
- Chapter 7: The journal *Public Policy and Administration*, for permission to use an article by Lucy Gaster published in autumn 1999.
- Chapter 8: Richard Diment, Chief Executive of the Ambulance Service Association, for information about ambulance services.
- Chapter 12: Barking and Havering Health Authority, for the support provided for the pilot reported in this chapter.

Lucy Gaster and Amanda Squires

Part I

Setting the scene

1

Introduction

Lucy Gaster and Amanda Squires

Exhortation and confusion

It is now rare for a government statement about public services not to mention the idea of 'improvement' and, often in the same breath, of 'quality'. This is helpful in underlining the importance of making public services better, but leaves great gaps as to what is meant, expected or possible.

Public services, in the UK as everywhere else, cannot simply be supplied on demand to whoever asks for them. Differences of definition and identification of need, conflicts of interest, constraints of finance, arguments about policy, and legal requirements must necessarily be taken into account in decisions about the extent, nature and focus of services to and for the public. Any discussion of quality and its improvement must be set within this context. The ever-changing policy environment in which service providers find themselves inevitably affects what they can do, what they think they can do and what the public and politicians *expect* they can do to improve their services.

From time to time since the early 1990s, exhortations to adopt particular quality systems have been heard, mainly from central government and to some extent in individual public services. More recently, under ever tighter inspection regimes, many services, especially those operating at the local level, have had their quality and organization reported on and in some cases labelled a 'success' or a 'failure'. The use of national league tables has meant that lists appear, which are eagerly scanned by journalists and the public, but where little information has been available about why an authority, hospital or school appears where it does, what the practical implications are for users, and what can be done to help. Even the criteria for such ratings are often obscure, relatively unquestioned and unrelated to the local context.

The net result is that while 'quality' is discussed at a very general level, no easily accessible overview exists as to what it might mean either in theory or in practice. This is not surprising, since it is in fact a very complex issue. However, it leaves politicians and managers in the public sector with few tools to know how to define quality, how to put it into practice and to measure it and above all, how to improve it.

Most public service organizations are large, complex and provide a wide range of different services. They increasingly need to be able to work with other organizations with different constraints, cultures and values to solve shared local problems. This makes it even more difficult to know where to start.

The aim of this book

This book looks at the theory and practice of 'quality' in public services. It is not a handbook, and does not pretend to know the answers. However, it brings together thinking and experience from many different sources, in the hope that the frameworks and models presented here, together with accounts of what has happened in practice, may provide ideas and handholds for those who are truly interested in understanding and improving the quality of public services.

The early part of the book is based on a previous publication (Gaster 1995a) where a comprehensive model for understanding 'quality' was developed. Subsequent experience has shown that this model (presented in Chapter 3 below) is reasonably robust, making sense to practitioners from a wide range of services, and provides a diagnostic tool for assessing what has been done and what needs to be done to improve quality.

As discussed below, public services are different from private services – even when they are delivered by private sector organizations – and therefore *quality* in public services also needs to be different. The idea of democracy is central to the discussion of quality. This helps to define who should be involved in debating and developing quality improvements, and it helps to define the process which itself needs to be 'democratic'. This means starting with the 'citizen' and not with the service provider.

This is very different from the 'managerial' view propounded by most of the quality gurus who, basing their assumptions about quality on experience in manufacturing industry, have generally seen 'quality' as a technical issue. For them, it is not the concern of politicians or, except in terms of 'satisfaction', of the public. It is also very different from the philosophy underlying the systems proposed and developed by those same gurus, whose view of 'customers' has in general been as relatively passive recipients, actual purchasers or occasional complainants. In that model, the only perceived power of the 'customer' is to take business to other providers – to 'exit' – and the aim of the quality manager is to prevent that exit if possible. Public service 'customers', on the other hand, cannot easily exit, having nowhere else to go, and their only alternative is to 'voice' their dissatisfaction (Hirschman 1970). A different relationship is therefore needed, which depends on the constructive use of such 'voice' and implies active participation. This is the *democratic* model.

This means that stakeholders' perceptions, experiences and relationships in different service situations must be understood and measured by providers, so as to be able to find out and then improve consumer and customer satisfaction (Price and Gaskill 1990). All forms of consultation and participation, including continuous consumer feedback through discussion, surveys, comments, compliments and complaints, and other routine intelligence can then be used to 'listen to the voices' and focus service responsiveness (Walsh 1991a; National Consumer Council and Consumer Congress 1995).

As well as seeing 'quality' as part of the democratic process, it should be seen as a whole system, that is *'holistically'*. This is very important to our thinking, and explains the emphasis on the need to make connections between the different aspects of quality – values and aims, standards, definitions, processes, monitoring, results and review – all leading to 'improvement'. Therefore the need to communicate and to develop a culture where these connections can be made is emphasized.

Finally, improving quality is a *long-term* process, requiring understanding and commitment, innovation and, possibly most important of all, attention to detail. One weak link can bring down a whole service. So ensuring that the links are strong, and that all 'stakeholders' have a clear idea of their role and responsibilities and can effectively contribute, is essential for success.

What is quality?

A major problem with the concept of quality is that the term has informal and widespread use, is dynamic and contextual and, like health, 'is difficult to define but easy to recognise' (Bird 1985). But without such definition it cannot be improved or measured. As a first step, we take a common-sense look at the interchangeable terms of 'qualities', 'of quality' and 'quality' (this issue is explored in detail in Chapter 3).

The *qualities* of a product or service are its attributes or characteristics, which may or may not satisfy the needs of an individual (Seedhouse 1994). These attributes may be *'of quality'*, commonly taken to mean that they are 'good', or even 'exceptional'. However, criteria to support such a definition may be obscure and will almost certainly be different for different people. Thus, if an individual need is not satisfied, the 'quality' feature – 'responsiveness', for example – may not be perceived as a (high) *quality* attribute by that individual. Conversely, the specified attribute may be commonly considered to be of poor quality, but if it meets the individual need or exceeds original expectations – speed of response, for example – it may be experienced as a (high) quality attribute by that individual.

The nature of products, services and public services

Products

Products, or goods, are tangible, movable and not usually consumed at the same time as they are produced (Walsh 1991a). Although they may also include a service component in the form of sale and after sales support, a product is likely to be obtained by the purchaser through a single, complete contact with the chosen *end supplier*. Quality characteristics are likely to include convenience, control, choice and effectiveness ('fitness for purpose'). For these tangible goods, the desired characteristics can be sought in advance of the experience, for example, test driving a car before decision to purchase (Walsh 1991a). They are consequently known as 'search' goods.

Many ideas about quality were originally developed in the private sector, initially in manufacturing industries in relation to the need to improve 'products'. An early aim was to reduce or eliminate wastage by ensuring that all the items manufactured actually conformed to their specification, which would have been developed from the expressed needs of customers (for example, assembly plants) and technically defined in relation to the purpose for which the item was being made (for example, engineering parts). The elimination of 'variance' was therefore crucial. This improved profit margins and reliability, enhancing the capacity of each firm in the production chain to survive, both financially and in terms of reputation inside the industry and in the eyes of the public.

Thinking about this gave rise to quality systems such as 'quality control' whereby all specifications were checked at the *end* of the production process to see whether they had been met.

The introduction of 'quality assurance' enabled component providers to reassure the customer that processes were in place to ensure that specifications *would be met*. 'Total quality management', whereby the whole organization focused on continuously improving the product to meet customers' changing needs and to retain market position, and 'business process engineering' (re-organizing internal processes to support production of the product/service), were also developed, thus moving from a focus on *process* towards a focus on *organization* (see also Chapter 4).

Services

Services differ from goods in the purpose for which they are produced, and how they are produced, consumed and evaluated. Services are intangible, heterogeneous (due to changes in provider and user expectations over time), inseparable (requiring both a customer and a provider), invisible, fluctuating (in response to demand and supply), latent (sold before produced-consumed) and labour intensive (by user and provider) (Squires 2002).

When a service is sought, it should meet a need, just like tangible products. However, its intangibility produces different criteria for acceptable 'quality'. In addition to the criteria for tangible products (convenience, control, choice and effectiveness), reliability, responsiveness, assurance, empathy and surroundings are important for the customer (Parasuraman *et al.* 1988). However, the effectiveness of the service cannot be guaranteed in advance – merely 'assured' on the basis of proven expertise of the supplier at a previous 'service encounter'.

The service may be one in a series from the supplier, with choice or expectation strongly based on the *initial* contact. The need for investment in 'customer care' training, which aims to improve this interaction (and all subsequent ones), is almost infinite (but see Chapter 4 for the limitations of customer care).

For services, experience cannot be separated from the actual process of service delivery. Choice about whether to purchase therefore has to be based on information, not all of which is available in advance. For example, when planning to change banks, the potential customer may use counter services in a number of potential banks to compare the experience of front line service, if that is what is important to them. Services are consequently known as 'experience' goods. Qualitative information, especially from past experience (one's own or that of others) and from trial use are particularly influential in influencing these decisions (Zeithaml *et al.* 1990; Walsh 1991a; Reynolds 1994).

Public services

All societies have some form of public service provision for reasons of economics, risk and moral responsibility. In democratic societies, political parties will convert public opinion and political vision into a prospectus (manifesto) for voter support. Once elected, these statements may be adapted to become national policy, subsequently requiring further adaptation for national and local implementation. The voter (service provider, manager or service user) may or may not recognize or support the final policy as it affects them. They may not have read the manifesto or voted for the party subsequently elected to power, or voted at all. Nevertheless, all these decisions, however unrecognizable, can be justified by government as having been legitimated through the election process. Equally, those making decisions about policy and implementation are in theory accountable to the public through the structures and mechanisms of democracy (Parliament and so on). This is completely different from the private sector and indeed the voluntary sector, neither of which has such a route for public legitimation or obligation to account publicly for their actions.

Public services are paid for through general taxation and/or by means-tested payments, and not through individual payments made by choice. Profit motives that stimulate private sector performance are therefore absent in pure welfare systems. This generates a completely different relationship between service producer and service consumer. As is argued throughout this book, this gives rise to the need for continuous and active involvement by the public, difficult though that might be.

In addition, public services operate within a legal and financial framework that is very different from the profits-driven private sector. This means that services cannot be produced 'on demand', but need to be placed within a wider context of societal demand and supply, which must be decided politically. Movement towards 'means-tested payment' (some prescription, optical and dental charges, for example) have raised the expectations of those who now pay a contribution, even though the service provided remains 'non-profit' and is publicly subsidized.

Finally, a major difference between private and public sector services (with voluntary sector services coming somewhere in between) is the question of motivation and underlying values. Workers at all levels in public sector organizations such as local government and health still generally enter the service with a genuine intention to *serve* the public (Pratchett and Wingfield 1994). They are not doing it for their own advantage or profit. This is the 'public service ethos'.

However, public sector workers can be sucked into a more selfish and self-protective ethos, partly for self-preservation (Lipsky 1980), partly because of the tensions arising from the structural shift towards public commissioning and private delivery. At the same time, they have increasingly been expected to work jointly *with* the public to provide a 'seamless' service, rather than providing services *to* or *for* them (the paternalistic stance). This too creates a new set of expectations and pressures on 'custom and practice'.

A key element in the current quality debate is therefore how to preserve the positive aspects of the 'public service ethos' in a way that is sustainable in the changing political, policy and developmental environment in which public servants now have to work.

Within public services, general interest had been raised in the concept of quality by a combination of factors including economic competition, rising expectations, environmental concerns and the activity of quality gurus. The public service user also buys private sector products and other services. With the mixed provision of publicly funded services, this will be an increasing experience within the public sector. The past grateful acceptance of poorer provision in free welfare services has been overtaken by the ability to make direct comparisons between the sectors, despite their fundamental differences.

The basic challenge for providers of public services, working directly or through contracts, is to provide responsive services within the legal, financial and policy framework in which they are required to operate. But in the public sector, increased consumer satisfaction does not necessarily lead to increased efficiency, through economies of scale arising from higher demand, nor does it generate higher profits (income) as it does in the private sector (Pfeffer and Coote 1991). On the contrary, higher levels of satisfaction may increase demand but result in *reduced* quality because existing resources are stretched more thinly. Fear of 'extra' demand on resources can perversely act as a disincentive to finding out consumers' views or improving quality, leading to the common situation where many people who need and are eligible for a service are in practice excluded, consciously or inadvertently.

Why public services need to improve quality

'Quality' is important to public services for several reasons that build on each other:

- It is a way of ensuring that services are 'fit for purpose' and meet the needs, consistently and sensitively, of the immediate consumer and of society as a whole.
- Services perceived as good quality increase satisfaction for consumers, who derive greater benefit from the outcome, developing greater confidence in the services and in the organizations that provide them.
- Greater confidence and better (more appropriate) services encourage non-users to take up services to which they are entitled. The focus can then be on earlier and more preventative action (intervention) rather than crisis reaction, leading to better results and possibly using fewer resources.
- Greater confidence and trust in those who provide services is an incentive for greater consumer involvement and influence. This in turn may lead to wider involvement of people as citizens who, seeing real change and improvement, now believe it is worth exercising their democratic rights as voters and community members, working as partners with, rather than antagonists against providers.
- More user and citizen involvement and satisfaction, and the knowledge that they are doing a better job, leads to higher staff morale and creates incentives for new ideas, innovation and skills development, benefiting both staff and users.
- Attention to quality draws attention to the effective use of resources. While a programme to improve quality should never be a vehicle for

hidden cuts, initial savings from eliminating 'non-conformance' and ongoing savings from better coordinated processes can be used to achieve better and more effective outcomes both for the public and for the organization.

- If attention is not given to quality, poor performance could draw in external intervention and provoke structural change to remove services from democratic control.

With so many compelling reasons, it is perhaps strange that more public services have not implemented programmes to improve quality – or, more accurately, have not maintained and built on programmes introduced in previous years.

There are many explanations for this. Public sector managers – in the health service, in schools and in local government – have been beset by a stream of policy initiatives, some with very profound implications for their very survival. It is not easy at these times to think clearly and systematically about 'what is the business we are in, and how can we improve what we do?'

In addition, many quality initiatives have been introduced top-down, piecemeal, without a clear purpose and without a real understanding of what 'quality' in that sector or unique setting really consists of. They have been fashion victims and have suffered the same fate – built-in obsolescence. In some cases, the initiatives have been promoted by central government, using financial incentives. This was particularly the case with the NHS in the early 1990s, when different waves of quality systems from the manufacturing sector – quality control, quality assurance and Total Quality Management – were all encouraged in turn and backed by financial incentives, often after only a couple of years with the previous system. Yet experience indicates that five to ten years may be needed to achieve real change and to embed the type of culture essential for success.

In addition, many quality initiatives were associated with individual managers (rarely politicians, even in local government) enthused by ideas about quality, but often acting in isolation. Such initiatives tended to be 'add-on', not integrated with other parts of their organization and not sustainable after the individuals moved on to other jobs or other ideas. Sustained change in the culture of the organization was again missing.

The difficulty with such initiatives has been that staff lower down in the hierarchy have rarely been able to develop 'ownership' of the idea and practice of quality, nor have they been given the freedom and autonomy to try things out for themselves. The blame and fear culture of too many public service organizations has been a major barrier to progress in this field.

While we would not suggest that changing an organization's culture is necessarily going to bring about the improvements so badly needed in public services, we do feel strongly that the question of 'culture' is at the heart of this issue. If the organizational culture is inappropriate, if the leadership is remote and hierarchical, if front-line staff do not feel valued or involved and if the public is seen as a 'nuisance' rather than an ally (and an employer), it is difficult to see how 'quality' can be embedded in a way that is sustainable beyond the involvement of a few enthusiastic individuals.

Included in this book are examples of organizations which have understood that what they are trying to do is to implement a *philosophy* rather than just a *programme* or *project* of quality improvement. This is not to say that they are perfect, or that the public has become actively involved in the way that is needed. But we can be optimistic that it is possible to take a long-term and corporate approach to quality improvement, since some organizations are already doing it.

Values

The part played by 'citizens' and 'values' within the concept of quality is explored in Chapter 3. At this stage of the book, we need to explain why we see both as central to our own thinking and to that of politicians and managers of public services.

The delivery of services is not a value-free activity. Values are at the heart of the debate about the nature of democracy and therefore of the activities undertaken in the name of democracy. In the public arena, choices, conscious or unconscious, implied or explicit, are constantly being made about what services to provide, who should be allowed or persuaded to receive them, how much resource should be devoted to them, and how long they should continue to exist. It seems to us, then, that values should not be taken for granted, but should be elicited, explored and if necessary developed so that they are coherent, consistent and practicable – and are in fact put into practice.

Recent floods of 'mission' and 'value' statements have often appeared to be tokenistic, especially when they have seemed to be more about appearing to be 'correct' than about creating a basis for real change. But the fact that at least a few people have sat down and thought – and occasionally consulted – about what their organization is really trying to do and to be, is to be welcomed. The danger is if these statements are left on the shelf rather than put into practice, which is of course the challenge.

At the *psychological* level, it is particularly important for operational staff, who are mainly responsible for delivering and improving services, to be involved in the development of their organization's values. Too often they are cynical or even hostile to the 'espoused' values of management and policy makers. This can happen when there is insufficient communication and involvement, or if the stated values do not match what happens in practice. This is particularly striking when staff feel they are being treated and indeed valued differently from, say, managers or the public: there is a great and natural concern with 'double standards', as encounters with practitioners consistently show.

In the demanding and often poorly paid public services, job satisfaction is an important service value. The constraints that staff work to are often not fully understood by, or explained to, the public. And without some idea of the values underlying the day-to-day activities of a public service organization, it is easy for employees to lose a sense of purpose and commitment and for individualists to do 'their own thing' (albeit to a much lesser extent than in the past, when they were unconstrained by performance targets and indicators), rather than follow agreed and rational guidelines or standards where they exist.

Traditionally, this kind of autonomous and altruistic practice has been a cherished value of practitioners. But it raises problems of accountability and involving the public (who are often seen as 'ignorant' and 'dependent'). Professional judgements are certainly important, especially where hard evidence of what constitutes 'good practice' is limited, or where the situation is unique and complex. However, professionals still need to take other views into account, and this is what they are often bad at doing.

So at a *practical* level, individualistic or 'professional' values also raise the danger that people – the public – will be treated differently and possibly inequitably, depending on whom they encounter on the front line. This is not a case of different styles of interaction or desirable variation to meet different needs, but of idiosyncratic behaviour designed to give maximum satisfaction to the service provider. Inequity in public services may simply arise because of lack of evidence to indicate what *is* equitable. Other reasons include the overwhelming power of the provider, the power of the loudest voice (often of the least needy) and the gradual societal change towards the cult of the individual since the 1979 Conservative Government of Margaret Thatcher.

Also at a practical level, it is difficult to see how a service provider can define services and decide the standards for those services unless they are clear about their values. The basic quality question is 'What is the business we are in?' This must be preceded by the question 'What *kind* of organization do we want to be?' In the early days of the welfare state, the answer might have seemed obvious. Now, with increased awareness but also uncertainty about social, economic, environmental and political expectations and priorities affecting everyday policy and practice, the issues need to be thought through, debated and agreed in a way that might have seemed unnecessary a few years ago.

To turn round this state of affairs, providers will need to increase their specialist knowledge and change their behaviour and attitudes. They will need to work together across both occupational and organizational barriers to respond to the increasingly complex needs of their service users. Service users will also need to take responsibility for becoming better informed about their own expectations, wants, needs and about service provision and provider values.

A partnership with service users in developing the aims of the service could result in staff working with, rather than against, their clientele. Professionals, already experiencing excessive user demands, may reject partnership and power sharing as a bridge too far, but as Hugman (1991) suggests, mutual education between all stakeholders on the limitations and possibilities that affect progress towards agreed aims can be a first step.

A citizen-centred approach

Different organizations will have different sets of values. That is inevitable. However, one value needs to be common to all public service organizations pursuing quality improvement and that is 'citizen-centredness'. As already mentioned, public services have a different relationship with their 'customers', based on the democratic context within which these services are to be provided.

As seen in later chapters, a balance has to be maintained between general and specific need, between the provision of a service for the 'public good' and the meeting of particular needs. This means that, unlike private services, the 'customer' can never be 'king' (or queen). The 'public', who are being called 'citizens' here, has, though, a major role in determining the shape and quality of public services.

In considering how services should be designed and delivered, it is essential to move away from the 'we know best' professional and producer-dominated approach, to one that understands and, where possible, incorporates the needs and views of the public *as the public sees and expresses them*. Services designed in this way – combining the 'expert knowledge' of professionals, managers and front-line staff with the 'experiential knowledge' of consumers, citizens and communities (Barnes 1997) – will be more efficient and effective. They will also generate higher levels of satisfaction than those where the consumer has to fit into the box designed solely by the service provider.

This idea has, it is true, a somewhat idealistic, 'missionary' feel to it. Can the world really be changed to that extent? It is necessary to try. If this is not done, 'quality' improvements will simply be confined to tinkering with the present structure. Radical thinking would be excluded, and the result could easily be 'bureaucratic paternalism' (Skelcher 1992): 'the same, only a bit better – if only we had the resources!'

Bringing consumers and citizens (that is, people not necessarily actively consuming the said service, but with an interest derived from their role as taxpayers, voters and potential users or beneficiaries) into the equation implies a shift of power and a change in the locus of decision making. It suggests that service providers need to work with members of the public, individually or collectively, as 'partners' rather than adversaries or superiors. This again has major implications for the kind of culture experienced by public service providers. It suggests a debating, questioning, skilled and empowered culture, where service providers have genuine opportunities to find out the needs and concerns of those citizens most directly affected, together with the authority to listen and respond to the public's ideas and experience. For many public servants, this is still a rather new concept, not assisted by the 'blame and fear' cultures to which so many are increasingly subjected.

In a few instances a glimpse of the future public sector activist – the newly and early retired – is now being seen and heard (Herzlinger 1997). Such people are knowledgeable, will demand the best service and organization at times of need and have the physical, mental, financial and time resources and a lifetime of experience and contacts to enable success. The potential size of this group, who have much to give and little to lose, is an influence seriously underestimated by the services of which they are the largest users (see Chapter 10). These sectors risk not only losing a collaborator, but ultimately magnifying the problem by responding reactively, having lost the opportunity for proactive partnership. It is this potential to work *with* older people, the largest users of welfare services, actively meeting their needs, that largely focused the content of this book.

Structure of the book

The four principles on which this book is based are as follows:

1 'Values' are at the heart of a quality-improvement culture in public services.
2 Citizens are the starting point for thinking about quality improvements.
3 'Quality' must be treated holistically, and the connections between each element must be strong and clear.
4 Quality is an issue that needs both a clear theoretical base *and* practical experience.

In the next chapter, Chapter 2, the institutional context is set out, focusing on recent public policy developments that are likely to affect efforts to improve the quality of day-to-day services and suggesting ingredients for an organizational infrastructure that can support policy and practice to improve service quality.

Chapters 3, 4 and 5 propose a theoretical framework for thinking comprehensively about quality. Chapter 3 looks at the key 'stakeholders', considers how quality might be defined, and discusses the central issues of values and objectives. Chapter 4 examines the processes for developing and implementing a policy to improve quality, considering both 'ready-made' systems and some underlying principles and models that could help the development of 'home-made' approaches. Chapter 5 considers how quality can be measured and evaluated, and what the development of 'quality stand-ards' might contribute to this.

When considering how to progress the idea of quality in different public services, it is useful to know what has been tried in the past, and to understand the broader policy framework affecting such efforts. Chap-ters 6, 7 and 8 therefore provide brief overviews of developments around the quality issue in central and local government and in the health service.

It is now clear that established service organizations will increasingly need to work together – in 'partnership' maybe – in order to develop services that truly meet public needs. Chapter 9, by Carol Hayden, analyses the reality of partnerships and partnership working as experienced through the pilots for the 'Better Government for Older People' policy. She also suggests what a 'quality partnership' would look like.

The next five chapters, Chapters 10–14, have been written by practi-tioners trying to improve quality in the field. Where relevant, they too have focused on older people as a way of developing a common theme for this part of the book. However, although all the services described in this part of the book are highly relevant to older people, not all the chapters specifically focus on this part of the population: they are among many potential beneficiaries. Thus there is a chapter by Tessa Harding, which looks in detail at the position of 'citizens', relating this to several policy initiatives including the 2001 National Framework for Older People. Returning to 'Better Government for Older People', Pat Scrutton describes and analyses the particular experience of South Lanarkshire in relation to the improvement or change in key services important to local older people. Following that, and thinking about services that are very important for the overall welfare of older people, there are two chapters on quality in relation to health care (Amanda Squires) and to housing – the lettings and allocation process (John Crawley).

Finally, in this 'practice' section of the book, there is a chapter by Michael Greenwood (writing in a personal capacity) on the Metropolitan Borough of Tameside. This is one of the few councils known to have tried over several years to develop a corporate culture and practice of 'quality'. In this case the Deming model has been used systematically, and while it is too early to judge the impact on the outside world – that is, the local public – it may be significant that this authority has been a frequent 'winner' for several central government schemes aiming to recognize good practice.

The final chapter considers the political context in which this issue is being played out and reflects on the recent experience of 'quality in the public sector'. It identifies some key lessons for the future, making recom-mendations for action by the main groups of stakeholders – politicians, managers, front-line staff and citizens and consumers. It suggests what is needed to make 'democratic quality', or 'citizen-led quality' come into being consistently in public services as a whole. Is it a pipedream, or is it really possible?

2

The public policy context

Lucy Gaster and Amanda Squires

The 'modernization' agenda

The need for public services to change and improve has long been recognized by central government, though for different political reasons. The Conservative governments of the 1980s and early 1990s, motivated by the desire to 'roll back the state', mainly used methods to change the *structure* of the public sector and spend less on it. These methods included the introduction of the contract culture (Compulsory Competitive Tendering, or 'CCT', in local government), some privatization (prisons), some devolution (schools) and the 'internal market' (health). In all these, 'quality' was a specified but vague component.

Since 1997 and the election of a Labour government for the first time since 1979, the focus on public services has intensified, with a much greater stated concern for 'quality' and 'results' and with some 'extra' spending on health and education. Labour has apparently been more interested in the *process* of service delivery, introducing policies of 'Best Value' and neighbourhood management in local government, and emphasizing the need for more consumer choice and 'joined-up' services. Taken together, these measures were advertised as being part of the Labour Government's 'modernization' agenda (see Chapter 6).

However, the division between political ideologies is not as clear as might appear. Discussion of possible re-structuring in public services continues, and there is no political objection in central government, as far as can be seen, to increased private provision of publicly funded services.

Equally, it was the Conservative Government which introduced the Citizen's Charter in 1991 (Prime Minister John Major's 'big idea') and which, through legislation and circulars for community care, set out two basic principles that are now leading ideas for the public sector: 'needs-led' services and 'seamless' services. These policies aimed to improve *how* services were delivered to the public.

No assumptions can therefore be made about the political thinking shaping the nature, size, content and value of public services. Since the post-war consensus on the Welfare State broke down in the late 1970s (Deakin 1994; Levitt *et al.* 1995) there has been a great deal of uncertainty, with very fluid terminology to describe what is happening. It has been hard for service delivery agencies to find out what is expected and what will be rewarded or punished through the ever-expanding inspection regimes. A current example (2002) is the government mantra of 'improved public services'. The expectation raised during the 2001 General Election was that the Labour Government, after four years of announcing policies, was now moving to the process of implementing them. However, a strategy for carrying this out was not defined and, as seen in Chapter 6, the Cabinet Office civil servants responsible for creating the central drive for 'reform' (the Performance and Innovation Unit, the Office of Public Service Reform and the Delivery Unit) all appeared to be operating separately, working on very specific topics but with little overall sense of direction or coordination – or input from citizens and users.

All this means that, although there is great expressed concern about the state of (some) public services, contradictions and tensions exist, as one policy overlaps or supersedes another, and as one method is favoured at the expense of the previous one, itself relatively untried.

Some of these tensions can be identified as:

- *Values*: does the 'public service' or the 'business' ethos prevail?
- *Performance*: is it more important to get things right for the public, the profession, the courts, the inspectors – or (somehow) for all of these?
- *Innovation*: is it better to play safe and do what has always been done, or to try things out which might be successful ('beacons') or might be punished ('failing' institutions), as government inspectorates decide?
- *Visibility*: is being 'upward looking' to strategic direction (government) or 'downward looking' to operational activity (the public) best rewarded, and if so by whom?
- *Users and citizens*: is a 'needs-led' service really about listening and responding to the consumer, or is it about looking good on bids for government monies?
- *Joined-up services*: is there a real impetus to work in 'cross-cutting' ways, listening to users and radically changing the shape of traditional service provision? Or is it simpler, safer and easier to continue to work in the same 'boxes' as before? Are the (protective) forces of departmentalism

and professionalism simply too strong? Is the public actually ready for the consequences of such change (for example, closing the Cottage or War Memorial hospital to improve community services)?

The effects of policy on 'quality'

The question for this book is, how do these high level policies and ambiguities affect the development of high quality public services on the ground? Individual service agencies – local councils, hospitals and primary care, police, fire and ambulance services – are all affected at the local level by the knock-on effects of what is happening nationally. They are constrained by legislation, which can set out both what they *must* do (the statutory element), and what they *can* do (the discretionary element). They are affected by annual and, at central government level, tri-annual resource allocation decisions, and in some cases by the requirement to generate income.

Public service providers are inevitably influenced by the public climate of expectation – the culture – in which public services operate, both in developing local policies and in their day-to-day work. What is the message coming from central government? Is it assumed at the highest levels that public services are generally hopeless, and will only respond to kicks? Or is there some goodwill and understanding of how these services work, of the pressures they have been under, and of their own ability to improve if given the chance? (It hardly needs to be said that this book, written entirely by practitioners, is premised on the latter assumption.) Can central government demonstrate what it means by 'good practice' in its own work, or does it merely expect others to work in ways of which it is not itself capable? Is the relationship between central government and local practice dominated by mutual suspicion or by 'partnership'?

At the time of writing, the messages are thoroughly mixed. On the one hand, some good ideas (on paper at least) have emerged. The idea that services can learn from each other through 'beacon' and other schemes must be good. The idea of rewarding the best performing agencies with greater freedom to act is also surely beneficial. The idea of re-examining services from scratch, and involving service users in that process, as set out in the policy for 'Best Value', is thoroughly useful in the context of 'quality'. In the latter case, the practice, as discussed in Chapter 7, has unfortunately reinforced the mixed messages about what exactly the government wants or expects. Under the Best Value regime, organizations and specific services are being labelled by the Audit Commission as 'poor and incapable of improving'. This is bad for morale, and bad for innovation and experiment.

In healthcare, public participation is encouraged and complaints processes are widely advertised. Yet if there is a subsequent increase in the number of complaints, health providers are criticized, rather than investigated to find out whether the increase relates to unresolved existing issues or to new issues raised by a quality conscious and empowered public with a now receptive organization.

The policy environment is thus crucial to the development of policies to improve quality in public services at several different levels.

Three levels of 'quality'

Services can be considered at three levels: the *strategic*, 'macro' level; the *design*, 'meso' level; and the *delivery*, 'micro' level. If the quality of public services is to be improved, thinking and action is needed at all these three levels, with consistency between them. Yet the tensions identified above, and the policies that have created them, can cause divergence rather than consistency, particularly if local, participative processes are developed. These may raise expectations of what can be changed, yet in practice be constrained by non-negotiable legal or national quality standards.

Problems can arise at each of the three levels:

1 At the macro level, policy makers struggle with the next new policy and find it difficult to maintain interest in policies that have already been 'done'. They suffer, as was noted in a recent report (DTLR 2001c), from 'initiative fatigue'.
2 At the meso level, heads of services have to decide how they can best fulfil their targets and work within their resources. They may have little incentive to ask whether the services for which they are responsible actually meet real needs, since this could raise expectations and therefore demand.
3 At the micro level, front-line staff, generally at the receiving end of top-down policies, have to make sense of what is happening at both levels and filter this through to their day-to-day encounters with the public.

These dilemmas and tensions explain, perhaps, why so little clarity can be found about the fundamental issue of 'quality', much though the word is used in public discourse. Despite the best efforts of front-line staff, most of whom have a continuing commitment to provide a decent service, the public inevitably perceives confusion, mixed messages and no clear sense of direction. Rather than assuming that UK public services are as good as they can be, it is often a matter of surprise and gratification if they are.

What is the business we are in?

A positive climate for change needs to be created, at central government level, *within* services and at the very local (community) level. As

Chapters 10–14 show, there have been many efforts to do just this over the whole period of change since the early 1980s.

An important prerequisite for deciding what needs to change is a clear sense of purpose. Because most public service institutions were for many years working on an 'incremental' model, mainly doing what had been done before, with new services or ways of working being largely seen as 'add-on', the habit of defining objectives is relatively recent. It was only in the mid-1990s that, either as part of the 'New Public Management' process, or because they were under threat of extinction, many services began at last to consider their *raison d'être*. Constant pressure on resources has also underlined the need to be clear about priorities in a way that had possibly been evaded in earlier years, either because such pressure did not exist or because the choices were not so stark and it was possible to operate regimes of 'hidden rationing'.

While it is easy to be sceptical about the burgeoning pile of 'mission' and 'vision' statements that emerged at this time, the fact that some people were seriously considering why they were there and what they wanted to achieve, was significant. We discuss how this 'clarity of purpose' might be aided by 'clarity of values' in the next chapter.

What is important in terms of national policy is that if public service agencies do *not* have a clear view of why they exist and what are their intended outcomes, it becomes very easy to sway with the wind and to change direction each time a new policy is introduced. If clarity of purpose exists, it is much easier for local policy makers to determine how they will interpret national policy, and how they may use it to strengthen their own 'business'. It also makes it much easier for staff and the public to understand their own role and potential contribution and, if necessary, to challenge actual practice if it appears to be inconsistent with the stated goals. Finally, when commissioning services, the responsible institution can clarify to potential contractors what they are looking for and what would be acceptable – or unacceptable – in day-to-day service delivery.

Clarity of purpose is needed to determine both the *nature* of the service and *how* it is delivered – the 'technical' and the 'non-technical' dimensions of quality (see Chapter 3).

The characteristics of modern, high-quality public services

In order to survive and adapt to the requirements of the modernization agenda, it seems clear that public services must now take on certain characteristics that were not prominent in the past. Some of these characteristics arise from government and public expectations, some arise from the organizational need both to be able to respond to change and to put change into practice.

Three broad expectations have been created by the government's modernization agenda. These are:

1 The need to achieve 'results'.
2 The need to work in 'partnership'.
3 The need to 'consult' users and communities.

While it would be difficult to disagree with these expectations, we have made careful use of inverted commas to underline the fact that each concept is in fact not easy to define and is open to different interpretations. This would not matter if everyone recognized these differences, but in practice this is often not so. This leads to simplistic interpretations and/or disagreements between stakeholders when definitions do not match. We explore some issues arising from this later in this chapter.

A further set of expectations comes from the public. These expectations, which are closely related to the notion of 'perception' and 'satisfaction', are not in fact easy to interpret – my 'satisfaction' is not necessarily the same as your 'satisfaction' (Pirsig 1974; Donovan *et al.* 2001). However, leaving aside the immediate and important influence of the media (which may decrease satisfaction by pointing out all the worst aspects), and allowing for the 'deference' factor, particularly among older people and less educated people (which may increase satisfaction because of low expectations and dependency), research has shown that consumers particularly value (National Consumer Council 1986, 1991 and 1995):

- reliability
- good and relevant information
- speed/timeliness of performance
- access
- helpfulness.

These, it could be argued, are – or should be – all part of a 'quality' system, implying that modern public service agencies *must* develop policy and practice that acknowledges and where possible meets these expectations.

If public service organizations are to be able to respond to the expectations listed so far, some new(ish) skills and processes, which have not in the past been strong points in public services, will be needed. In the context of quality improvement, two that particularly come to mind are:

1 problem-solving approaches
2 change management skills.

In order to produce high-quality services, an organization needs to be 'high quality' in itself. While a single prescription for achieving this does not exist, the ideas identified in this section could give a useful lead, not only because government says so, but because, as we argue in the next three chapters, this is the way forward towards 'democratic' quality. Public service organizations will need actively to involve stakeholders, especially users, citizens and communities; they will need to work jointly with other organizations, maybe informally, maybe through a formal 'partnership'; and they will need to ensure that the intended results (as well as processes) are actually achieved and accounted for.

Following from this, it seems obvious that organizations providing public services in the future will have to look not only at the quality of their services, but at their corporate framework and infrastructure: do they have staff and organizational qualities and characteristics that will enable them to deliver the expected services?

A new organizational infrastructure

What we suggest here is a way forward for organizations responsible for public services – through direct delivery, commissioning or contracting – to be able to do what is now expected and required. Experience seems to show that although none of these are new ideas, and many have been taken up in different parts of the public services in recent years, it is still rather rare to find a 'whole organization approach' to the issue. Improvements and change tend to be patchy, reflecting long-standing divisions and differences within the complex organizations involved:

> We have inherited a set of structures, professions, skill mixes and job demarcations which have emerged as a series of responses to the needs of society . . . that have long since passed . . . If it were possible to start again with a greenfield site, it is inconceivable that we would create anything like the same organisational and professional architecture that we now have.
>
> (Wilkinson and Applebee 1999: 38)

Three reasons for developing a holistic approach stand out:

1 The public is not interested in the internal workings or structure of a council, a hospital or a police service. Whomever they encounter *is* the council, hospital or whatever – and the whole organization is likely to be judged by the experience of that one service or even one encounter. It is therefore vital that a consistent experience is provided right across the board in any one organization. To achieve this, a 'whole organization approach' makes sense.
2 Very few services are entirely self-sufficient – they generally consist of a series of actions, often the responsibility of different people, teams, divisions and departments (leaving aside external agencies, which will increasingly be part of the process). If we are to move away from the culture of 'more than my job's worth', 'it's not my responsibility', an integrated and cooperative approach is essential.

3 Most public service organizations have been trying out some structures and processes to help them to meet the changing demands on them. However, these have not necessarily been closely connected either with external policy requirements, or with other internal policy and practice. Our experience is that improvements have tended to be patchy and often isolated from each other – 'add-ons' rather than 'mainstream'. Because of this, organizational learning is often slow to take place and there has been much re-inventing of the wheel. This is another reason why an organization-wide approach to change is necessary.

Problem solving

It was suggested in Chapter 1 that the key to quality improvement is the development of an appropriate 'quality culture'. This is neither easy nor an overnight process. However, there are two elements which it is particularly important to get right in the early stages and which can form the foundation of an inclusive approach. These are the ability to identify and solve problems and the ability to implement change effectively and sustainably.

'*Problem solving*' is an activity which is either taken for granted or, in too many cases, does not happen. It is a process with several stages and was the underlying concept in Deming's approach to reducing variance and improving quality in manufacturing (Deming 1986) (see Figure 2.1).

The cycle goes as follows:

- *Act*: The first stage is to review existing practice. An explicit attempt is made to identify the exact reason why, for example, there are frustrating blockages inside the organization, or why 'mistakes' are made, why backlogs and waiting lists exist, or why objectives are not being achieved. Such an analysis is based on evidence such as statistical data, consumer

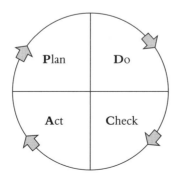

Figure 2.1 The Deming cycle.

feedback, staff interviews, observation and so on. Careful consideration is given to whether there are several causes of the problems and, if so, which are the most significant. The analysis is *not* based on assumptions about who is to blame, or 'instant analyses' of the first piece of 'evidence' that comes to hand. A decision to 'act' is then taken.

- *Plan*: Having identified the problem, the second stage is to consider possible solutions. This is the stage of 'option generation', where the widest possible thinking is needed for imaginative and appropriate solutions. As with the first stage, the key is to take a rational approach, to learn from similar situations, and to consider a full range of alternatives, considering the consequences (results and impact), benefits and possible disadvantages of each one. This approach rules out 'instant solutions' and requires the involvement of as many stakeholders as possible, both to generate ideas and to ensure 'ownership' of the resulting decision.
- *Do*: The third stage is the 'implementation' stage. Here, the idea would be to ensure that responsibility for action is clearly allocated, shared and *supported* appropriately. It does not involve telling people to 'get on with it', with impossible timescales and inappropriate tools.
- *Check*: The last stage is to assess whether the intended results have been achieved, again by systematically collecting evidence, both quantitative and qualitative, and to ensure full participation in an evaluation process.

A range of tools exists to identify and measure the cause and effect of variation and to solve quality problems (see Chapter 4 and Annex 4.2). Although little used in the public sector to date, many of these generic tools are applicable. The Tameside approach based on the Deming system incorporates many of these ideas, as will be seen in Chapter 14.

Working groups can be particularly useful in bringing together the main stakeholders, harnessing ideas and ensuring continuous ownership of the process of problem solving and improvement. They could take the form of 'quality circles', which have a particular structure and form, or they could be less formalized task or action groups with a remit to report back with suggestions for improvement and to take action forward and monitor progress in a particular area of work.

Problem solving in Tameside relates specifically to the improvement of selected services. In this chapter, we suggest that it can in fact be applied to the working of a whole organization, so as to consider its structure, decision-making processes, use of resources and relationship with the community. The reason why we emphasize it is because we fear that this approach is still not endemic in many – or even most – public service organizations, which continue to use the top-down, instant solution approach that has doomed so many policy initiatives to failure.

It could be argued that problem solving takes more time (staff time and chronological time), which is at odds with the difficult political time targets set centrally and locally, and it would not be realistic to say that corners will never be cut. Equally, it could be argued that since information on which decisions must be based will never be 'perfect' (there will always be elements of uncertainty), this highly rational approach is irrelevant and even inapplicable. The counter-argument is that it is better to use any evidence that is available, rather than going too quickly for the first – or fashionable – solution. It is then a matter of judgement – for politicians as well as managers – to decide how to use that evidence (Stewart 1998a).

So we are advocating the 'normalization' of the problem-solving approach – building it into the culture. The success of this would be tested in actual behaviour: a decision taken in the traditional way (top-down and instant) would begin to *feel* uncomfortable or even wrong. Of course, staff and other stakeholders (particularly users and citizens) must be fully trained in the skills and techniques so that this becomes day-to-day practice.

A systematic, problem-solving, enquiring, rational and, it is to be hoped, experimental and innovative approach to the development of policy and practice should produce ideas about what needs to be done that are different from what was done in the past. It would be worrying if this was not so, and might lead one to ask whether enough options really were considered.

However, it is one thing to come up with solutions, another to implement them. This is the stage where, unless care is taken, all the forces of 'dynamic conservatism' (Schon 1971) will come to the fore. The aspect of this that concerns us is the ability of the organization as a whole to change – not for change's sake, but because it is necessary for responsive development and indeed survival. The second important ingredient for an appropriate organizational infrastructure for quality is, then, the ability to manage change.

The process of organizational change

Organizational change is a process which, like problem solving, requires a systematic and inclusive approach. Although the need for change is well-known in the public sector, it is not easy to put into practice: there are a great many pitfalls.

First, all stakeholders' needs and concerns, including those of service users and citizens, must be identified. This is crucial to success. All those involved need to understand the process of change and be able to identify and appropriately deal with potential barriers in their unique organizational culture. Who will (or thinks they will) gain or lose prestige and resources?

Second, it is important to understand the different stages in the process of organizational change, as shown in Figure 2.2.

The following paragraphs examine each of these stages in turn.

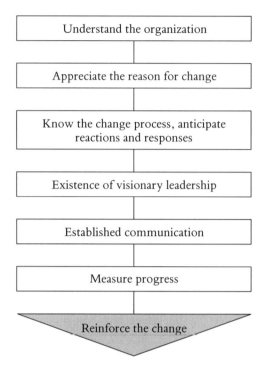

Figure 2.2   The process of organizational change.
(Adapted from Clarke 1994)

Understand the organization

Employees actively seek environments that have similar values to their own (Handy 1985), further strengthening the culture of the organization (Lewin 1952). Being clear about the true values of employees and therefore of the organization is an essential prerequisite for successful change.

Appreciate the reasons for change

Both the external and the internal environments influence change. External pressures include competition for scarce resources and the introduction of new policies. Internally, Greiner (1972) suggested that 'endogenous' changes are influential. These changes occur as an organization goes through predictable phases of evolution and revolution as it ages and grows, with different tensions at different times: creativity or leadership; direction or autonomy; and delegation or control.

Know the process, anticipate reactions and responses

The process

The process of change can be at two levels. First-order change is confined to tinkering, for example, reorganizing office layout. Second-order change is a strategic, fundamental approach, for example, posing the question: do we *need* the office at all?

In order to achieve a process of change that meets its objectives and is therefore regarded as successful, three sets of actors are needed (Conner and Patterson 1982):

1 *Change sponsor*: who has the power to legitimize change
2 *Change agent*: who is responsible for the change process
3 *Change target*: who is required to alter their personal knowledge, skills, attitudes and behaviour.

If 'participation' is now to be the way of life for public services, the targets for change will include both service providers (main targets) as well as users (minor targets).

Reactions and responses

Over time, values, beliefs and assumptions produce actions that become natural and comfortable habits. It can be 'agony' to change them (Heller 1986). However, in most organizations there are also people who are eager for change: they can see the advantages, and they may have been unhappy with the 'custom and practice' of former times. Such people often become change agents, promoting and actively participating in change.

There can therefore be a range of responses to organizational change (Rogers and Shoemaker 1971):

- *Innovators* are quick to adopt new ideas and change accordingly.
- *Early adopters* follow closely behind the innovators, but try to conform with social norms.
- *Early majority* take on change once it has started to become accepted.
- *Late majority* are more conservative and wait to see all the effects before adopting change.
- *Laggards* are very suspicious of change and are slow to adapt. They need exceptional leadership.

Rogers and Shoemaker found that 70 per cent of people fall into the categories of 'early' and 'late' majority.

Management needs the skill to enable (empower) staff as the major 'change targets' to want to drive themselves – as 'innovators' and 'early adopters' – towards the new vision. Such passion 'adds value' to the organization, product or service, and to the individual. If these empowering solutions fail, this will show up in grievances, high staff turnover, poor efficiency, low output and anti-management feelings (Coch and French 1952).

Given the complexity of, and stamina needed for successful change, it is not surprising that it continues to remain elusive for some. Machiavelli was under no illusions as to the problems of change management when he wrote *The Prince* in 1513:

> There is nothing more difficult to execute, nor more dubious of success, nor more dangerous to administer than to introduce a new order of things; for he who introduces it has all those who profit from the old order as his enemies, and he has only lukewarm allies in all those who might profit from the new. This lukewarmness partially stems from fear of their adversaries who have the law on their side, and partly from the scepticism of men who do not truly believe in new things unless they have actually had personal experience of them.
>
> (Machiavelli 1513, *The Prince*)

Visionary leadership

All organizations possess variable levels of administration, management and leadership, but change needs leaders. For success, these leaders will need to demonstrate the new culture in everything that is done in a consistent and committed way. While leaders provide the vision for change, managers have to provide the physical effort of implementation. Where organizations fail to manage change successfully, an important cause is imbalance at the top, being either over-managed or under-led or both.

Communicate

Key organizational stakeholders must collaborate to find what needs to be done to meet the new organizational goal. Thereafter, the resulting mission, vision and strategy must be clarified and communicated so as to ensure consistency in both policy and action by all participants. The main benefit of good communication for the organization undergoing change is feedback to inform management decisions, in the true spirit of a quality organization. Such feedback must be heard and seen to be acted on if it is to be useful to the process of change.

Measure progress

Change should have achievable (and challenging) objectives. Such objectives, agreed with stakeholders, can include changes in the organization's culture, structure, processes and outcome. They need to be documented in strategic plans, and are inevitably unique to each organization. They should be clear, measurable (quantitatively and qualitatively) and well communicated. Progress needs to be monitored and documented so that identifiable rather than assumed progress is recorded.

As with 'problem solving', the process of organizational change can be presented rationally, but is hard to put into practice. The history of organizational change in the public sector shows that, once the immediate political pressures are relaxed, old-style behaviour can emerge very quickly. Where change has been successful, usually as the result of exceptional local leadership, further time (commonly five to ten years) is needed to embed the new style into the culture of the organization (Peters and Waterman 1991). It is extremely important to try to prevent backsliding at the departure of a key individual.

Having considered what organizations pursuing quality improvement should be *like*, the next three sections consider what they should *do*, in the light of government and public expectations.

Consultation and participation

We noted problems of definition for 'consultation', 'participation' and 'partnership', ideas which are now common within the public sector but which are open to very different interpretations in practice.

Participation and consultation – 'involvement' is another word currently in use – form part of the same model, in that they are concerned with forms of participative democracy, involving users, citizens and communities in decisions affecting their lives. A basic distinction can be made between them (Wilkinson and Applebee 1999: 128):

- '*Consultation*' is a process of eliciting and listening to people's views and feelings about services, projects and proposals. This provides information that is (or should be) taken into account when the decision makers are deliberating and making decisions.
- '*Participation*' is based on the assumption that those affected by a situation are best placed to determine how to change it and make implementation work. It implies dialogue, leading to greater involvement both in jointly generating greater understanding of shared concerns and, in some cases, in the decision making itself.

In most cases, a process of 'empowerment' is needed to ensure that local people can participate on equal terms with professionals and politicians. Participation needs to be voluntary, based on equality of contribution, mutual respect and bridge-building between groups.

The well-known 'ladder of participation' (Arnstein 1969) draws attention to the fact that what goes under the label of 'consultation' or 'participation' may in fact be 'manipulation' and 'control', when those carrying out the consultation are in reality looking for approval or rubber-stamping of a decision they have already taken. Unfortunately, this 'talking shop' approach has been a common experience for many local communities, leading to considerable scepticism and lack of trust in the decision makers (Commission on Poverty, Participation and Power 2000).

Other levels on Arnstein's 'ladder' usefully distinguish different aims when 'consulting'. These can be summarized (Gaster and Taylor 1993) as:

- *Information giving*: for example, through publicity, advice, councillors' surgeries (the information – reports on past performance, proposals for the future, etc. – needs to be honest and as full as is necessary for local people to be able to discuss and form a view about it)
- *Consultation and feedback*: gaining people's views, for example, through market research, satisfaction cards, focus groups
- *Advisory*: for example, through standing groups, such as user groups or citizen forums, or inviting non-voting cooptees to join existing committees, etc. Advice is given and suggestions are made by residents, but there is no commitment that these will be accepted by the decision makers
- *Some control*: joint planning groups, neighbourhood forums with delegated budgets
- *Power sharing*: joint management committees or local boards of citizens with delegated powers.

These five levels – which are generally applied to *collective* decision making, but could also be used in the context of service delivery to *individuals* – have different implications for the amount of influence or control residents may be able to exercise. Because the aims of consultation policies are often very vague, it is often the case that none of the participants are clear about which level is intended. As might be expected, this leads to frustration both among local people and among those carrying out the 'consultation', while elected representatives have an exaggerated fear that they are losing their legitimate power to 'unelected people' in what they see as a 'zero sum game'.

It is therefore important for the organization as a whole to have a clear idea, transparent to the local community, about:

- Why and on what issue it is consulting
- The degree to which local people should be involved
- What methods of consultation/participation will best suit the situation
- Who takes the final decision
- How the decision is fed back to those who were consulted.

It is vital that public involvement is embedded in the organizational values and strategy of public service organizations, including contractors actually delivering services. The dangers of lip-service, tokenism and double standards are too great if the organization is not fully committed and geared up for this. It is also essential that staff and decision makers are trained and supported to use the appropriate skills – listening, negotiating, using straightforward language, preparing venues and agendas, community development, etc. – to make it work.

Partnership

The same could be said of '*partnership*', which also calls for new attitudes and new ways of working. 'Partnership' is increasingly seen as an adjunct to, or even a replacement for contracts. Indeed, some of the considerations set out below could also apply to contractual working, where one (or more) organization works with the 'client' or 'purchaser', each having very specific roles and being bound by legal documentation. The key to either type of relationship is to build up cooperative working for the benefit of the public, and to diminish or eliminate confrontation from either side.

There is no single meaning of 'partnership', although, like 'consultation', it is often referred to as if there were. This issue is explored in considerable detail in Chapter 9, but it is appropriate to introduce the concept here, as an important part of our desired organizational infrastructure.

It is possible to work in 'partnership' – formal or not – at all three levels discussed earlier: macro, meso and micro. Local Strategic Partnerships, for example, have been promoted by central government as a way to combat social exclusion. Many other partnerships have been set up for particular strategic purposes – so many, indeed, that many people involved in public services can hardly keep up.

These *macro*-level arrangements are necessary as a framework for the practical day-to-day work of organizations, if only to give a lead, set an example, and coordinate different strands of policy and action. However, it could be said that the *meso*- and *micro*-level partnerships, or joint working arrangements, are more important for the effect they have on people's lives. If, as has been too often the case, health, social services and housing (at the least) are not working effectively together to provide community care, it is the community, and individuals within it, who suffer. Getting these relationships right, as Chapters 9 and 11 show, can be immensely fruitful, achieving far more than the 'sum of the parts'.

Service users also have a contribution to make to this new culture. The concept of 'co-production', where users and producers work together as equal partners to generate solutions and provide services, is useful here. It means that mutual knowledge and respect can be harnessed constructively (for example, carers working with professionals). This would be a welcome change from the past, where consumers were expected to behave in a manner acceptable to a (monopoly) service provider.

It is self-evident that joint working, under whatever rubric, needs very clear objectives. If the objectives are not clear, 'partnership', like 'participation', can degenerate into a 'talking shop', with falling commitment and the 'real' work taking place elsewhere. To achieve real partnership, attention needs to be given both to the *process* of developing joint working, and to the degree of *closeness* it is intended to achieve.

Taking the latter first, another 'ladder', this time a 'ladder of partnership', can help. This was developed in the course of research on the relationship between local government and the voluntary sector (Gaster *et al.* 1999), where the voluntary sector's need to retain independence as well as to work together effectively meant that there was considerable caution about how close to become or even whether to be 'partners' at all. Equally, it became clear that if crucial information was not being released by one or more partners, the basis for a good relationship did not exist. The key to all this was the development of mutual trust and understanding, which depended not only on present practice, but also on what had happened in the past. People have long memories.

The 'ladder' includes five levels. These could indicate progression over time or, like the ladder of participation, they could suggest different types of relationship which would not necessarily change. The levels are:

1 *Information exchange*: mutual learning, openness about decision making, access to databases
2 *Planning action*: debate local needs and priorities, identify services where cross-boundary working could be effective, agree responsibilities for action
3 *Implementing projects and service plans*: take action, jointly and separately, monitor and review, mutual feedback on results
4 *Coordination and cooperation*: appoint coordinator(s), who bring together and draw on partners as needed, nurturing a developmental and co-operative culture and involving/supporting new partners
5 *Collaboration*: separate and distinct roles but shared values and agendas, pooled budgets, blurred boundaries, dynamic to meet new needs.

Clarity and agreement about which type of partnership suits particular needs, and what is practicable, needs to be part of the preliminary negotiation. Indeed, as the experience of Better Government for Older People partnerships shows (p. 167) the process of developing a partnership is crucial to its success. This itself needs several stages:

1 Pre-partnership: 'recruitment' (skills needed, political consideration of inclusions and exclusions, reaching out to potential partners) and 'courtship' (who's who, what might each potential partner contribute, what kind of representation would be appropriate, who wants to join?)
2 Signing up: to what, for how long, with whom?
3 Developing ground rules (ethics and behaviour), getting to know each other
4 Getting going: who does what, joint problem solving, action planing, overcoming barriers
5 Keeping going: do we trust each other, are we achieving anything?

6 Constant review: involving stakeholders and considering the past, present and future
7 Leaving or sustaining the partnership (time-limited or long-term relationship?)

In practice, more stages may be needed, for example if new partners join. But the main requirement is a developmental process at or very near the beginning, and the need to support the less powerful partners (in terms of budgets and clout) to play a full part and not to feel patronized.

'Partnerships', like any form of human relationships, can be fragile and emotional, but they can also produce results that would not otherwise be achieved. Whether formal or informal, or even in the form of contracts, they are essential for jointly solving the problems of how to deliver services that meet real needs.

Achieving results

'Results' are the third main component of the government's modernizing agenda. The ambiguities around this are different but just as important as those relating to 'participation' and 'partnership'.

First, it is necessary to distinguish between results in terms of 'outputs' and 'outcomes' (effects/impact).

'Outputs' can be classified as the immediate results of a particular action: a family is re-housed, a street is cleaned, a broken leg is operated on. These rather specific examples can be observed and counted. This is the kind of 'result' most commonly used for official performance indicators, although even here there is always the danger of the 'measurable' taking precedence over the 'unmeasurable'.

'Outcomes' are the results, usually taken over a longer term, which do or do not contribute to the achievement of overall objectives, whether these are the organization's or the service recipient's. Quality of life or economic well-being, good health or living in a safe community are some possible outcomes. These may be collectively negotiated, or they may be more subjective, important to individuals, but difficult to measure and compare. The main difficulty with this type of outcome is that it can be difficult to specify, it will vary with the changing needs of the service user, and it may take time for the results to become observable and measurable. Also, because the types of outcome listed here are usually the combined result of a mixture of actions (and inactions) by official bodies and by people and communities themselves, the relationship between cause and effect may be very unclear.

The question, then, of *which* results are to be used to assess the modernization programme itself or its ability to deliver good quality services needs to be carefully thought through and debated.

This leads to the second area of concern: *'whose* results?' In a political climate where organizations are judged 'successes' or 'failures' – with specific rewards or punishments accordingly – it would be a matter of considerable concern if the results were solely those deemed suitable by Whitehall, the Commission for Health Improvement (CHI) or the Audit Commission. Despite national 'consultation' exercises, the danger persists that local service providers will continue to regard these central criteria as inappropriate. As numerous media stories show, such indicators are open to manipulation by those who want their organizations to come high rather than low in the league tables.

For quality improvement, the crucial 'results' are those that are meaningful to local users and communities (see also Chapter 5). They should be assessed through the use of a combination of qualitative and quantitative measures. The importance of being able to achieve tangible results and to measure and account for what is done is unquestionable. How this is carried out in practice needs to be thought through very carefully. The widespread cynicism of both staff and the public and low morale induced by central targets and performance indicators needs to be replaced by constructive and honest evaluation of progress and actual 'results' that are meaningful to all the key stakeholders.

Conclusions

This chapter has examined the policy context in which UK public service organizations are working. Even before the arrival of the current 'modernization' agenda, central government as well as local bodies were concerned about the use of resources to produce the best possible services. This issue is now far more explicit. However, with honourable exceptions, central government policies tend to work at a level of generalization and exhortation, with surprisingly little regard for *how* public service organizations – councils, health services, police, schools and central government departments and agencies – are to move from 'here' to 'there' (but see Chapter 6 for an analysis of what is being done in this respect).

Looking at the trends of both central government expectations (not necessarily the same thing as policies) and considering what the public most values from public services, it seems clear that it is not just a matter of tinkering with existing structures and practices. There really is a need for a much more radical approach to change, aiming to create a 'quality infrastructure' that can deliver 'quality' services (*high* quality of course in both cases).

We have identified five building blocks for creating this infrastructure and its accompanying citizen-oriented culture. These are:

1 To make 'problem-solving approaches' normal at every level, addressing real problems and creating better and more imaginative solutions.

2 To introduce and sustain 'change management' methods and skills to ensure organizational capacity and readiness for change.

3 To develop a clear and honest local strategy for public consultation and participation and ensure organizational capacity to make it work.

4 To engage stakeholders, understand different viewpoints and create clarity of direction and synergy through partnership working. This must be seen as mainstream, not 'add-on', with agreed purposes, processes and levels of involvement.

5 To be oriented to achieving results, but think carefully and consult locally about what the best results would be for local people and communities.

These ideas are not particularly radical or strange. Many organizations are developing them in whole or in part. However, if they are seen, not as something that will enable an organization to do its job better – to carry out its 'business' – but merely as a way of placating government and keeping out of trouble, they will not contribute to enduring high quality services. Taking into account the complexities of modern services and the complex needs of individuals and communities, a 'whole organization' approach does seem to us to be absolutely essential.

Having looked at the policy and organizational context, the next three chapters introduce a model of quality which is also 'holistic', bringing together different strands of policy and action on quality itself, and linking this firmly to the 'citizen'.

Part II
The theory

3

The conceptual framework: stakeholders, values, objectives and definitions

Lucy Gaster and Amanda Squires

If improving quality was easy, everyone would have done it by now. So what are the basic ingredients of a discussion of quality? Where do we start?

The questions to which answers are needed are:

- How is quality defined?
- How is it measured?
- How is it put into practice?
- How is it maintained?
- Whose quality is it?

From these arise other questions, notably:

- What is the business we are in, what are we trying to do?
- How can all these issues be linked together?
- What choices do I have for how I (and my organization) go about it?

A model for 'quality'

A model (Figure 3.1) was developed in the 1990s, which attempted to take a comprehensive and coherent look at these questions (Gaster 1995a). It is based on both primary and secondary research on quality and on discussion and debate with a very large number of practitioners encountered in post-graduate and post-experience teaching programmes.

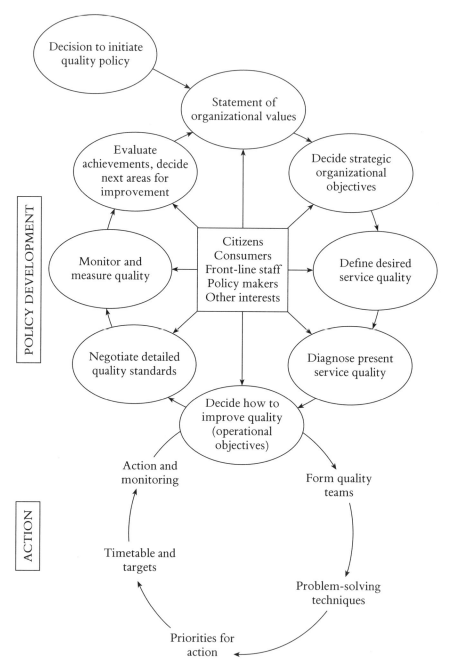

Figure 3.1 A model for service quality.
Source: Gaster 1995a.

The framework is based on a classic 'policy-implementation' cycle. It was initially stimulated by the preoccupation of many people delivering public services in the early 1990s with how to measure quality, this in turn having been triggered by a concern that quantitative indicators did not tell the whole story (and even distorted it). The question therefore became: what is it that we are trying to measure? And this in turn led back into issues of standards, targets and the very nature of quality. Underlying these was the question of what kind of services was the agency aiming to deliver – what were its objectives? And how are objectives formulated? Explicitly or not, objectives and hence practice are necessarily based on values (Lawton 1998), generally a mixture of political, professional, managerial and 'street-level bureaucrat' concepts (Lipsky 1980): what *kind* of organization are we trying to be?

So the 'policy' segment of the cycle identifies the values, objectives, nature and desired level of quality. This is matched by an 'implementation' stage, incorporating systematic problem solving and an action-oriented approach, sometimes 'off the shelf', sometimes home-grown. Finally, a process of evaluation needs to be built in (not added on) so as to achieve a learning cycle that leads to further thinking and action.

At the heart of the model is the range of 'stakeholders' who are or should be involved at each stage. This underlines the fact that if the public, as consumers, citizens or communities, are only brought into the cycle at the measurement/monitoring stage (as is still very often the case), it is far too late for them to influence key decisions such as the nature and characteristics and standards of the service to be delivered to, for or with them. They, and other key actors such as front-line staff and elected councillors, all need to be brought into the picture as soon as possible. Otherwise 'quality' becomes yet another management tool, prey to the management fashions that so beset public services, and not embedded in the culture and politics of the organization (see especially Chapter 10).

The 'rational' model presented here can therefore be used:

- To demonstrate relationships between different parts of the policy process
- To clarify why particular activities, such as performance measurement, should not be tackled in isolation from values and objectives
- To provide a weapon against 'ad hocery' and fragmentation and promote integration and collaboration.

The aim of the model is both to provide a tool for systematic analysis of what is actually happening in any one organization or service, and to enable practitioners to identify where to focus their efforts in order to achieve a complete cycle. It is based on the belief that if 'quality' is presented and experienced in a fragmented way, for example through performance targets and indicators, or as encapsulated in selected quality systems (quality assurance, customer care, etc.), or indeed simply as 'service' or 'citizen's charter' standards, the effectiveness and impact of the change, both on the commitment and involvement of staff, and on the services and their recipients, will be weakened.

The much longer experience of the private sector, which has also seen many management fashions come and go, appears to bear this out in many instances (see, for example, Quality Focus 1999). A holistic, 'customer-driven' approach, built up over a long period (three to four years at least), which combines strong leadership, clear goals and employee involvement, are the minimum requirements for a successful TQM (Total Quality Management) or CQI (Continuous Quality Improvement) programme.

The private sector experience of TQM is instructive: despite very strong, almost missionary beliefs in its efficacy, it has failed again and again. The combination of factors necessary to make it work have simply not been in place. And even if it had been generally successful, it has its limitations as far as its applicability to the public sector is concerned. Where it has failed it has generally been implemented top-down, is highly managerial, and lacks *active* consumer participation (Morgan and Murgatroyd 1994). It has not achieved the necessary culture change. A public sector model needs to go further, incorporating public sector values, taking a democratic approach which involves citizens and communities as well as consumers. And, if it is to be truly 'needs-led', it should combine top-down with bottom-up development and implementation (Gaster 1996a).

Other models originating in the private sector, such as the EFQM model (European Foundation for Quality Management) currently being advocated in the context of 'Best Value' and 'Modernizing Government' and BPR ('Business Process Re-engineering'), fashionable two or three years ago, have similar theoretical and practical limitations (Gaster 1996b). Nevertheless, an eclectic approach can both avoid the pitfalls and draw on the most useful and relevant aspects of these and other models, while ensuring that they are applicable to the very different ethos and setting of public services.

Whose quality?

Before looking at the policy/implementation elements of the quality model presented in Figure 3.1 above, the question of involvement needs to be considered. Who are the 'interests' or 'stakeholders', and what kind of involvement would be appropriate?

Starting with the concerns of local people, can they as users help to shape the services being delivered? How can these needs and concerns be balanced with those of the wider community? Public service quality can never simply be about 'satisfying' or 'pleasing' the 'customer', since it has wider responsibilities laid on it by society, which lead both to a range of public expectations and to a set of organizational constraints of a legal and financial nature. So it is important to consider the full range of interests that may be involved in developing and maintaining good quality in public services. The main questions are:

- Who is concerned; that is, has an 'interest' or a 'stake'?
- Who are the direct and indirect beneficiaries?
- Who is involved in ensuring and developing the quality of the service?

Within this, a key question is how to balance the complex needs, wants and demands of individuals, communities and society as a whole, with the capacity, resources, legal requirements and technical abilities of organizations and individuals responsible for achieving good quality services.

It is therefore important to think as widely as possible about who might, at some stage of a service, want or need to become engaged in service quality. It is important not to limit the debate to active participants (as the language of 'user-involvement' and consumerism does). To express this, the word 'interest' may be preferable to 'stakeholder', although in recent years it has been increasingly hard to resist the use of 'stakeholder'.

Interests can coincide – they can be 'synergistic', working together to produce more than the sum of the parts. If, however, there are major differences in culture, language, priorities or purposes, one of the elements in a negotiation is to recognize and live with the differences as well as to note the areas of common concern. Interests can also be oppressed and repressed: it then becomes the job of the manager to uncover those interests and enable them to be expressed (Williamson 1992).

Starting from the citizen

In this book, the citizen has been identified as the key stakeholder in quality. Moving away from the highly consumerist philosophy of the previous (Conservative) government, the current (Labour) government has clarified, through its policies on social exclusion and a commitment to citizenship education, that public service providers need to think beyond current users, and to involve their whole communities. This makes a lot of sense when considering quality. It allows for the inclusion of 'non-users', 'excluded users' and even 'future users', acknowledging that people have an interest in many aspects of public services, whether or not they are using them at the time. Indeed, to confine decisions or influence to current users only runs the risk of reinforcing past patterns of service delivery – the very ones that have often been found to be inappropriate or inaccessible to many people who need them.

One way of approaching this is through the concept of the 'citizen question'. This derives from work in the Nordic countries to develop 'citizen services' (Gaster and Rutqvist 2000), and is set out below:

> A 'citizen question' is a question defined by the citizen, either as a direct recipient or applicant for a service, or as an expression of wider concerns, for example about equity, access or priorities. The 'question'

can take any shape or form, ignoring present patterns of provision. It can be posed collectively or individually. Citizen questions are more likely than not to challenge present practice, and more often than not they will require an integrated response, cutting across organisational, bureaucratic and professional boundaries.

(Gaster 1996b: 5)

Individual 'citizen questions' would be questions like 'What do I do and what services can help me when I retire/become disabled/have a child/move house' and so on (the Service First Team's work in the Cabinet Office on 'life episodes' began to consider just these questions, Service First Unit 2000). *Collective* 'citizens' questions' would be posed in terms of crime and safety, local environment, 'why are there so many holes in our roads, how can we improve our area?' In all cases there is no single service that can answer these questions. In the past, they would have been 'passed round the houses'. Now there is more awareness within public service agencies of the need to respond but, so far, relatively little capacity and few incentives to do so. This – the need for cooperation in almost all aspects of service delivery – is a (*the?*) major problem for quality improvement.

How can citizens be involved and make sure their questions are answered? What rights do they have to do so?

Administrative law gives individual citizens the right to challenge decisions by statutory authorities through the use of judicial review. However, this is a complex, expensive and time-consuming process, very much a last resort. Citizens can be involved in services more constructively and continuously, through processes of participative democracy. However, their right to be involved needs to be acknowledged by service providers.

Two kinds of citizenship '*right*' can be identified. *Procedural* rights derive from a relationship – mainly as a service user – with a particular service or element of the State. They seem mainly to be expressed through the right to redress if things go wrong. *Substantive* rights emphasize the participation of the citizen in shaping the common purposes of society. They can include civil rights (to vote and pay taxes) and, more controversially, social and economic rights (to have a house or a job) (Seneviratne 1999). From these rights come *entitlements* to services, which may be received automatically, or they may have to be pursued more actively through various methods of participation and persuasion. And *duties* – to pay taxes, obey the law and, more controversially, to contribute to society – are also involved, as Tony Blair has frequently emphasized.

Although the 1991 Citizen's Charter (see Chapter 6) in practice focused more on current users of services than on citizens or communities, its introductory leaflet stated that 'We all pay for our public services through our taxes. We therefore have a *right* (our emphasis) to expect that they will do what their name suggests – serve the public.' This is a potentially useful statement, but a long way from being put into practice.

The rights derived from citizenship are particularly important for excluded groups. They can base demands to be involved not on the patronage or goodwill of the service provider, but on their own rights. Practically, citizens may find it difficult to become involved in service quality – consultation and participation tends mainly to focus on current users – and an explicit organizational commitment to *citizen* involvement is needed, aiming to improve accountability and to empower those whose voice is not normally heard.

This kind of commitment is not cost-free, and the potential benefits need to be clear. A citizen-based policy means involving 'hard to reach' and 'excluded' groups, gaining a wider perspective on what services are needed and knowing better the kind of services that will meet those needs. These benefits can then be weighed against the investment of community development and other support that will be needed, as well as the time to enable consultation and participation to take place. If this is not done, it will simply feel like an extra pressure for officers and managers struggling to respond to endless policy initiatives, in the face of reduced resources and increased demand.

Differentiating users

'Users' are not a homogeneous group. Public services come in several broad categories, which generate different kinds of relationships between service providers and service users. The seven types of service are:

1 *Universal* services provided to everyone (street sweeping, rubbish collection, environmental maintenance and improvements)
2 *Demand-led* services (housing repairs, advice, information, primary health care)
3 *Rule-based* services available to those deemed eligible (welfare benefits, council housing, shelter for the homeless, age-related health screening)
4 *Rationed* services based on resource availability or assessment of 'need' (day nursery places, home helps, housing, most forms of health and social care)
5 *Compulsory* services, aiming to benefit or protect individuals or society or both (school education, some social services, food standards and health and safety, police and prisons, sectioning under the Mental Health Act)
6 *Preventative* services (community development, youth services, community safety, environmental and public health services)
7 Services available by *choice* for all to use as they wish, sometimes for a charge (leisure services, libraries, transport).

Most public services fall into one or more of these categories. While the contracting-out process complicates consumer understanding of who is actually providing the service, the underlying nature of the services remains the same whether provided directly or through contracts.

So users of rationed services will be in a very different position (as 'applicants' or 'supplicants') from users of universal services (complainants?) and again from those being compelled by law (reluctant users) or receiving health or social care (dependants). It cannot be assumed that most of these users will assert their needs truthfully and openly to the provider, particularly when actually receiving the services: they may, as 'survivors', feel able to express their views more honestly later on, when they have less to lose.

Consumers in any case have different attitudes to public services, often highly variable. Some may trust the professionals and 'the system'. Others may be more suspicious – 'don't let them get away with it'. Nevertheless, the right to a decent, preferably high-quality service, and the right to complain if the service is not good enough, is – or should be – inalienable. The problem is that, despite the alleged growth of 'consumerism' during the 1980s and 1990s, far too many consumers do not exercise their rights and still feel fearful of what would happen if they complained. Since it is only recently that many public service workers have begun to see the public, not as a 'nuisance', but as people they are working *for* and with (as well as their paymasters), such beliefs are rather well founded. And the widespread use of the word 'customer' should not be used to disguise the fact that most people have very different relationships with the public services: exercising consumer – or 'customer' – influence by withdrawing custom and going elsewhere is not normally possible.

In addition, there are vital differences of interest between current consumers and those who are not using the service. People may not be using the service because they are not eligible or have been refused, or they are on a waiting list; or they may be unaware of their rights, ignorant of the service, or excluded through discrimination. They may also be future or past users ('survivors').

Such 'non-users' may be difficult to contact. It may seem simpler to consult current users. Yet if these are disempowered, inarticulate, young, old, poor, disturbed, geographically remote or being compelled to use the service, this too can be difficult and expensive in time and money. Nevertheless, since the alternative is only to hear the voices of the articulate and those with a grievance, it does seem important to try. The key point is to avoid simplistic and tokenistic consultation, which merely alienates those whom the public service provider is trying to involve and produces little real change (Commission on Poverty, Participation and Power 2000).

Councillors and appointed Board members

In local and central government, councillors and ministers have normally been elected on the basis of a manifesto, itself derived from national political positions: their basic values are (partly) legitimated through the election process. In the rest of the public sector – the 'Quasi-governmental organizations' (Skelcher 1998) – 'Board' representatives are appointed, some from local authorities, some from voluntary organizations, increasing numbers from business, and a residue of the 'great and the good' and/or people who put themselves forward to be selected by central government. Whether elected or selected, such people will be expected to work to 'political' values – with a small or a large 'p'.

It has been striking that quality initiatives in local government have generally been given their first impetus by managers: councillors have not been very visible in this debate (Gaster 1997). Yet councillors must have a part to play in the development of quality policies. Councillors must make strategic decisions and develop policy; they can facilitate the exercise of citizen and consumer rights; and they can act as advocates – for people in the community and for the authority as a whole (Gaster and Taylor 1993). Under the political arrangements introduced by the 1997 Labour Government (DETR 1998), they are now also expected to act in a 'scrutiny' role and as community leaders (Sullivan *et al.* 2001a).

Councillors are perhaps the only people who can legitimately bridge the gap between policy and practice, and between officers and the public, and who also have the power to bring about change. It is ultimately the councillors, in local government, who have the power and the responsibility to make the policy decisions on which the whole system rests.

Chris Skelcher (1998: 1) points out that the 70,000 men and women appointed to quasi-governmental bodies (quangos) 'take decisions on the nature, distribution, funding and prioritising of many of our public services'. Despite their weak lines of accountability, quango members are responsible for many services in just the same way as elected councillors, both as purchasers and as providers. However, while some appointees feel a sense of accountability to the public, the public has no acknowledged right to hold them to account and they have no formal methods of being 'accountable'.

Board and management committee members may be appointed to 'represent' a particular constituency or particular interests, such as black and ethnic minorities. Such Board members can be placed in a very awkward position, constrained by 'commercial confidentiality' from reporting back to those they are expected to represent. A study of Training and Enterprise Councils' policies for people from ethnic minorities (Boddy 1995) illustrated how difficult it was for black Board members either to influence policy or to relate to their local black communities.

Front-line workers

As Lipsky (1980) pointed out, in a hierarchical culture the interests of the front-line staff are different from those of staff in other parts of the organization. Devolved decision making and the flatter organizational structures increasingly favoured as part of effective public management could in time reduce some of the tensions. But involvement of front-line staff – the street-level bureaucrats – is important because they have probably the most accurate idea within the organization of the concerns of current consumers. If they are community-minded, or are natural networkers, as many front-line managers are, they will have a wider view of the needs and expectations of the communities they serve (Gaster 1995b).

In recent times, there have been many press articles about the low morale of public service workers. A paper on 'public satisfaction' published by the Performance and Innovation Unit at the Cabinet Office (Donovan et al. 2001) reports research in the private sector that makes a clear link between whether staff feel valued and whether customers are satisfied with the service. If staff do not feel valued, the service suffers and consumers are less satisfied. Recent research in the public sectors of European Union countries strongly reinforces this point (Pillinger 2001).

This is a lesson that needs to permeate thinking about public service quality. Ideally, front-line staff need to be praised and valued for providing responsive services and encouraged through constructive criticism and training to build on their strengths and to address their weaknesses. Constant public denigration, as has been palpable for many years with regard to the teaching profession, only serves to discourage new entrants and to force experienced people out. Even if, as in the recent past, the identification of 'poor' services has attracted government attention and investment, such denigration does little to improve the self-esteem of service providers. Nor does it seem to enhance the service in the eyes of users: their expectations continue to be low.

Recognizing and valuing front-line staff is important and overdue. Otherwise front-line staff may simply transmit their own feeling of helplessness to the public (James 1989). This does not mean that their views can in any way be taken to represent those of consumers and citizens. Whatever front-line staff report about consumers will have been filtered through their own values, perceptions and experience, positive and negative (Czepiel et al. 1985). As an interest group, however, they need to be genuinely regarded and listened to, in conjunction with other key groups within and outside the organization.

Trade union interests

Trades unions are often neglected in the discussion and practice of quality. In a period of major change, where jobs are under constant threat and hard-won skills appear to be challenged, industrial relations have to be particularly constructive if quality policies are not to be seen as yet another attack on public service workers. The mixed economy of social welfare has underlined the vulnerability of hard-won working conditions right across Europe (Pillinger 2001).

The 1988 Local Government Act (compulsory competitive tendering) galvanized the public sector unions into seeing quality as part of the competitive edge for direct-service organizations (Paddon 1992). The idea that providing a high-quality service might not only preserve public sector jobs but also increase job satisfaction and appreciation from the public – and, in the longer run, keep down costs through less re-work – may increase union commitment and understanding. It all depends on how the policies are introduced. The same may be said of the Best Value policy, now beginning to filter into the day-to-day work of local government and other public sector providers. Full, constructive discussion about the likely impact of quality policies on work practices, training and jobs is certainly possible.

Managers and professionals

Public service managers do not have to espouse 'business' values, but they will almost certainly be concerned with the values of efficiency and economy. These can appear to conflict with other values, such as sensitivity, flexibility and responsiveness. Whether these tensions can be constructively handled is likely to depend on the management style adopted, 'macho' or 'enabling'.

'Professionalism' – always hard to define – can be viewed positively or negatively by the outside world. Traditional professional values are now being challenged, by new business practices, by the contract culture, by the removal of restrictive practices and by crises varying from childcare cases and medical malpractice to corporate scandals. While the basic ingredients of 'professionalism' may continue to be autonomy, integrity, fairness, relationships based on trust, and agreed (by professional bodies) standards of performance, recent studies have shown that 'the roles, skills and attributes of professionals are increasingly contested and indeed challenged by the new methods of judging "performance"' (Sullivan and Gaster 2000). Professionals may bring high-quality, ethical standards and high levels of commitment to their employing organization. Or they may appear defensive, arrogant and protective of their status at the expense of the organization.

Managers and professionals are extremely important – vital – to the successful introduction and implementation of policies to improve service quality. If they are not on board, acting as change leaders and change agents (see Chapter 2), it is likely that the policies will make no progress and have no impact. It is therefore crucial for top managers and decision makers to involve managers at *all* levels, as well as the key professional groups, in developing the policy and working out how to implement it. Too often, organizational change has been stifled at the middle management level, and this is often because they have not understood the policy or seen what benefits it could bring to their own service areas.

More positively, professionalism can include the ability to think freshly about professional goals and values, and to welcome, anticipate or initiate change. Similarly, managers can and often do take up new ideas and become the 'change agents', leading (challenging?) an organization into new ways of thinking and behaving. How the organization handles this challenge – accepting it or rejecting it – will influence the decision of such visionary managers either to continue to be involved, or to withdraw and take their energies elsewhere.

Balancing the interests: a question of power and participation

If, as is argued in this book, defining and implementing quality is a matter of negotiation, it might be assumed that, once the main interest groups are defined, each will have more or less equal power. This is patently not the case.

Power comes from different sources: from position – board member, senior officer, recognized community leader; from professional status; and from the positive or negative strength of individual personalities – a leader or a bully. Power (or influence) also derives from past performance, from acknowledged citizen and consumer rights, from knowledge and from acting collectively. The latter is the power that, in relation to public services, consumer and residents' groups have been building since the 1970s. It is particularly important because it can help combat the fragility of some interest groups, especially consumers, who inherently have less power than others.

As well as acknowledging power differences, it is essential, in the absence of 'choice' or 'exit', to encourage the use of 'voice' (Hirschman 1970), not only for consumers, citizens and communities, but for other weaker groups, in particular front-line staff.

There is an increasing literature about the principles and practice of consultation and participation (see, for example, Richardson 1983; Lowndes et al. 1998; Gaster 1999a). Anyone – providers *and* users – involved in improving quality in the public services needs to be well educated in these matters. Ground rules are important: how to run a meeting, how to deal with conflict, how to network and ensure equal participation, how to support weaker or less powerful groups. Identifying key interest groups, enabling them to be effectively involved, and redressing imbalances of power are all part of the process of developing a suitable organizational culture for quality.

As noted in Chapter 2, public service managers and service practitioners will thus need many new skills for the management of quality, in particular those of consultation and participation, on top of the ability to deliver the service to the required standard.

Values and objectives: using the model for quality

Having considered the 'interests' or 'stakeholders' and what they might each bring to the question of quality, we now turn to the issue of quality itself. How, in a complex public service organization, can decision makers, managers, staff and the public understand and link the different elements identified in this model? The rest of this chapter concentrates on objectives and definitions: what kind of organization, and what kind of quality needs to be developed? Underlying these questions, often hidden and unexplored, is the important question of values. What and whose values are the drivers behind everything that the organization is doing or is striving to achieve? This, as emphasized in Chapter 1, is the starting point for the whole quality cycle.

Values in quality

The question of values covers not only how quality is defined in an organization, but how it is interpreted and, most important of all, how it is implemented. This is demonstrated through, for example, how staff and consumers are consulted, who gets listened to, the style of leadership and other cultural factors.

Values come in different shapes and sizes. Some, like equal opportunities and empowerment, are big, all-encompassing, difficult for anyone to disagree with but difficult to practise effectively and credibly. Others are more specific, relating to the particular position and role of an organization and the individuals working for it.

As the previous section of this chapter shows, different 'stakeholders' or 'interest groups' – politicians, managers, professionals, consumers or citizens – will bring different values to the question of quality. The values that dominate are likely to make a considerable difference to the kind of 'quality' experienced by the public.

At the same time, general societal values exist, which may be espoused by some or all of the stakeholders and are likely to be common between different public service organizations. In a democratic society, these values – not all of them compatible with each other – are likely to include:

- the three 'E's of economy, efficiency and effectiveness
- equity, equality and diversity
- democracy, accountability, empowerment and community orientation
- variation, standardization and choice
- working together, partnerships and cooperation.

Economy, efficiency, and effectiveness influence how organizations behave, and how they approach the question of quality. These three values need to be differentiated from each other. If 'economy' values are emphasized, high turnover and quick throughput will be the name of the game. If 'efficiency' values are emphasized, the more 'difficult' or 'hard to reach' people could receive lower priority so as to achieve short-term targets. If 'effectiveness' goals are emphasized, the impact of the service over a longer period than a single accounting year should be the prime consideration.

Equality – of opportunity and of access – focuses on needs and rights. An organization with a strong value of equality and diversity will make every effort to ensure that people *can* obtain access to assessment for the services they need. It will actively acknowledge the right of all its citizens, including those generally under-represented within the decision-making structures, to make demands, complaints and suggestions about services. It will be concerned for its own staff, ensuring that its composition reflects the local population, and acknowledging the rights and needs of employees.

Equity is a question of distribution, which can be measured and monitored: who actually uses services on the basis of assessed need (rather than demand) against agreed criteria and who does not? Do users receive the amount of service they *need*, rather than a standard amount? An organization with a strong value of equity will make sure it knows the needs of all those whom its services are intended to benefit and responds to those needs.

Equity, equality and diversity are intimately linked with the question of 'whose quality?' An organization that has values of equity and equality will have a different view of who should be consulted, involved and responded to from one which does not have those values.

Similarly, public service quality policies based on an ethos that stresses *public accountability, democracy and community*, which actively tries to involve consumers and citizens, will feel very different from a purely managerial ethos – which is what very many 'quality initiatives' are.

Standardization in the public sector used to be justified on the grounds that it is fair – 'we treat everyone in the same way'. If there was variation, it might mean that some people would get a better service than others or, put another way, that some people would get a worse service than others. This, in a publicly accountable body, was thought not to be acceptable.

Now it is recognized that treating everyone in a standard way can be very unfair. People's real needs differ enormously, and they react to similar treatment in quite different ways. Equally staff need the flexibility to respond to different needs in different ways. *Responsiveness* to needs, and *sensitivity* to and respect for people as individuals are now seen as essential ingredients for many areas of public service. They ought to lead to flexibility, choice and, the logical consequence, *variation*. The question is how to balance these new values with the old ones of fairness and equity.

In the 1990s, pressures from central government legislation and the *contract culture* left little room for *flexibility* and *initiative* among the workforce. The move towards a 'business culture' forced workers and departments back into the boxes from which, through generic working and localized working (decentralization), many were trying to escape. This trend towards re-specialization and departmentalism is a matter of concern to both local services and central government. The rhetorical emphasis now is on 'working together': *'joined-up' working, partnerships and cooperation* (Cabinet Office

1999a; DETR 1999a, 1999b). If these values come to dominate, they will lead to a very different configuration and quality of services from what exists now.

Values, then, are a key component in considering quality. Values affect what an organization does, how it works, its organizational culture and its day-to-day practice. Some values encourage involvement in and ownership of policies, others generate fear, distrust or cynicism. Some values encourage cooperation, teamwork and working with difference, while others foster competitiveness, individualism and standardization. Some values may look good on paper ('espoused values') but are not actually practised ('values in use') (Schein 1987).

Objectives

From values, objectives can be derived. It is the combination of values and objectives that defines the 'business' that public service organizations are in.

The process of developing and publicly expressing *strategic objectives* is one way of helping people know what to expect, and of helping staff know what they should do. These objectives, sometimes externally imposed, sometimes home-grown, derive from values, even if these are not explicit. They could and should be providing a clear sense of direction for the organization. They can also guide how quality is defined, and form a base-line for diagnosing whether it can be or is being achieved. Such objectives may cover the organization's role in the local community; they will take account of legal and financial constraints; and they will normally reflect any agreed priorities of politicians and managing boards. Strategic policies provide important clues in the search to define what services are for – the 'fitness for purpose' of quality. They can also provide a basis for account-ability and, by providing a starting point for internal planning, they provide a framework within which flexibility and discretion can be exercised.

Policy units tend to be at the centre, committees operate centrally, so do management boards and the like. It is often assumed that 'strategy' is decided at 'the centre' and 'operations' take place lower down or at the periphery. With the increasing interest in devolved management, and revived interest in decentralization and localization, both strategic and *operational objectives* can in fact be developed at different levels.

In decentralized organizations, *local strategies and objectives* can be developed (Gaster 1992; Taylor 2000; Sullivan *et al.* 2001). These, like corporate or central strategies, need to be placed within a framework of values, they need to take a long- or medium-term view, and they need to be operationally possible. The advantage is that they can respond to local needs and involve more people, especially local residents, in their construc-tion. Current policies for community well-being, neighbourhood manage-ment and social inclusion point the way towards further emphasis on the local dimension in future years (Social Exclusion Unit 1998, 2001).

What quality? – definitions

Once values and objectives have been identified, it is time to consider the nature of quality itself. How has the problematic issue of definition been approached by key thinkers and researchers, and how might this translate into practice?

Defining quality in public services is no easy matter. Services are not like manufactured goods, where quality processes and definitions are relatively straightforward. They involve individual transactions which, whatever the attempts to standardize them ('Have a nice day . . .') will, except in the most routine of services, each be different. Not only that, but the essence of quality in services, and especially the public services, is that these differences are an inherent part of the service itself: responding appropriately to different needs is, most people would agree, a sign of a good quality service. In the past, individuals have too often been treated as though they were machine parts on a conveyor belt.

Chapter 1 set out the differences between 'goods' and 'services', and between public and private services. Definitions of public service quality must take account of these differences. Quality has been defined in three rather different ways.

1 Focusing on the *nature of a service* and breaking it down into a variety of quality 'dimensions' (Donabedian 1980, 1982, 1985; Stewart and Walsh 1989; Walsh 1991a).
2 Focus on the *perceptions and the experiences of consumers*, expressed in the notion of 'satisfaction' (Maister 1985; Parasuraman *et al.* 1985). Quality is about closing the gaps between expectations and experience.
3 Focus on the *active involvement of the public* and other stakeholders: a negotiated or democratic definition of quality (Pfeffer and Coote 1991; Centre for the Evaluation of Public Policy and Practice 1992).

Each of these three approaches is helpful. They combine the idea of being quite specific about the characteristics needed with the need for the service to be satisfactory and the fact that some characteristics need to be 'traded off' against others: the final definition has to be 'agreed' through a process of negotiation, taking into account both producer and consumer/citizen views.

Working within the legal, financial and policy frameworks in which public services must operate, our suggested definition of quality is:

> A negotiated and agreed set of characteristics, ensuring services that are fit for purpose, delivered in a user-friendly way in a decent environment, with consistent and rising standards, and changing over time to meet new needs and aspirations.

Definitions based on the nature of the service

Working in a healthcare setting, Donabedian (1980, 1982, 1985) identified three broad dimensions of quality. These were:

1 the 'technical' dimension: the application of science and technology to a problem
2 the 'non-technical' dimension: the social/psychological interaction between practitioner and client
3 the amenities, or settings of the service.

Donabedian felt that these three dimensions of quality were interdependent. The technical efficacy of a service is directly affected by how it is delivered, while the environment – the layout of a ward, its cleanliness, the arrangement of visiting times and possibilities for privacy – can all contribute to a quicker or slower recovery (including the possibility that the environment or treatment by staff is so poor that patients discharge themselves too soon, or do not return for follow-up treatment).

For local government, John Stewart and Kieron Walsh (1989) suggested that quality should reflect both whether (or how far) it satisfies users' requirements and whether (how far) it meets the public purposes for which it was designed. They note that users' requirements may vary and be in competition with each other and that some services may never meet users' requirements since they exist to meet public (i.e. collective citizens') purposes expressed through legislation and election manifestos. They also suggested three dimensions for analysing the quality of individual services, similar to those of Donabedian.

1 The 'core service': does the service do what it is designed to do, does it meet the requirements of those for whom it is designed?
2 The 'service surroundings': is the service supported and enhanced by its surroundings or local environment?
3 The 'service relationship': does the relationship between those providing the service and those receiving it enhance the experience of the core service?

Further thinking has produced an important fourth dimension (Gaster 1999b):

4 The democratic aspect: are consumers and citizens involved, and if so, how?

The *'technical'* or *'core'* quality equates quite well with the concept of 'fitness for purpose': what is the service *for*, what does it *do* and how is it *used*? Another way of describing this is 'conformance to specification', assuming that the specification itself has been negotiated and agreed in the light of known needs, rather than the service producer's assumptions.

'Non-technical' quality – the service relationship, the social/psychological interaction between producer and consumer – is a key, possibly *the* key, to the technical quality actually achieved. The visible, most obvious

aspect is the relationship with the external consumer. However, because most services involve several different but linked stages, it also includes relationships between internal 'producers' and 'consumers'. The quality of the formal and informal relationships between colleagues, teams, departments and agencies – the 'internal customers' – along the 'service chain' (see Chapter 4) can have very positive or very negative effects on the quality of the service as a whole.

Czepiel *et al.* (1985) examined the interaction between producer and external consumer in some detail. They also considered 'process design' and relationships between the 'front line' and the 'back line'. The back line is the part of the organization that the external consumer does not see. In a contract relationship, it includes the contractor organizations.

Front-line encounters with the public are often of very high quality. The problems often arise from poor relationships with the 'back line' and other organizations (Gaster and Rutqvist 2000). Many public sector services now need to be delivered, not through traditional hierarchical and departmental networks, but through cooperation with other organizations, contractors and partners. These are each driven by their own values and objectives. How these can best be harnessed and matched for the benefit of services as a whole now constitutes an important element in 'non-technical' quality.

The *service setting* can enhance or undermine the rest of the service. It is particularly relevant to the front line and, now, to electronic government: websites, cyber-cafes and so on. It is from the experience of the organization's boundary with the outside world that the whole organization will be judged. What 'message' is being given to people encountering the organization for the first (or the 100th) time?

Richard E. Wener (1985) identified three levels of what he called the 'environmental psychology' of services. Although he, like all the contributors to Czepiel *et al.*'s book, was talking about the private sector, his ideas are clearly transferable to other sectors. The three levels are:

1 The ergonomics: heat, light, warmth, noise, furniture design: quite simply, are callers made comfortable?
2 The social ecology: is there enough privacy, are people crowded together, or are they possibly too distant from each other (behind a desk, on a platform).
3 The meaning: what are the messages being given as to the behaviour to be expected? Do the staff fear you, or are you supposed to fear them? Are you socially desirable, or not? How are the staff themselves expected to behave? Is the situation under control or is there too much stress present?

Environments influence how people feel and how they behave. A bad environmental setting can produce consumers who are angry, fearful or disoriented; in the same setting service providers can be defensive, frustrated and disorganized. None of this is likely to lead to a high-quality service. An unwelcoming setting, especially for a service that people do not necessarily want and may feel stigmatized in using (social services, prisons) will lead to low-level service encounters, where constructive listening and dialogue are impossible and contact is kept to the basic minimum.

A good environment and good non-technical quality can make the technical quality better, more effective. They are not substitutes for it. High levels of technical quality, where workers know what they are meant to be doing and do it to the best of their ability, are essential to the quality of public services. However, in all public services, the need for understanding, respect, explanation and where possible, choice, puts a high premium on the interpersonal qualities of the service, especially where resource constraints, government policies, the (recent) need for evidence of effectiveness, and the national economic situation can severely limit the services that can in practice be provided.

The quality characteristics of most services can be contained within the first three dimensions of quality described above – the technical, non-technical and 'environmental' dimensions. Starting with frameworks of service and organizational objectives, and taking into account the range of values that the organization explicitly or by implication embraces, the detailed characteristics of each service can be pragmatically defined along these dimensions.

The fourth, 'democratic' dimension applies across all three of these dimensions: all can be discussed and negotiated with users, citizens and other key stakeholders as part of the democratic process.

Definitions based on consumer expectations and/or satisfaction

Instinctively, there is a close relationship between *satisfaction* and quality: if we are satisfied, the service must have been perceived and experienced as a high-quality service. If this is the case, all that is needed is to satisfy consumers, and 'quality' is automatically assured. By this definition, the quality of public services could simply be measured through levels of stated user satisfaction, from which satisfaction 'targets' could be set (Donovan *et al.* 2001). For public services, however, three problems arise:

1 What satisfies me will not necessarily satisfy you, because I might not have been looking for the same things from the service.
2 'Satisfaction scores' are therefore difficult to interpret, and cannot easily be used to identify possible service improvements.
3 Many public services (see list above, p. 45) cannot by their nature be seeking consumer 'satisfaction'. There is even the danger of seeking popularity and lack of hassle at the cost of other public purposes and values.

There is a strong relationship between need, *expectations* and satisfaction. Needs create expectations, based both on perceptions and on direct experience (Maister 1985). If both needs and expectations are properly understood, action can be taken to create accurate or realistic expectations, not so much to manipulate people to feel 'satisfied' (though that is a danger), but to close the gap between expectations and experience.

Kano *et al.* (1984) categorized needs as 'basic', 'expressed' and 'unanticipated'. Service providers' responses were respectively categorized as 'expected', 'wanted' and 'exciting'.

- *Integral, 'basic'* needs are generally unnoticed by users, as those are the assumed responses that may be technical and defined by experts, for example, that all safety checks on an aeroplane have been made before take-off.
- *'Expressed'* needs are those identified by the consumer. They must be heard and understood by the service provider so as to develop a response, which should also include a response to unexpressed basic needs. Desired responses, which are foremost in the user's mind, are generally functional and symbolic. They will have strongly contributed to the decision to engage in the activity, for example, the aeroplane takes off and lands on time and luggage is intact.
- *Unanticipated* needs are identified through responses over and above those wanted and expected. These may be exciting for suppliers to pursue and can elicit an excited response from users, so long as the integral basic and expressed needs are met, for example, the in-flight service provides choice and variety not previously experienced or anticipated. Satisfaction with this aspect will be diminished if the flight proves unsafe, arrives late and/ or luggage is damaged or lost.

Only the meeting of expressed needs has the potential consistently to achieve mutual satisfaction, underlining the importance of encouraging articulation of needs by users and their representatives. If basic needs remain unmet, the risk of falling into the pit of dissatisfaction is forever present, irrespective of other needs that may be met. When unanticipated needs are met in addition to those expected and wanted, customer satisfaction is maximized (Kennedy 1991).

Yet levels of 'satisfaction' can differ dramatically between population groups. High levels of satisfaction can simply be the result of low expectations, or the 'halo' effect of being treated well, even if you do not get what you want. This kind of 'satisfaction' does not lead to service improvement, and indeed can make the service producer complacent. Conversely, low levels of satisfaction may reflect high and possibly unrealistic expectations.

People most likely to say they are 'satisfied' (Calman 1987; Craig 1990; Beaumont 1992) are:

- older people, women and those who are married
- lower socio-economic groups
- minority groups (ethnic, social and physical).

These characteristics equate with the least influential and those most in need and dependent on the service (Hardy and West 1994).

The 'dissatisfied' tend to be disproportionately influential (Locker and Dunt 1978) and most likely to complain (Calman 1987; Craig 1990; Hall *et al.* 1990; Allen 1992). They are:

• higher socio-economic groups with higher expectations and capacity
• carers, who will fight more for a third-party than for self
• young users who are less tolerant of poor services
• those who were refused what they felt it was their right to expect.

The characteristics of the dissatisfied are significant. Each of these groups is likely to increase in size in the light of demographic, epidemiological, social and political change. Of particular note are the carers, who will form an increasing part of health and social care provision within the policy of community-based care.

Although 'voice' is virtually the only option for the dissatisfied in public services, complaints reflect only the tip of the iceberg. For example, 40 per cent of NHS patients have wanted to complain at some time, but only 4 per cent took action (Newman and Pyne 1995) – but *all* the dissatisfied probably relay their story to at least ten other people. Some reasons why so many dissatisfied people fail to complain include their own perceived powerlessness (it won't make any difference if I do), barriers (of knowledge, discrimination, procedures), personal reasons (not a complainer, other problems) and low expectations (all services are like this anyway). It is unclear whether deciding to complain is or is not linked to the seriousness or consequences of the event (Cole 1994; Mulcahy and Tritter 1994; Williams 1994). Individuals seem to have a personal tolerance level – the actual nature of the final straw is probably irrelevant.

Building on the idea that satisfaction and actual experience often do not match, the Parasuraman-Zeithaml-Berry explanation of service quality (1985) identified key gaps in the organization of services that would affect their ultimate quality (see Figure 3.2). Because services are intangible, heterogeneous and largely inseparable from the client (the client affects the service and is part of it), they suggest that attitudes, expectations and perceptions are all crucial both to the final outcome and to the process of service delivery. These attitudes, perceptions and expectations are formed in many different ways, and affect both consumers and, at a series of stages, the service producers. At *each* stage, there may be a gap between expectations, perceptions and the ability to deliver the right service.

The more often – or the longer – a service is used, the smaller will be the gap between what people expect and what they actually get. This does not in itself define satisfaction, of course, since expectations are themselves moulded by previous experience. So a previous bad experience can lead to an expectation or a fear that similar treatment will be meted out next time. And expectations, even those based on knowledge and

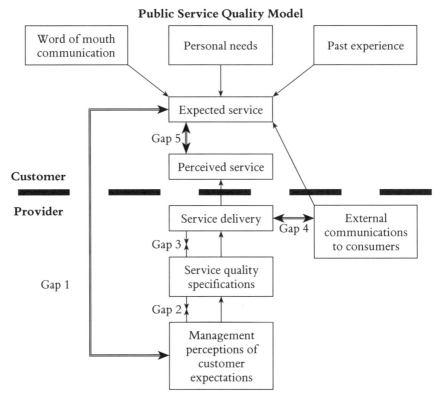

Figure 3.2   The Parasuraman-Zeithaml-Berry 'gaps' model of quality.
Source: Parasuraman *et al.* 1985.

experience of the service, may still be low: the service may be historically of poor quality (does not meet its specification), or consumers may have low self-esteem.

Also, feelings are important. Services are often sought at a time of maximum vulnerability. This affects both expectations and perceptions: you may expect little, be unable to assert what rights you have, but are disproportionately grateful if anything is done at all. It is only after the service has been received, when you have left hospital or had your home repaired, that the sense of powerlessness, dependence and gratitude may be shed.

Who should define public service quality? The democratic approach

In the private sector, the main aim of quality improvement policies is to gain competitive edge. The focus can be relatively simple: maximizing customer satisfaction by meeting their requirements (Oakland 1989).

In the public sector, which is paid for by, and has duties to the wider community, and where 'customers' cannot normally take their custom elsewhere, the picture is far more complicated. It is not simply a matter of meeting expressed needs, but of finding out unexpressed needs, setting priorities, allocating resources and publicly justifying and accounting for what has been done.

The first half of this chapter analysed the array of 'interests' involved in public services. The idea that quality definitions should be negotiated becomes self-evident. It is all the more important because different expectations and perceptions affect the very survival of public services. If they are not known or understood, no one will defend them.

A debate about what constitutes the quality of a service makes explicit the fact that not all needs can be satisfied. It also clarifies the actual nature of the service, including its 'non-technical' characteristics and its 'service setting'. It is a process that could make uncomfortably clear what are the real priorities of each party to the negotiation, but could also lead to honest and clear agreements, and a sense of ownership of the result. 'Ownership' cannot guarantee that a policy will be successfully implemented, but the overwhelming consensus among quality 'gurus' and writers on organizational change is that implementation is seriously impeded if commitment and understanding have not been sought.

In principle, then, the definition of quality could be negotiated with users and citizens. In practice, there are some obvious difficulties, not least the possibility of 'participation fatigue', where voluntary and community groups are constantly being requested to send a representative to every working party in sight. The time and cost of participation is a real problem for any organization involved in it. It is far greater for those with few resources, dependent on volunteers or a few precariously paid staff (Martin and Gaster 1993).

Conclusion

This chapter has introduced a model that can be used both to draw together the key elements of service quality, and to help identify the main 'interests' or 'stakeholders' who need to become involved.

The importance of 'values' as a starting point for considering service quality in a single organization has been emphasized. These, if they are made explicit and fully debated between the stakeholders, provide a sound basis for defining strategic objectives and, from there, how quality itself can be defined.

However, it is not easy to define quality, and no consensus exists. The 'best fit' seems to be a combination of the three 'dimensions' of quality: technical ('what?'); the non-technical ('how?'); and the environmental ('where?'). And because of the nature of public services and the need for 'voice' (not just in the form of complaints), a fourth, 'democratic' dimension needs to be added: can the *public* now be the driving force behind the definitions and practice of good service quality?

In this context, the notion of 'satisfaction' has to be approached cautiously. There is often a gap between expectations and perceptions or experience, and what people really mean when they say they are 'satisfied' needs to be critically examined.

There is, then, a need for dialogue and negotiation between the main parties to service production and consumption. This includes not only immediate consumers, but also the wider community. Because public services cannot meet all basic and expressed needs or demands, 'trade-offs' are needed between quality characteristics. Public service organizations make the ultimate decisions, but their decisions will have greater legitimacy, ownership and commitment if they are democratic and participative.

Public service managers face a whole range of dilemmas and contradictions when trying to improve the quality of their services, not least because of the economic and political climate in which they have to survive. They need to be clearer than ever about the nature of their service, about their 'stakeholders', about the quality characteristics that need to be improved or conserved, and about the public sector values and objectives that inform the negotiations about what is important. Having achieved clarity of values, purpose and how to define quality, they also need to be able to put it into practice. Implementation, and how service quality can be assessed and reviewed, are the subjects of the next two chapters.

4

Implementing quality

Lucy Gaster and Amanda Squires

Introduction

The aim of this chapter is to enable public service managers to think about implementing quality policies in their own services. It extends beyond the stage in the model for quality (presented in Figure 3.1 in the previous chapter) where values, strategic objectives and definitions have been tackled, to the phases of diagnosis and implementation. It considers how to analyse existing approaches and systems for implementing quality policies, and suggests some models which could be helpful in practical implementation.

Discussions of 'implementation' are bedevilled, like so much of the debate on quality, by problems of definition and language. This is important because, as discussed, so many quality *systems* (that is, a set of methods and tools) have been confused with quality *principles* (that is, the overall philosophy within which specific systems, methods and initiatives may be deployed). There is, then, a hierarchy of action for quality management, from individual initiatives to corporate culture, through which successful organizations will travel. In this chapter, the aim is to be as clear as possible about which level is meant. The definitions are given in Table 4.1.

For example, the route of travel for an organization might be that based on individual *initiatives* (surveys, complaints analysis) from which the board formulates a *policy* to pursue quality management. Research could indicate that the *principles* of Total Quality Management are compatible with the organizational culture, and that of the various possible *approaches* to TQM, that developed by Deming is the most suitable. A *programme* is

Table 4.1   Implementing quality management: five levels

Level	Definition
Policy	The corporate decision to implement quality management throughout an organization.
Principles	The philosophy within which action is taken for quality management, e.g. TQM, CQI or organization specific.
Approach/ system	A set of activities designed to put the philosophy into practice, e.g. quality control, quality assurance, Deming's quality cycle. Off-the-shelf or a locally designed *combination* of methods may be used to implement specific parts of the approach, e.g. external consultant's own system, ISO 9000.
Programme	The organizational structure, responsibilities, procedures, processes, training and resources for implementing the approach.
Initiatives	One-off ideas, projects, tools and methods to solve particular problems, e.g. surveys, customer care.

Adapted from Pike and Barnes 1996.

then developed for communication, training and appointment of departmental leads to take the approach forward. The specific tools and techniques to be used may already be *in situ* (surveys, complaints analysis) but may need revision as well as expansion to include more staff. Training in additional tools and techniques may also be needed.

Most quality systems embraced within the public sector since the early 1990s originated in, or were adapted from the private sector. When these were developed during the 1930 to 1970s, their main context was manufacturing. Their main purpose was to combine proven initiatives into a programme to identify 'failure', to reduce variance and to maximize standardization within the prescribed specification. Later, the combined results of the programmes developed by, and associated with the so-called quality gurus, led to an organizational philosophy aiming to encourage all staff actively to strive towards improvement of the product so as to 'exceed customer expectations'.

The question has to be asked whether quality management developed for the private sector can be successfully transferred to the public sector? Because of the differences between the public and private sectors discussed in Chapter 2, caution is needed when considering what is transferable between sectors and what is not. This leaves wide open the opportunity for developments specifically for the public sector.

The problem is compounded by a shortage of detailed and systematic research into whether quality systems or programmes, once introduced, do or do not improve the actual quality of the service. In the public services, research has tended to test users' opinions, without relating these to service production or quality systems or to the views of other stakeholders; or the characteristics of different quality approaches have been analysed (British Quality Foundation 1996; Cabinet Office 1999c); or the number of organizations introducing specific quality approaches and initiatives has been counted, again without relating them to the service produced (Local Government Management Board 1993, 1996).

Recent research looked at the impact of the 'Excellence' model in the public sector. This model (see Annex 4.1) was strongly endorsed by the Cabinet Office (see also Chapter 6), but the research concentrated more on the processes and problems of its introduction and its organizational impact than on the effects of the use of the model on the quality of the services produced (PricewaterhouseCoopers 2000). Results for the public sector were not yet available and could not be assessed. Similarly, the relationship between the Excellence model and the introduction of the Best Value regime in local government (see Chapter 7) was examined by the Improvement and Development Agency (IDEA 2001), but, again, the conclusion was that the organizational impact (positive and negative) could not be readily assessed, and it was too soon to say whether it had improved service delivery.

In the private sector, it is equally difficult to find evidence of the direct *effect* of a specific quality system or programme on the actual products, goods or services. Implementation has largely been a matter of faith, even though the beneficial effects on internal costs and profits achieved by 'getting it right first time' could be a major benefit in itself – to the producer, if not also to the consumer.

It is therefore important to consider the issue of transferability as objectively as possible, taking into account the nature of public services, local circumstances and the need to keep 'the citizen' at the centre.

Assessing quality activities

Quality activities designed to improve services in some way, whether explicitly under the heading of 'quality' or not, come in many shapes and forms. Sometimes they take place within an encompassing policy, sometimes they are the result of individual or departmental enthusiasms and values. In order to make sense of them, and to help decide which can be transferred into a particular public service context, the following questions can be asked.

Is the quality programme or system underpinned by values consistent with those on which the definition of quality is based?

A quality system loses credibility if values are inconsistent. For example, in the early days, many 'customer care' programmes fell by the wayside or were implemented in the face of tremendous staff cynicism because front-line staff were asked to value 'customers' while they themselves, as *internal* 'customers', felt ignored and under-valued. Similarly, local authorities and other purchasers often require contractors or grant-aided voluntary organizations to have in place quality systems and monitoring which they do not themselves have.

Are the objectives clear? What are the intended improvements, and are these (reasonably) consistent with other organizational objectives?

Objectives for quality management may be obscure or inconsistent with other strategic objectives. They may derive from the latest management fashion, from the performance requirements of top managers (to get a tick in the box), or from external forces such as the demands or expectations of central government (see Chapters 2 and 6). If this is the case, they are likely to be perceived as tokenistic, an add-on set of activities with a narrow range of potential beneficiaries, among whom may or may not number the public.

Does the quality approach/system arise from an organizational diagnosis?

Does the approach/system build on strengths and address weaknesses that actually exist? Does it acknowledge the constraints placed on most front-line staff, or the skill and commitment that many staff already bring to their work as a matter of course? Is it, in other words, 'fit for purpose'? Systems imported wholesale from outside may not take account of specific circumstances, particular existing culture, organizational capacity and competing initiatives, and run the risk of failing to build on previous work inside the organization.

What sort of timescales are involved?

Short-termism can lead to early judgements and early disappointment. Clarity about planned timescales helps to reduce uncertainty and to understand what is achievable at different stages.

Which key interests have been or should be involved at each stage of implementation – and how?

Policies and programmes for quality management by definition imply the need for change. It is the staff who must take responsibility for such change, so their involvement is essential.

Other interests need to be brought together – a 'stakeholder analysis', in current jargon – not merely as an intellectual or token exercise but as a practical measure. However, time is needed to develop group cohesion and to provide support to certain stakeholders (users and front-line staff, voluntary organizations and community groups) so as to balance different levels of power, different expectations and experience (see Chapter 3). Mutual trust and understanding need to emerge before real progress on standard setting, service design and monitoring or policy advice can be made.

Where is leadership and support coming from?

External consultants have often been used to develop programmes to introduce new systems. They will have been very enthusiastic about 'their' system. When they leave, the project may collapse for lack of internal leadership and because other agendas encroach (Morgan and Everitt 1990). Leadership and support from politicians, board members and managers are essential for giving staff the confidence to try out new techniques, to 'make mistakes' without undue blame and to be clear about the overall purpose and potential benefit of what they are trying to do.

What aspect of service is the quality programme intended to improve?

Quality activities need to cover both the full policy/implementation cycle (Figure 3.1) and the four dimensions of quality – technical, interpersonal, environmental (ambience) and democratic – suggested earlier (Chapter 3). New systems may be presented as a panacea – the introduction of BS 5750/ ISO 9000 for example. Later on, they can be seen for what they are: a starting point only. Particular approaches will suit the needs of an organization at a particular time, but their limitations, potential benefits (and costs), intended coverage and links with longer-term strategies need to be carefully considered.

Are measuring, monitoring and evaluation systems and tools consistent with the rest of the programme?

Considerable risks of distortion exist if too much emphasis is placed on quantitative indicators or on the requirements of external registration, measurement and audit tools applicable to different services. Measurement (the collection of data for performance indicators) may be – and often has been – the first 'quality' activity in an organization. Too often this process has been disconnected from the question of what sort of services consumers and citizens really need or want, or what quality standards would be realistic and achievable. Measurement then becomes a 'game', a tickbox exercise and not a comprehensive 'quality' activity.

Off-the-shelf quality systems and approaches

Systems for quality management may be 'off the shelf' or they may be 'home-grown'. In the early 1990s, when people in the public sector were only just beginning to consider 'quality' in detail, there was a great temptation to try to apply ready-made systems. At that time, in the absence of in-house approaches, tools and techniques, many people thought there was a good chance that change would be achieved by these methods. In the health service, some government monies were made available for a succession of initiatives (see Chapter 8). In most other public services, the costs of trying out new methods had to be absorbed within those services. A leap of faith (reinforced in some cases by contract conditions) was required for what was sometimes a considerable investment. The reward would be competitive edge, the winning of contracts, better services, better morale and improved public satisfaction.

Three reasons why this considerable amount of work appears to have produced relatively little public recognition (see Chapter 1) are:

1 Too many initiatives and systems were introduced as part of a management fashion, rather than being embedded in, or relevant to, what the organization was trying to achieve.
2 They were too dependent on enthusiastic individuals, and too isolated from other teams, divisions and departments: very few public service agencies could be found which were taking a corporate approach to quality improvement (but see Gaster 1997; Homa and Bevan 1997; and Chapter 14).
3 They only covered part of the work needed to achieve real change, focusing for example on front-line behaviour ('customer care'), management processes (quality assurance), etc., but not on the organization, on stakeholders' interests, or on the service process as a whole.

Many of the ready-made systems were in fact less 'ready-made' than at first appeared. Different interpretations of Total Quality Management, Business Process Re-engineering, or quality assurance have meant that, for politicians, workers, managers or service users trying to understand and weigh up the pros and cons of different philosophies and approaches, there are real difficulties in making rational decisions. Nevertheless, each approach contains some common features, which are summarized in Annex 4.1 to this chapter. (Readers are also referred to the Appendix at the end of this book, 'The language of quality', which sets out many of the terms common in discussions of quality in the public services since the mid-1980s.)

Quality control

Quality control, based on post-inspection to identify faults and 'mistakes', was the start of the manufacturing quality revolution. It can be useful, but

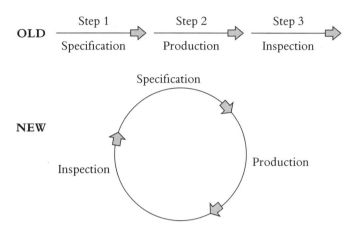

Figure 4.1 Linear and circular quality control.
Source: Shewhart 1939.

is limited when it comes to services: the fault or mistake in a product can be rectified, but the service 'mistake', once done, may be difficult to undo. This affects people's lives, and the consolation (or trauma) of being able to make a complaint or to take the authority to court may be trivial compared with the damage done, especially when the user is at their most vulnerable. It is also expensive, since it assumes that faults will happen. The cost of quality control therefore includes the cost of 'putting things right' – that is, doing things twice.

It is important, however, to be able to learn from the 'mistakes' identified in the quality control process. As Figure 4.1 shows, information needs to be fed back into the production process (the 'circular' approach), rather than simply accepting that there will be a certain percentage of errors, but then doing nothing about it, except perhaps to apologize or, in the case of manufacturing, to replace the faulty good (the 'linear' approach).

Quality assurance

Quality assurance is 'broadly the prevention of quality problems through planned and systematic activities (including documentation)' (Oakland 1989: 10). This approach has largely been equated with certificated systems of, first, BS 5750 and then ISO 9000, which tend to emphasize systems and procedures, rather than outputs and outcomes. Caricatured, this can mean that perfect systems can be developed – to produce goods or services that nobody wants or needs.

Certificated systems of quality assurance are expensive to introduce and maintain and, while they have been widely used in trading standards departments and in blue-collar services where routine actions dominate, they may place far too great a burden on small contractors, such as voluntary organizations. Indeed, the voluntary sector has developed its own quality assurance system, 'PQASSO' (Charities Evaluation Service 1997), which allows structured development over time in a way that is consistent with voluntary sector values and practical constraints.

In services provided through contracts, certification of a supplier's quality assurance system by an independent accreditation body gives assurance to the purchaser (Wall 1995), reducing the need to do their own inspection of the area covered (Moores 1993). The supplier's costs may be increased, but the purchaser makes a saving on their own inspection costs.

However, the certificated quality system chosen needs to meet the requirements of all participants – purchasers, suppliers and service users. With quality assurance, there is a major risk that the process of documenting procedures (this is a large part of the popular ISO 9000 quality assurance system) will fossilize existing ways of working and even lead to the return of debilitating bureaucracy (Healey 1996). However, this can be avoided through active staff participation, while the actual process of certification can help to develop an organizational culture that would support a broad approach to quality improvement (Scrivens 1995).

Quality assurance does not have to be carried out through a set system such as the International Standard. It can be internally developed, to suit the needs and situation of each organization. While it can in practice be a mechanistic process aiming to satisfy contractual clients rather than service consumers, it could be developmental and preventative, ensuring the analysis of the service process, identifying procedures to ensure consistency, and providing staff with appropriate training and tools for self-evaluation.

Total quality management

Total Quality Management (TQM) is a philosophy that aims to inspire the behaviour and interactions of people in work situations, through their attitudes, aspirations and motivations, to produce a good quality product or service (Pike and Barnes 1996). It has evolved from the combined approaches of quality 'gurus', which were analysed by Bendell (1992) and are set out in Table 4.2.

As pointed out in the Appendix, TQM, even more than QC or QA, can be interpreted differently. This means that comparisons between organizations claiming to be implementing 'TQM' will probably come up with different processes and behaviours depending on the approach they are pursuing. Nevertheless, some common elements of TQM exist. They include (Morgan and Murgatroyd 1994):

- top management commitment, promoting a culture of quality, employee empowerment, team working and a long-term perspective

- organizational commitment to change the culture
- consistency of management message.

The time needed to achieve and sustain such cultural change is estimated as being between five and ten years (Peters and Waterman 1991).

Table 4.2 Common factors of TQM advocated by quality gurus

1 Management commitment and employee awareness	Deming, Peters, Crosby, Moller
2 Facts and figures including costs of quality	Juran, Crosby
3 Cross-functional teams	Peters, Crosby, Ishikawa
4 Tools for problem solving and continuous improvement	Ishikawa
5 Technical tools	Taguchi, Shingo
6 Management tools	Crosby, Ishikawa, Fiegenbaum
7 Customer focus	Juran, Crosby, Peters, Deming

Source: Bendell 1992.

TQM was the subject of many missionary claims in the 1990s (Morgan and Murgatroyd 1994). Nevertheless, it has been difficult to find working examples of successful implementation in the UK private sector and few, if any, public sector organizations have explicitly embraced it, perhaps because it is so comprehensive, long-term and undoubtedly difficult to put into practice. An exception is the National Health Service, where TQM was launched alongside the 1990 NHS reforms (see Chapter 8). Research by the Audit Commission indicates that, among managers and at least a proportion of the clinical NHS workforce, there was considerable success in transmitting and learning the concepts of quality management. However, the research found that 'there is little firm evidence of returns in terms of better patient care' (Foster *et al.* 1994).

The main difficulty with TQM is the lack of active involvement of 'customers' (consumers and citizens) and the need for continuous, high-level support and commitment. This is difficult at a time when public sector managers are under great and continuous pressure from a never-ending stream of central government policy initiatives and performance requirements. There are also particular problems in that fluctuating political influence affects clarity of goals, compromising the long-term perspective necessary for the TQM philosophy and for measuring the effects (Osborne and Gaebler 1993; Redman *et al.* 1995).

Continuous quality improvement

'Continuous quality improvement' (CQI) is yet another 'comprehensive' quality philosophy. Pike and Barnes (1996) use the term synonymously with TQM. Reynolds (1994) differentiates the two, seeing TQM as a philosophy for *managers* to meet *customers'* needs and CQI as a philosophy for *everyone* to meet *all stakeholders'* needs. Reynolds also suggests that the exclusion of 'management' in the headline language of 'CQI' may make it more palatable to some staff, giving it a more dynamic vision: refreshing the concept of quality with a new title may even revive those who have become complacent about TQM. The use of the term 'CQI' could encourage professional staff to acknowledge changing needs and to work on continuous improvement of their autonomous practice. An alternative view is that the appearance of yet another change of language may produce despondency among staff, tired of an avalanche of 'new' quality policies, approaches and initiatives. Messner (1998) has pointed out that culture change remains a requirement, whichever term is used.

Customer care

'Customer care' could not be described as a quality system or philosophy like QC, QA or TQM. However, it has been prominent within public services for some time as the first, main and sometimes only quality initiative undertaken to improve services, and needs to be considered here. We would suggest that, taken in conjunction with other approaches, and embedded as part of wider organizational change, it can have considerable value in changing how the public are treated at the front line, as well as internal customers throughout the organization. However, it is an activity where a 'good idea' has often suffered from the way it was put into practice.

The introduction of a customer care programme in a particular service or organization could signal the beginning of a process aiming to change public services from being 'producer-led' to being 'consumer-led'. In the early 1990s, however, 'customer care' training was introduced top-down and targeted solely on front-line staff. Thinking deeply about 'quality' as a concept was not on the menu. Such programmes therefore tended to put the front-line staff under the spotlight, made them feel that management was more concerned about valuing the public than valuing them, and failed to address underlying problems in internal systems and back-up which would have enabled them to provide a better service.

The effect was simply to teach staff how to be better gatekeepers. It set them up as scapegoats for failings elsewhere in the organization. In addition, consumers, who were assumed to be passive rather than active, were not involved in contributing to the training. Senior managers sometimes appeared to be more concerned to enable staff to minimize trouble from the public, rather than creating a culture where public needs and demands were both listened and responded to. All this led to considerable cynicism among staff, for most of whom this was the first experience of anything under the 'quality' label. The unfortunate consequence was that they were sceptical of, and resistant to, later initiatives, some of which might have had a real impact on services.

More positively, some customer care programmes were part of a wider 'learning organization' strategy, including consultation with consumers, standard-setting procedures and action to remedy failure. And it is likely that some public sector customer care training programmes triggered new thinking about services, which could have led to a more comprehensive approach to quality improvements.

The 'Excellence' model

The Excellence model is an approach that has been strongly promoted by central government, both for overall quality improvement in the public services (see Chapter 6) and for implementing the Best Value policy in local government (see Chapter 7). It is a model that was developed by the European Foundation for Quality Management, publicized in the UK by the British Quality Foundation: its formal title is the 'EFQM Excellence model' or the 'Business Excellence model'. The model (see Figure 4.2) contains nine elements, which together are thought to make up the totality of service delivery. They are divided between 'enablers' (leadership, policy and strategy, people (staff) management, resources and processes) and 'results' (customer satisfaction, 'people' (staff) satisfaction, impact on society and 'business results' or 'key performance' results). Each of these elements is assigned a percentage, to illustrate its importance in the whole picture.

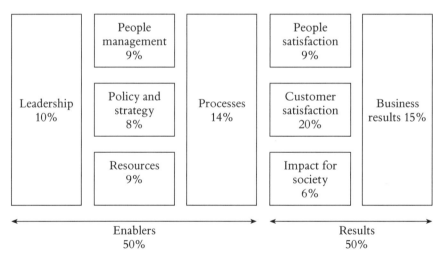

Figure 4.2 The Business Excellence model. The European model for TQM.

The main difficulty with this model is the spurious number-crunching. Also, while it has been somewhat over-sold as a complete system, it is in fact not much more than a diagnostic tool. This may be helpful as a starting point, but it will certainly not improve service quality on its own. A great deal of action, using a wide range of approaches and quality tools, also needs to be incorporated. Like most of the other systems and tools described in this chapter, the Excellence model also runs the danger of becoming purely a management tool, unconnected with other stakeholders and implemented top-down, without adequate staff or public understanding or involvement.

Horses for courses: matching the approach with the organization

Each organization needs to understand the range of different approaches that might be pursued. Preventive action is, in the long run, cheaper than corrective action, but in practice a mixture of approaches will be needed at different times or for different services. For example, a health care organization may pursue TQM by using the Juran approach (see Chapter 12). Another organization, such as local government, can aim to develop organizational and corporate quality using the Deming approach (see Chapter 14). Both will have considered the suitability of each approach for their own organizational culture.

Despite the differences, three common features of most quality implementation systems can be identified:

1 cultures
2 structures
3 techniques.

Each of these is now discussed in turn.

Organizational culture

The culture of an organization is represented through the values and customs to which all employees are expected to conform, as much through techniques of socialization as through more explicit training and induction programmes.

A study of four local authorities taking a corporate approach to quality improvement (Gaster 1997) identified the following features of a 'culture for quality':

- Sustained commitment from the top
- Communicating with and valuing staff
- Communicating with and valuing the public
- Seeing 'change' as a normal part of life
- A desire to do things better
- Willingness to experiment, to say you do not know the answer and to put things right

- Taking responsibility
- Making connections, working across boundaries.

All writers on quality, whether writing about the public, private or voluntary sectors, have stressed the need for an appropriate culture. The first step is to decide to move away from a blaming, macho and hierarchical management style. The second step is to analyse the present culture in some detail – existing tools for problem solving and organizational analysis can be useful here (see Annex 4.2 at the end of this chapter). The third step is to consider what approach to take.

A 'tight-loose' approach (Figure 4.3) encourages devolved and decentralized decision making within a well-specified policy framework. It thus incorporates the basic features of a desirable culture. This ensures that the organization knows where it is going, but at the same time frees staff to act on their own initiative, to experiment, innovate and self-evaluate.

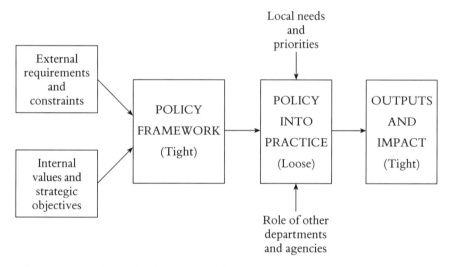

Figure 4.3 The 'tight–loose' model.

The 'loose' part of the 'tight-loose' model is where implementation of policies takes place. This requires decision-making authority to be devolved to the level nearest the point of decision (the subsidiarity principle). Staff – and the public where democratic decision-making structures have been developed – need to be supported, trained and trusted to make decisions, acting within the 'tight' policy framework in order to achieve 'tight' outcomes, both of which may be specified internally and/or externally.

A tight-loose culture takes time and energy to develop. Management–employee relationships need to be developed through collaboration, working in teams and multidisciplinary groups, and with an 'enabling' style of leadership. Clear commitment, understanding and a sense of direction from the top are vital, otherwise groups can become isolated and disheartened. A culture of mutual trust, where communication is open, honest and explicit, is vital.

The tight-loose model appears to have considerable spin-offs, not least the increase in confidence and accountability of front-line workers and managers and the release of energy at the top to think about policy, strategy and the long-term future.

Organizational structures for quality

The structures within which public services have been delivered in the past have tended to be large, divided into departments and sections, bureaucratically and/or professionally hierarchical, and difficult for the outsider to penetrate, whether as consumer, resident or potential co-worker. Quality improvement in the public sector will only succeed when departments break down or cross these traditional barriers, so as to make the service to the consumer more comprehensible, better integrated and more sensitive to the needs and desires of those who pay for the services – the public.

As noted in the discussion of 'culture' above, it is also important, through the 'tight-loose' model, to maximize the decision-making authority of those with responsibility for delivering a service or part of a service and to gain the committed involvement of staff. Finally, it is vital to achieve some form (or forms) of participation by the public.

A well-established organizational structure that encompasses these characteristics is 'decentralization'. This has evolved in UK local government and to some degree in the health service (Ham 1992) since the early 1980s, applying to sub-localities or neighbourhoods, and involving localized, integrated service commissioning and delivery, coordinated local management, and new structures for public participation and representative democracy (area committees, neighbourhood forums). It can be argued that a close relationship exists between quality, decentralization and devolution, since these policies are all aiming to design and deliver services most appropriate to citizens' needs and to involve citizens in that process (Gaster 1991a, 1996a; Gaster and Rutqvist 2000). However, decentralization is not a panacea, whatever form it takes (and many different models are possible). It is a means to an end, not an end in itself. It may be one of several options available to meet different policy objectives (Gaster and Hoggett 1993).

Local offices – one-stop shops – can provide services that cover part of, or the whole of, a service chain (see below), depending on the length of the chain and the facilities provided locally. Workers in local offices or local management structures will need to be good at bridging organizational gaps and making the links along the chain. This requires new skills – or rather, a new combination of skills – such as negotiating, influencing, coordinating, managing, working with politicians and enabling public participation (Gaster 1995b; Sullivan *et al.* 2001).

Another structural method is to set up a completely new organization, formed by merging two or more former services, which it is now recognized will be better delivered as a single service. Many structural reorganizations, in local and central government, in health services and elsewhere in the public sector, have in the past tried to do this. Unfortunately, many of these initiatives were blighted, partly because the objectives were not clear or understood by staff or the public, partly because little attempt was made to merge the former cultures or to develop a new one that would carry implementation forward.

A current example of 'new' organizations is the 'Care Trust', where social services and health services are being brought together to deliver community-based services in a way that has not happened before. Such an innovation could be really helpful to patients, carers and staff alike, but only if it is accompanied by cultural and organizational development. Then the spirit as well as the letter of the reforms may perhaps be put into place. But this, as most structural reorganizations have found, is not at all easy.

A structural analysis tool (see Annex 4.2) may be helpful in understanding the current structure and deciding on the necessary changes.

However, changing the structure will not be enough on its own. As already noted, the culture needs to change too, and staff and managers need a working set of tools and techniques to enable them to deliver the hoped-for improved services.

Quality tools and techniques

Within any quality system, different techniques and processes may be used (see Annex 4.2 and Table 4.3). They can serve three main purposes:

1 diagnosis of what is required
2 maintaining quality
3 application of 'best practice', learning from others.

For *diagnosis*, writers on TQM and continuous improvement stress the use of *problem-solving* techniques to assess the present state of play and to identify which problems can most profitably and practically be tackled (see also Chapter 2). Some of these techniques are identified in Table 4.3. They can be particularly useful at an early, diagnostic stage in the quality process, though it may be necessary later to go back to the diagnostic and problem-solving activities, as a check on what is happening, or if something is not working out as planned.

For the *maintenance* of quality, *quality working groups* can be particularly useful in bringing together the main stakeholders, harnessing ideas and

Table 4.3 An analysis of tools and techniques for implementing quality improvement

Technique	Type of activity	Characteristics	Problems tackled
Problem solving	SWOT analysis	Analyses strengths, weaknesses, opportunities and threats	Analyses current level of 'quality' and factors affecting possible improvements
	Pareto analysis	Method of identifying chronic problems underlying poor service (the 20 per cent of factors causing 80 per cent of the problems)	Identifies priority areas for action
	Bar charts, scatter diagrams	Counts incidences of identified activity/product	Identifies variations from the norm
	Brainstorming	Gather group ideas quickly, without qualifying comments	Helps group think about possible solutions, develop imaginative options
	Process mapping	Charts the individual processes through which each act of service has to pass	Makes explicit what is happening, may identify unnecessary actions or provide the basis for suggesting redesign
	Fishbone diagram	Maps men, methods, machines, materials used in production process	Used to suggest possible remedial action in any of the four areas
	Force field analysis	Identifies organizational positive and negative forces and their respective strengths affecting the ability to achieve change	Identifies areas for action in order to achieve specified result
Working groups	Quality circles	Voluntary peer groups of six to ten employees develop solutions to problems	Bottom-up process for identifying work-based solutions to quality problems
	Task and action groups	Groups (e.g. 'diagonal slice') of stakeholders to identify problems and possible solutions	Useful in complex organizations, bringing together people with different interests and roles to develop comprehensive solution and carry it forward
Learning from others	Benchmarking	Structured process to identify elements of service production process which can be compared with other organizations' approaches	Check how we are doing and gain ideas for change and improvement
	Research, seminars, workshops	Evaluate own policies and practice and, where relevant, enable learning to take place between organizations with similar remits	Opportunity to reflect, learn and consider next steps

ensuring continuous ownership of the process of improvement. They could take the form of 'quality circles', which have a particular structure and form (see Appendix), or they could be less formalized task or action groups with a remit to report back with suggestions for improvement and to take action forward in a particular area of work.

For the *application of 'best practice'* (to avoid reinventing wheels), 'benchmarking' can be useful. This involves close examination of another organization's methods, providing an analysis of processes in service production. Some areas of activity (the processing of routine requests for action; efficient reception activities; managing a residential home) could well have parallels in very different kinds of organization. The main difficulty, compounded by the issue of commercial or competitive confidentiality, is whether organizations are willing to reveal how they do things. Benchmarking was introduced to public services in the early 1990s (Bullivant and Naylor 1992) and taken up in a big, though slightly different, way through the Best Value process, where it has not been found to be easy (IDEA 2001; and see Chapter 7).

The 'quality chain'

A tool for analysis

It seems clear that the process of implementing quality policies is largely about understanding and making connections. This is particularly important in those large organizations where departmentalism and hierarchy has dominated, and where individuals, teams and departments either know very little about what their colleagues do, or are resentful or suspicious of the intervention of others. The same issues increasingly apply to the question of working across boundaries beyond one's organization, through contracts and partnerships. Here it is even more important to know, understand and respect the contributions of others to what, from the consumers' and citizens' perspective, is or should be a complete 'seamless' service.

A useful tool for thinking about this is the 'service' or 'quality chain' (see Figure 4.4). The quality chain is 'the linkage of internal or external support services, all of which must be of high quality if the service to the public is also to be of high quality' (Audit Commission 1993: 9).

The service chain (or quality chain) is a way of mapping the activities involved in delivering a service, the constant point of reference being the citizens' needs and concerns. It is closely related to 'process mapping' (Deming 1986), but with as much if not more emphasis on the 'who' as on the 'what'.

The idea of a 'chain' underlines the need for attention to detail at every stage. It is a way of making links which, from the individual or departmental perspective, are not always obvious or understood. It helps front-line staff to understand what goes on behind the scenes, and back-line staff to understand how they are contributing to the front-line service, highlighting the interdependence of each apparently separate action. This leads to the idea that for each stage of a service process, there is a producer and a consumer. Understanding this provides a starting point for diagnosing the service as a whole and for considering whether its current design is appropriate or should be changed or improved. From this diagnosis, options for action can be generated, both for redesign when necessary (Gaster 1996b) and to strengthen the weak links.

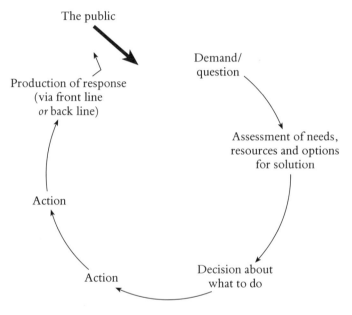

Figure 4.4   The service or quality chain.

Some chains may be relatively short. A council tenant may report a broken window, for example. After a visit or phone call to a neighbourhood or housing office, the repair is logged into the system. Then come inspection and analysis of what needs to be done; ordering any supplies; arranging access for the workforce; carrying out the job; and possibly post-inspection. Each of these is a link in the service chain.

However, even in this relatively short chain, plenty of things can go wrong, since each activity may be under the control of a different person or organization (especially if the service is operated through contract). Depending on the relationships, the service chain can either be a 'cooperative' chain or a 'blame' chain. Sadly, there are too many of the latter in existence still in UK public services. This is highlighted by the longer, more complex chains, such as those involving health or community care. Here the numbers of stakeholders – partners and residents as well as users and front-line staff – are greater and therefore even more vulnerable to weak links. In such situations the consumer may be the only person aware of the total inter-agency chain.

Improving service design: a dynamic process

Saying what the service consists of, which is what the analysis of the service chain is all about, is helpful as a launch pad for the next phase, which is to address the weak links in the chain and to improve the service design. Within this concept of linkages and weak points in a chain comes the notion of service 'gaps', developed initially by Parasuraman, Zeithaml and Berry (1988) in the mid-1980s (see Figure 3.2, p. 60). These are the gaps between what is expected and what is actually done, both between the consumer and the organization and *within* the organization itself. They found that if the reasons for the gaps – the weak links in the chain – are differences in perceptions, attitudes and expectations, the solution is not to change rules and procedures but to focus on clarity of goals, commitment to quality and improved communication. Workers' feelings about whether they have some control and discretion about what they do was found to be particularly important:

> We propose that when employees perceive themselves to be in control of situations they encounter in their jobs, they experience less stress. Lower levels of stress lead . . . to higher performance. When employees perceive that they can act flexibly rather than by rote in problem situations encountered in providing services, control increases and performance improves.
>
> (Zeithaml *et al.* 1988: 42)

These ideas were elaborated for the public sector by Speller and Ghobadian (1993) (see Table 4.4 and Figure 4.5 below). They identified two additional internal gaps arising from the need for 'seamless services' and 'responsive providers', which reflected the need for good communication and understanding between different layers of management and the front line.

The additional information provided by this model (gaps 6 and 7) promotes the idea that the staff who deliver the service in both the 'front line' and the 'back line' are integral to the process. They therefore need appropriate training, development, management, and the opportunity to communicate up, down and across the organization. This reflects the Juran approach to Total Quality Management, where quality is intrinsically linked with every stage of the business process.

The 'gaps' model confirms the need for a new, preferably 'tight-loose' organizational culture described earlier in this chapter. This is a useful basis for redesigning the services themselves, while the concept of the 'service chain' keeps the user at the forefront. The question to be answered is: are the needs of consumers – *and* citizens – being met? Is the process right? Are the right people involved?

Rather than tinkering at the edges and merely 'improving' what already exists, the analysis of service chains and Parasuraman's 'gaps' (Parasuraman *et al.* 1988) provides the basis for innovative and fundamental redesign – if it is needed.

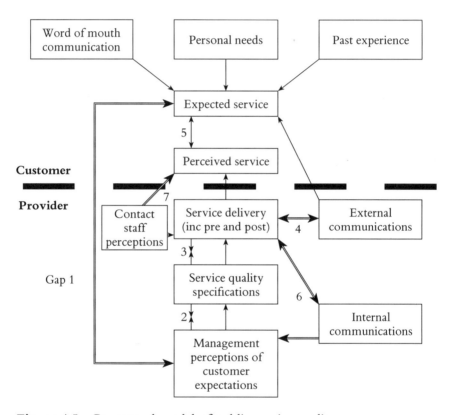

Figure 4.5 Conceptual model of public service quality.
Source: Speller and Ghobadian 1993.

Table 4.4   The public service 'gaps' model

Gap	The problem	Cause	Solution
1	Management perceptions	Management do not understand correctly what customers expect from the service	Marketing, research, consultation
2	Service quality specification	Not translating knowledge of customers' expectations into service quality specifications, standards and guidelines	Service design
3	Service delivery	Guidelines or specifications for service delivery are not adhered to	Human resource management, training and development, quality systems
4	External communications	Failure to communicate effectively to customers about the service	Public relations
5	Customer expectation/ perception gap	Customer expectations based on word-of-mouth, need and past experience and related to the five criteria	Understand and respond to expectations
6	Internal communications	Failing to listen to contact staff about what the customers think of the services delivered	Staff communications, human resource management
7	Contact (front-line) staff perceptions	Failure to empower staff and train them in delivering service to customers	Human resource management, training and development

Source: Speller and Ghobadian 1993.

Conclusion

In this chapter, we have presented the 'implementation' part of our model for quality (Figure 3.1, Chapter 3). We have suggested how the complex but often over-simplified question of quality 'systems' could be approached. We have considered how to assess the applicability (transferability) of ready-made systems, and have put forward some key elements of home-grown or bottom-up systems, such as the 'tight-loose' model and the 'quality chain'. And we have stressed the need for an appropriate and participative organizational culture.

Within the broad framework presented in this and the previous chapter, service providers need to make detailed decisions about how to design, change and improve new or existing services for the benefit of the public. We recommend what might be called 'rational eclecticism'. This would

Annex 4.1 Key characteristics of quality systems

Type of system	Value base	Purpose	Main characteristics	Aspect of 'quality' covered	Timescales	Leadership/ support	Key interests	Monitoring	Concerns/issues
Quality control	Putting things right afterwards	Identify errors and variations based on specification and put them right: 'inspect quality out'	Post-production inspection, rectify errors	Technical dimensions of product or service (fitness for purpose)	Immediate results	Line management, top down	Management; production workers	Continuous inspection/ sampling	Useful for routine services, may reassure consumers; consumers not actively involved; unsuitable for personal services; cost of rework expensive
Quality assurance	Getting things right first	Avoid mistakes, ensure adherence to specification: 'build quality in'	All aspects of production system must be documented and implemented consistently	Process of production	6 months – 1 year	Top down	Management; production workers	Handbook used to check processes	Emphasizes systems and procedures at expense of outputs and outcomes; important trigger to thinking about processes of service production; high set-up costs
Total quality management	Quality is everyone's business	Continuous improvement and zero defects; delight the customer	Whole system approach	Technical, non-technical dimensions; systems and procedures	Long-term – 3–5 years	Generally top-down; Continuing top leadership essential	Senior management; employees	Not known – improved product/ service and customer satisfaction?	Comprehensive system, needing long-term commitment and leadership; pressure to standardize could drive out innovation; lack of customer/public involvement
Business Excellence model (EFQM)	Comprehensive and coherent	To achieve business success through diagnosis and action	Nine-element model for analysing organizational quality	Processes and results	Not known – 1–5 years?	Top management; work teams	Employees; management	Results of the BEM diagnosis	Mainly a diagnostic tool, could provide basis for action; spurious numerical values for each aspect of 'excellence'. Lack of employee ownership; lack of public involvement

involve deciding on the main building blocks needed for particular, local services, actively involving the key stakeholders, particularly citizens, and developing processes, structures and cultures that are both innovative and draw on past experience, including ready-made models.

The next chapter – the last of the conceptual chapters – considers the two final elements in the model: the question of standard setting; and the issues involved in monitoring and evaluating service quality.

Annex 4.2   Tools for quality

Seven original tools for quality

1 Cause and effect or 'fish bone': identifies potential causes of a given problem and their interrelationships
2 Check sheets: data collection for objective measurement of change
3 Control charts: display of data showing variation against acceptable limits after elimination of special cause using Statistical Process Control, the statistical calculation of control
4 Histogram: graphic display of check sheet data in adjacent bars
5 Pareto: sequential data display by frequency. Commonly 80 per cent of problems come from 20 per cent of the processes
6 Scatter diagrams: diagrammatic display of relationship between cause and effect
7 Stratification: classification and separation of data for further analysis

New tools for quality

- Affinity: cause/effect issues grouped for local action
- Arrow diagrams: flow chart of tasks
- Matrix data analysis: adds weighting to complex matrix relationships
- Matrix diagram: relationship implications between two characteristics
- Process decision progress chart (PDPC): tree diagram with anticipation of problems at each decision
- Relations diagram: refined cause/effect analysis for complex interrelationships
- Tree diagram: project planning by asking 'how'

Examples of management tools appropriate for quality

- Benchmarking: examination of, comparison with and learning from the methods of another organization
- Business re-engineering: outcome-led forward and backward process mapping
- Delphi technique: whereby surveyed experts put topics in priority order, repeated for the top priority until the required length of list is achieved

- Departmental purpose analysis (DPA): the objectives of all departments are in line with objectives
- Diagonal ranking (whereby an individual can indicate their preferences on an infinite number of paired issues, the aggregated scores of all participants forming the final decision)
- Failure modes and effects analysis (FMEA) probes PDPC and prioritizes and costs risks
- Quality function deployment (QFD): customer wishes are checked at each stage of system design
- Taguchi method: any variation from specification is regarded as a loss and requires investigation back to basic design

Examples of social science tools appropriate for quality

- Critical incident technique: why certain opinions held
- Interviews: face to face or phone, based on sound methodology
- Surveys: statistical analysis of questionnaires developed through sound methodology

Sources: Lofland and Lofland 1984; Turrill 1986; French 1988; McIver 1991; Bendell and Merry 1992; Cole 1994; Joss and Kogan 1995.

5

Standards, monitoring and evaluation

Lucy Gaster and Amanda Squires

This chapter completes the examination of the model for quality introduced in Chapter 3 (Figure 3.1). The two final elements are 'standards' and
'monitoring and evaluation'.

Quality standards, especially when imposed from above, may be felt
mainly as an irritant and a diversion from doing the 'real job'. However,
standards of some kind, negotiated with users and citizens, reflecting real
objectives and targets, and attainable – but not minimalist – within a given
period, are crucial for improving service quality.

Similarly, the normal reaction to being monitored and evaluated is to
avoid it if possible. With the current experience of external performance
indicators and the fear of being labelled a 'failure', as well as the direct
experience of churning out dubious data for indicators that do not reflect
the things that are really important for the public, no wonder cynicism
exists.

Again, though, this does not have to be the case. Evaluation, particularly but not exclusively 'formative' evaluation, is an essential and
constructive feature of any organization genuinely wishing to improve the
quality of its services. Only by doing this, in a way that is consistent with
the overall policy for quality, can a check be made on what has changed,
and ideas generated for what to do next.

Standards

Standard setting is an important part of the process of redesign and continuous improvement. Consumers' needs and public expectations are constantly changing. The result of the analysis and development activity described in the previous chapter should not therefore be limited merely to compliance with existing specifications. It needs to be used to improve quality at least to meet, if not exceed, rising and expanding expectations. This involves setting and then raising standards and targets, which become minimum standards as each new level is reached. This ascending motion has been depicted (Figure 5.1) as the onward progress of the Deming Cycle, ratcheting quality up the incline of expectations, and securing each improvement to a particular standard, backed by an audit and review programme (Koch 1990). This should ensure that *basic* needs continue to be met while *higher* needs are explored (see Chapter 3 for an analysis of different kinds of 'need').

Consideration of service standards raises several questions:

- What level should be aimed at: high, low or somewhere in between, reflecting current reality or expressing future intentions?
- What are they to be used for: to give rights of redress, to enable employees to know what is expected of them, as the basis for service specification?
- Who is involved in their development, how are they built up, is there motivation to improve the standards once set?
- Where should an organization start when beginning to set standards?

Early thinking about service standards was somewhat overshadowed by the advent of the Citizen's Charter in 1991 and the consequent production

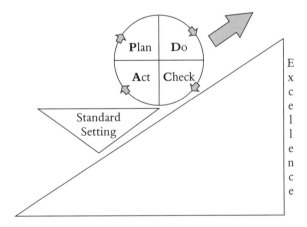

Figure 5.1   Ascending quality improvement.
Source: Koch 1990.

of innumerable 'charters', 'promises', 'guarantees' and 'standards'. Too many of these were meaningless not only to the public but also to staff: neither had been involved in their construction.

Much more important for service quality is the evolution of local standards, which reflect a true debate between stakeholders, identifying what is important and possible at a particular time and place. These standards take the form of a written statement available to both staff and the public. They can include basic principles about how the service will operate, together with specified targets as the basis for public redress and to provide criteria for measurable achievement. They are a first step in making explicit to staff and the public what the organization is setting out to achieve. While they may simply reflect the statutory *minimum* required by law, they could also be *aspirational*, showing what the organization is aiming for through its quality improvement programme.

Standard setting is – or should be – quite a risky process. Standards may challenge well-established 'custom and practice', and they may be genuinely difficult to implement when different elements of the service are being delivered by different parts of the organization or through contractors and partners. A good deal of spadework is needed to make standards a credible and useful part of the quality implementation process.

Standard setting as part of the quality cycle

If standard setting is to be a participative process, integrated with the quality implementation cycle, it could be useful to start with services with which participants are familiar, for whom the service is important and where a structure for participation already exists. Some early local government standards were negotiated in this way for swimming pools (Islington) and street lighting (Bradford). The aim was to be realistic, to develop attainable standards and to identify the role the public could play in ensuring that they were achieved. These were consumer-led standards, specifying what was important to the public and what should be done (by the council and by the public) when things go wrong. They were not the familiar kind of standard, which claims that 'X per cent of the lights (trains, etc.) will be working X per cent of the time'. This only causes annoyance for the public and cynicism among staff. It is also subject to much manipulation to ensure that the standard is met, often at the expense of more important things, like whether the trains are clean, are easy to book, have comprehensible fare structures, depart on time, or have enough space for passengers.

It will be obvious that not all stakeholders' wishes can be fulfilled. However, it is helpful to think about what the service *should* be like, both long term and short term, and to identify the real priorities of each group. Short-term targets (in practice, the published 'standards') can then be negotiated, taking into account the realities of legal, financial or political constraints. 'Trade-offs' and efforts to empower the weakest voices will be needed at each stage of this process.

Standards can be used to provide the 'tight' part of the 'tight-loose' framework (see Chapter 4) for local managers to make their own decisions as to how to achieve the standards required. Other aims include:

- empowering the public to ask questions and challenge existing practice
- providing better information for the public so that they know what to expect
- extension of individual consumer rights (complaints, redress)
- improving consistency, speed and overall quality of services
- providing the basis for inspection, measurement and regulation
- winning awards.

Rewards and punishment

Much depends on the level of credibility of the organization and the commitment and sincerity with which the standards are implemented. After ten years of charters and standards, it is still difficult to know whether published standards – central or local – are having any effect either on how services are delivered or on public expectations and behaviour. It is certainly easier and therefore tempting to develop easily quantifiable, top-down and producer-dominated standards and measures. Yet these could easily distort the service in a particular direction.

It all depends on the ideology behind the standard-setting process. If it is believed that people will not act unless they are financially rewarded (through performance-related pay or special awards) or threatened (through competition), then standards and the targets derived from them would need to be quantitatively measurable. Performance-related pay and the government's use of league tables in many areas of public service reflect this ideology.

If, on the other hand, it is assumed that staff are motivated to give a good service because they are committed to the idea of public service, then increased job satisfaction and better results will be the main incentive. In that case, qualitative public and management feedback will be a far more effective spur to action than a financial bonus arising from the fact that all telephone calls have been answered within three rings, or letters responded to within a set number of days (never mind what is actually said to the caller/writer).

For the public, standard setting may be a useful way of ensuring financial redress if things go wrong. If the customer (or passenger, or water user) finds out how to claim, they can get financial compensation or its equivalent in vouchers. For those public services that most closely resemble private sector services, this may be acceptable. However, given the choice, many 'customers' would prefer a different kind of response. Many people, especially those who are poor or socially excluded, do not have the time, finance, energy, clout or expertise to complain and claim (although others may use a lifetime of experience to complain very effectively). They may, too, be denied compensation because of the complicated rules – a further disincentive to complaining in the future.

Other people retain a notion of public services being for the general good. These 'customers' would prefer organizations to demonstrate an intention to learn from mistakes and improve their services, rather than paying compensation. And taxpayers do not want to pay for things twice.

Standards are certainly not a substitute for a properly thought out quality policy. They can, however, be important symbols and tools of just such a policy.

Measuring, monitoring, evaluating quality

Measurement of services and of performance are currently a major public policy topic and of great public interest. In simple terms, it is important to know the difference between a good and a bad service. Consumers and the general public want to know about how the services they need are performing and what they are like to experience, but they generally have to rely on obscure, partial, purely quantitative figures of doubtful utility for this purpose. Service producers want to know what local people think of their services, in order to make improvements.

The two key questions for those trying to improve their services' quality are:

1 What do I need to know so as to make sure the service is being delivered to the correct specification or standard? (the accountability and control question)
2 What do I need to know so that the service quality can be improved? (the development question)

Measurement on its own cannot improve quality. It needs to be part of a policy and a culture that welcomes and uses the results of measurement to assess and develop the level and type of quality required by the organization's values and objectives. Performance measurement for quality, in the climate within which most public service workers now operate, needs to have very clear benefits: to staff, to the public and to the organization. It needs to be closely connected with and relevant to everyday tasks, and the results have to be available in a form that is useful, comprehensible and timely. If quality measurements are not useful to front-line and back-line managers, to workers, consumers and the public at large, they will be subject to the same levels of suspicion, the same avoidance tactics, and the same manipulation as has so often been reported for the measures of quantity that already dominate performance measurement (Pollitt 1988; Carter 1989, 1991; Bouckaert 1990).

Key issues

The main issues in measuring quality are as follows:

- *What is being measured?* The main focus needs to be on the definition(s) of negotiated quality adopted (which may be published as 'standards'), and on whether strategic objectives are being achieved.
- *What types of measure* should be used – quantitative or qualitative or both?
- *Who needs to be involved?* The involvement of the public and of front-line staff is vital. Involving other stakeholders, for example purchasers and providers (see Chapter 12) is complex, but essential and achievable.
- *How will the measurements be used?* Different purposes – judgement or improvement – affect what is measured and how this is done. Respondents may give different answers according to how they think the information will be used.
- *When should measurement take place?* A common objection to measurement is that it is not timely: the policy has not had time to be implemented, problems have been encountered, new staff have been taken on board and so on. Conversely, political or management pressure for 'results' means that judgements of 'success' or 'failure' may be made too soon, failing to take account of the relatively long timescales needed for implementing quality policies. Measurement of services only at the time of delivery may be inappropriate.
- *What criteria are used* to judge whether the data collected shows an improvement in service quality – or not? Do these criteria change, for example as expectations and standards rise over time?

What types of measure should be used?

The main disadvantage of relying on quantitative data is that of the 'measurable driving out the non-measurable' (Bovaird 1975): only those aspects of a service that can be counted are measured. These may not be the most important ones, especially in the eyes of consumers (although they formed the basis of the citizen's charters); consequently, numerical measurements are never comprehensive.

However, the fear that qualitative methods are not reliable and valid in a way that quantitative methods claim to be can inhibit their use. In practice, as shown both in the long years of opinion polling since the 1930s and in recent developments in the measurement of quality itself (Parasuraman *et al.* 1988), items included in opinion research and the scales attached to them can be tested for both reliability (do they produce consistent results?) and validity (do they measure what they purport to measure?).

A qualitative approach can involve, not just opinion polls – which suffer from the fact that they tend to focus on the doubtful concept of 'satisfaction' (see Chapter 3) – but an active dialogue between providers and the public. This can be in the form of panels and focus groups, observations and audits, ongoing consultation methods and quality action groups. Internally, the diagnostic problem-solving techniques advocated in Chapter 2 and listed in Chapter 4 can be used to find out existing levels of quality, the location of weak points and the desirability of different options for action.

All these techniques explicitly and overtly depend on human judgements which, if care is not taken, can be rubbished as 'anecdotal'. It is therefore a good idea to use several different techniques to assess the quality of the same service. This 'triangulation' method is familiar to researchers using qualitative methods. By interviewing or observing different groups of 'actors', a series of perspectives can be obtained and compared, giving robustness and credibility to the findings. Such findings can also be integrated with those produced by regular (or one-off) statistical data, again for the purpose of cross-checking and assurance of reliability.

Inputs, throughputs, outputs and outcomes

Measures of the quality of what goes into the service (inputs) as well as the process (throughputs) and eventual results (outputs and outcomes) are all desirable.

Inputs include both expenditure and the training and experience of staff. Adequate resources and high-quality staff are essential ingredients for high-quality services.

Throughputs relate to what happens while the service is being performed. The commonest type of indicator is the headcount. If high numbers bring rewards in the shape of extra resources or extra individual pay and promotion, the incentive is strong to move people quickly through the system. Users feel as if they are on a conveyor belt. Yet spending more time on someone – keeping a patient in hospital a little longer, for example – and therefore treating fewer people could result in reduced resources unless or until there is public recognition that preventative work is more cost effective in the long run. However, the perverse effects of throughput measurements should not prevent a search for measures which relate to the quality of the *process* – of people's experience once they are in the system ('non-technical', interpersonal and environmental quality).

The immediate *results* (outputs) of a service can be measured quite easily in terms of numbers: how many operations were done, children taken into care, homeless people housed (or not)? The quality is more difficult to assess. Was it the right operation, was it right to take the child into care, was the homeless person dumped in a 'sink' estate? Were actual needs met, as far as the agency was able?

Outcomes, or 'effectiveness', are difficult to assess. It is not always easy to determine what *is* the intended outcome. Is it improved 'quality of life' and if so, how is that measured? Is it that people got what they wanted? Would councillors see it in terms of improved turnouts at elections? Would professionals judge quality effectiveness in relation to the achievement of their professional expectations of what they were trained to do?

Whatever is decided, an added problem is that it is difficult to distinguish the contribution of a particular service to an overall situation where many other factors may have been at work. A further question is, when is an outcome an outcome? How much time needs to elapse before the effect of a service can be judged? Yet it is this, in the end, that could be taken as the key test of quality.

How should quality measurements be used for evaluation?

Quality measurements can be used for evaluation in two ways: 'summatively' – to make a judgement; or 'formatively' – as part of a learning process. When monitoring and measuring services, it is important to be clear which purpose is the primary one. This, as noted earlier, will affect the attitudes and commitment of those involved and possibly the quality of the data. Higher levels of accuracy and honesty are likely when those collecting and supplying the data know that the results will be useful to them in some way.

Summative evaluation can be used:

- to decide whether standards are being met
- to provide a baseline for judging the current level of quality
- to make comparisons between similar organizations or from year to year (but care needs to be taken that the units of comparison and methods of data collection are actually comparable)
- to enable the organization to win contracts or obtain funding both by demonstrating what it does and by exhibiting a willingness to be evaluated.

Formative evaluation can be used:

- as feedback to service providers and as an incentive for improvement
- as a developmental and learning tool, to help decide where improvements need to be made
- as an aid to empowering public and staff (information is power – if presented in an accessible form).

These uses of quality measurements are not mutually exclusive. In the present climate of performance measures and league tables, the balance is tipped towards the summative and controlling use of measurement. A policy for quality would emphasize the developmental use of measurements and indicators as part of an ongoing programme of (self) evaluation and development.

Involving users and citizens in monitoring and evaluating service quality

It is probably in the area of quality monitoring that the greatest progress (though not nearly enough) has been made in actively involving users and citizens. With community development and other expert support, local groups can devise questionnaires and carry out surveys. Citizen involvement requires a lot of work to build up credibility, confidence and equality (Beresford and Croft 1993), but tenants on housing estates (Smith 1992; Spray 1992), or 'survivors' of the mental health services (Barnes 1997) have at different times and in different places become successfully involved in this way.

Even where users are not involved in the design of the monitoring process, their views can be canvassed. This is an essential part of quality measurement. Questionnaire surveys are possible – and common – but personal and group interviews and dialogue may provide far more telling information. Efforts are beginning to be made by the Audit Commission to ensure the systematic and non-tokenistic inclusion of users and citizens in their inspections and audits (Audit Commission 2001b). This creates a useful precedent for 'normalizing' this approach.

But if consumers become more actively involved, especially if they are interviewed while they are still receiving the service in question (as those with a long-term relationship with services must be), they need to be sure that the information will not be used to their disadvantage and remains confidential. Outside facilitators and trained service users can help, both to encourage current users to speak out, and to run effective and participative group discussions. Interviewees must also be confident that it is worth taking the trouble to respond to requests for feedback and information. They should in turn receive feedback.

Complaints and, if the worst comes to the worst, litigation, are also an important source of information about what people think of services. By definition, they are always in the form of negative feedback and they are individualistic. They also depend heavily on whether there is a climate where complaints are listened to and acted on, and whether a system exists that is easy to use and positively encouraged. Research carried out in the 1980s (Seneviratne and Cracknell 1988) showed that, as far as local authorities were concerned, this was rarely the case. However, this may have improved in the light of recent official encouragement to set up complaints systems. The danger, as we point out in Chapter 3, is that complaints are still seen by managers as something to avoid, rather than actively encouraging them. In this climate the reaction, as with litigation, is to become defensive and hostile to the complainant. Ideally, complaints should be responded to quickly and positively, perhaps even exceeding public expectations in the process.

The Citizen's Charter made much of the importance of complaints as a measure of quality. The Audit Commission (1992), devising the first set of indicators, was cautious about their use. Complaints can indicate both good quality and bad quality. One aim of a quality policy could be to generate public confidence to complain, so high numbers of complaints on new topics may reflect higher expectations and higher quality, showing that previous issues have been resolved. Complaints statistics, taken on their own, must be treated with great caution. Comparisons, even between departments of the same organization, may not be possible if there are different local policies and action regarding complaints.

Inspection and audit

The audit or inspection approach is not new. However, in the 'regulatory state' (Henkel 1991), it has become increasingly prominent as a method of monitoring and evaluation. There are two main disadvantages, arising not so much from the *principles* of audit (publicly funded bodies must account for their actions and finances) but from the practice, particularly as it affects day-to-day services.

First, such audits have mainly been the province of external bodies who may not appreciate the local culture and context within which services are delivered. This does not facilitate integration with a local policy for quality, resulting in lack of ownership by key players, notably staff. Yet they are very powerful influences on the future of the service or organizations concerned, particularly where central government has the power to insert new management in the case of 'failing' schools, hospitals or, in extreme cases, local authorities.

Second, even in the new regime of Best Value (see Chapter 7), users and citizens have until now rarely been actively involved, except perhaps tokenistically as part of the 'show' on the day of inspection. They have not generally helped to design reviews, and there is little evidence of participation in the process leading to formal reports and inspections.

Internal audits (reviews) are now encouraged in local government and related services through the Best Value regime. However, the final say still rests with the Audit Commission, and it is hard to say how far these reviews are making a real contribution to *quality* improvements, compared with the economy and efficiency of the reviewed services.

The costs and benefits of quality

Part of the monitoring and evaluation of work to improve quality must necessarily include the consideration of costs and benefits. Competitive organizations need to balance the effectiveness of any initiative or new system with its cost. The cost of quality improvement is no exception.

As with other quality issues, available analyses are mainly drawn from manufacturing. For example, the negative cost of quality is described as when 'the goods come back but not the customer' (Deming 1986: 175).

In services, as shown in Chapter 1, the consumer and the service are inseparable. The service cannot be 'sent back'. In public services, consumers often *have* to go back, whether they want to or not. A previous bad experience makes this return disgruntled, reluctant, and with low expectations. Because the service depends on the interaction with the consumer, its (non-technical) quality may well be impaired as a result. And in the service sector, the cost of a poor experience not only includes the costs of putting things right, but possibly having to meet the consequence of having got things wrong before (as so many child and hospital enquiries confirm). Of course, it is also possible that greater needs must now be met as a result of the previous service failure. All this can be very expensive, in resources and staff time and morale (and of course user time).

The conversion of service failures into financial data can convince management of the need for change (Moores 1993). It has been variously calculated that 5 per cent, 25 per cent and even 40 per cent of negative quality costs to an organization can initially be saved through continuous improvement measures (Jordan 1992). However, this level of financial benefit cannot usually be sustained. Cost-focused senior management can then become disillusioned with 'quality' in succeeding years, leading to a decision to halt quality programmes and projects. Yet five to ten years are needed for consolidation and culture change, by which time the benefits should be clear.

The calculation of quality costs is complex. Four categories are generally used (Table 5.1): *negative* costs of external and internal failure, and *positive* costs of prevention and inspection and appraisal. The ideal would be to reduce the negative costs of quality by increasing preventive costs and minimizing appraisal costs. In a non-quality organization it is common for 75 per cent of costs to be on negative issues with 5 per cent on prevention and 20 per cent on inspection and assurance (Anderson and Daigh 1991), clearly indicating that attention needs to be focused on negative costs such as negligence and process failures.

To the preventive costs listed in Table 5.1 can be added the costs of stakeholder participation. 'Quality' is not cost-free, but neither is it simply a matter of adding extra resources. Resources need to be used as effectively as possible, through local policies, programmes and systems both to improve quality and to make the best use of existing resources.

It is, of course, vital that public service managers and politicians and board members are aware of the real costs of quality improvement, insofar as they can be estimated. They also need to be aware of the potential long-term financial benefits derived from, for example, less rework, higher public satisfaction (and fewer complaints), high staff morale, and better use of resources to produce consistently acceptable quality services.

Table 5.1   The costs of quality

Costs of quality	Example	Cost calculation
External failure costs	Complaints	Estimate time to deal with and make good. Consider potential complaints – one letter represents up to 27 who did not write
	Negligence claims (litigation)	Base on worst case scenario
75 per cent of quality cost	Lost custom	Competition risk
		Re-attraction costs up to five times more than retention
		Reputation – one dissatisfied user talks to up to 15 others
Internal costs	Waste, duplication, delays, down time, correction, re-inspection, rework, diversionary activities, urgent calls	Use of a flow chart can estimate the problems and amount at each stage and cost.
		Such costs are usually hidden within the budget, are often difficult to calculate and may even be valued by peers
	Costs of non-conformance	Rework, disposal, customer relations
Prevention 5 per cent of quality costs	Planning, design, education, training, market research	Analyse and cost the removal of main cause
		Cost all activities undertaken to prevent defects in creating a product/service and during the business cycle
Inspection and assurance 20 per cent of quality costs	Surveys, audit, analysis, documentation, testing, maintenance	Costs of determining conformance to specification

Sources: Crosby 1980; Lisswood 1989; Ovretveit 1991; Baines 1992; Naumann 1995.

Conclusion

Measuring, monitoring and evaluating are complex issues in their own right. Perhaps the most important message from recent experience is the need for stakeholder involvement at all stages of the process. This, of course, links with the overall model for quality presented in this book, which sees stakeholders, especially citizens, as the starting point for the whole cycle.

There is a real danger that this element of the cycle could be hijacked by external inspection bodies. These can, of course, bring a wider experience to the process, and can be helpful in suggesting areas for improvement. In the current policy climate, however, it is probably rather difficult for such inspectors to develop and gain the trust of those being inspected, and it is likely to be a somewhat confrontational business. More positively, the central part that users and citizens can play in monitoring and evaluation is beginning to be recognized. This could lead to a sense of 'ownership', not just among the public but, if a policy and culture of participation is well embedded, among staff as well. It can also give credibility and legitimacy to the results – including the costs and benefits – far more effectively than through monthly statistical returns to Whitehall.

Quality standards were popular in the 1990s as a way of getting started on 'quality'. They can be used to show staff, the public and other stakeholders what is intended, and they provide a basis for measurement and accountability. Unfortunately, early quality standards were too often top-down, minimal and quantitative. We suggest that a more sophisticated approach is needed whereby, once more, users and citizens (and other stakeholders) are actively involved through a process of negotiation. The results can be presented in terms of both 'ideal' (long-term) and 'achievable' (short-term) standards. As with all the other aspects of quality, attention to detail and clarity of purpose are essential. In some organizations, developing quality standards may be a useful way of getting going. In others, especially where services cut across departmental and organizational boundaries, it may be more important to get the quality infrastructure right first.

Organizational culture is central to the constructive development of standards, performance indicators and methods of monitoring and evaluating progress. This is an issue that permeates all discussion of quality improvement and is an essential component in the overall thinking about how to achieve changes on the ground and make a real difference for users, citizens and communities.

The next three chapters bring together what has been happening in three important areas of public service: central government, local government and the health services. Here it is possible to see that various phases of thinking about how to introduce quality approaches have emerged since the early 1990s. It is not easy to assess their actual impact on the intended services, but each chapter suggests some ideas about this too, taking into account the model for quality offered here.

Part III

Learning from each other – overviews

6

Quality in central government

Lucy Gaster

Introduction

This chapter looks at how one part of central government in the UK has considered the question of 'quality' in public services since 1991, the year when the Citizen's Charter was introduced. This review is not and could not be comprehensive, since it is not within the scope of this book to examine the work of separate Departments and Government Agencies in improving the quality of the services for which they are responsible. Instead, it aims to give a flavour of the level and nature of political commitment at the very top, from the Prime Minister and the Cabinet Office. Even here, given rapid structural and policy changes since 1997, the description is limited, only covering activities identified either through the Internet (reports and other material) or through personal interviews held in early 2002.

The chapter concentrates on central government's efforts to encourage the development of quality-related activity by public servants – all 5 million of them. It makes no attempt to analyse other policies and activities affecting the structure of the public sector. There has been plenty of discussion elsewhere of the relative benefits and effects of contracts, privatization, public-private partnerships and other policies, introduced by governments of all political persuasions to 'improve' the quality of public services (see, for example, Walsh *et al.* 1997). As said in Chapter 1, a great deal can be done to improve quality *from within*, working with partners and with the public. This is the focus of this chapter, which tries to record the government's own efforts in exactly this direction.

Three main phases in the government's approach since 1991 can be identified. They are:

1 The Citizen's Charter (1991–97)
2 Modernizing government (1997–2001)
3 Improving public services (2001–)

The overall approach and underlying rationale of each phase, where these can be identified, together with the government structures and activities to support them, are described in this chapter.

The role of the Cabinet Office in government

The Cabinet Office was established by Lloyd George in 1916. In 1987–88 it had a budget of £49 million. Its responsibilities were to coordinate policy briefing for the Cabinet and Cabinet committees, to coordinate the security and intelligence services, and to prepare for economic summits. It also covered Civil Service security, top Whitehall and public appointments, honours and official histories (Hennessy 1989).

Although at the time of writing, Peter Hennessy recorded the existence of six secretariats, roughly mirroring the main activities of government, he also noted that it was 'a rapidly expanding power'. The source of its power was its closeness both to the Cabinet and, in particular, to the Prime Minister (with some tensions between it and the Prime Minister's private office). Hennessy described it as

> the crucial junction box of the central government system. It does not command the money lines like the Treasury. But when it comes to formulating policy at the critical stage before it goes to Ministers collectively, all wires lead to [it].
>
> (Hennessy 1989: 390)

The role of the Cabinet Office appears to have shifted substantially during the 1990s. It still contains six policy secretariats, but has accumulated a swathe of 'cross-cutting units' (e.g. Social Exclusion Unit, Performance and Innovation Unit, Women and Equality Unit). By 2001, it was also responsible for public service delivery (following the 1999 Modernization White Paper, see below), as well as Civil Service corporate management, the Centre for Management and Policy Studies and the Government Information and Communication Service (Cabinet Office 2002). Further structural changes were introduced in summer 2002, with the arrival of the new Permanent Secretary, Sir Andrew Turnbull. The effects of these changes on the Cabinet Office's approach to quality improvement could not be analysed here. At the same time, the name of the 'Performance and Innovation Unit' became the 'Strategy Unit'.

The Cabinet Office now therefore has to balance policy formation with policy implementation – or rather, with exhortation and persuasion to implement. In this, it is competing with two other powerful organs of government: the Treasury and Number Ten. The Treasury, through its post-1998 Public Service Agreements and its increasingly hands-on role in the delivery of cross-cutting policies such as 'Sure Start', has been developing new relationships with the 'delivery' departments (Deakin and Parry 2000). Already by 1989, when Peter Hennessy was writing, there was a clear tension between the roles of the Number Ten secretariat and the emerging role of the Cabinet Office, particularly regarding their access to the Prime Minister and their respective influence in policy making. This tension has not diminished since 1997. It is therefore difficult for the outsider – and probably for insiders too – to know where decisions are or should be taken, and who, among these competing bodies, has responsibility for action.

As the following sections will show, for the issue of quality, the Cabinet Office appears to have been mainly responsible both for policy formation and, increasingly, for implementation, aiming to spread influence not just across Whitehall but also across the whole of the public sector. The Cabinet Office has thus acquired responsibility (and accountability?) for results, without much formal power to deliver them. It still relies for its effect on the persuasive authority of closeness to the Prime Minister, the 'championing' (when it exists) of individual Cabinet Office ministers, and the goodwill of ministries. This, in the 'silo' culture of the Civil Service, could be a serious weakness.

Nevertheless, it is in the Cabinet Office that much of the 'corporate' work on public service quality has been taking place. This is examined in the next three sections.

The Citizen's Charter 1991–97

When it was introduced in 1991, central government expected the Citizen's Charter to do two things (HMSO 1991). First, public services were to be *developed and improved* along four main themes:

1 standards
2 quality
3 choice
4 value

Second, public services were to be *judged*, through performance indicators, league tables and through a new award, the Charter Mark.

Charters and standards

The 'standards' were the most prominent and superficially the most successful aspect of the Citizen's Charter in its early days. These were to be published and prominently displayed at the point of service delivery, and were to include courtesy and helpfulness from staff, accuracy in accordance with statutory entitlements, and a commitment to prompt action. Standards would, it was assumed, progressively improve as services became more efficient.

The first action by the newly formed Citizen's Charter Unit at the Cabinet Office seems to have been a round robin to all government departments requesting information about current service targets. These were then transformed into 'charters' for key areas such as health (the Patient's Charter), public transport (the Passenger's Charter), school education (the Parents' Charter) and about two dozen others (HMSO 1992).

This approach underlined the individualistic approach of the government at that time. It was assumed – although they conferred no extra legal rights – that the publication of these charters and standards would encourage current service users to exercise their rights and to seek redress – use their 'voice' – if things went wrong. Not surprisingly, service managers, particularly in transport and the utilities, found that the easiest way out of this was to issue vouchers, in the hope that the complainant would then go away.

Individual complaints were thus central to the philosophy, but they were not seen as a trigger for improvement (see Chapter 5). Instead, the government's preferred methods and mechanisms for improving services were measurement and inspection; regulation of privatized utilities; privatization and 'market testing' (that is, compulsory competitive tendering for an increasing range of services formerly provided directly by public sector organizations); and devolved management in the form of 'Next Steps' agencies (HMSO 1992).

It is easy to be cynical about this stage of development. Most of the published charters were simply the minimum targets to which services were already committed. They did not represent radical thinking about where the service should be going, they were entirely top-down, and they did not involve consumers or citizens in any way (Prior et al. 1993) although they did raise awareness as to entitlements. The mechanisms for change seemed to be part of the same ideology that had driven Conservative policies towards public services in the previous twelve years.

Nevertheless, the government version of charters and standards, the highlighting of the role of 'users' (however limited), together with the Audit Commission's introduction of 'Citizen's Charter Performance Indicators' and a requirement to report annually on their achievement, probably acted as a spur to making some service providers think about what the public needs to know about their services. It may also have stimulated awareness of consumers' and citizens' rights to public (or recently privatized) services.

There were inherent tensions within the Citizen's Charter, as Kirkpatrick and Lucio (1995) point out. They argue that, because of its individualistic nature, the policy was a political attempt to divert public attention from public services and resource issues. At the same time it was both aiming to increase the user 'voice' and to promote value for money and efficiency (largely measured through response times).

Could it achieve all these somewhat different aims? The answer is that it could not. There was too much to be changed through one mechanism and one small unit in Whitehall, especially after politicians' eyes were taken off this particular ball in the attempt to survive as a government. However, the Citizen's Charter seems to have been very successful in one respect: the Charter Mark.

Charter Mark awards

Charter Marks were introduced in 1992. Unlike most other quality accreditation or award schemes, Charter Marks focus on the experience of users, rather than on internal systems (in 2002, they were extended to internal support services, in recognition that front-line services cannot operate without them). They could be won – and lost – in all public services with direct contact with the public, including utilities and Next Steps agencies ('executive non-departmental public bodies', as they are now known), and in voluntary organizations receiving 10 per cent of funding from public sources. By 1996, 451 had been awarded, and the threat of removal had caused British Gas to withdraw. In subsequent years, ever increasing numbers applied (1202 in 1998), some for the second or third time, providing some evidence of continuing improvement (Cabinet Office 2000b).

The scheme drew attention to the experience of consumers at the front line, and services (which could be nominated by the public) were judged as shown in Table 6.1 (2002 criteria are in the second column).

Table 6.1   Charter Mark criteria, 1996 and 2002

1996 criteria	2002 criteria
Standards	Standards
Information and openness	Be open and provide full information
Consultation and choice	Consult and involve
Courtesy and helpfulness	Encourage access and the promotion of choice
Putting things right	Treat all fairly
Value for money	Put things right when they go wrong
User satisfaction	Provide user satisfaction
Improvement in quality	Innovate and improve
Enhancement to services	
	Work with other providers
	Use resources effectively

Sources: HMSO 1996; interview at Cabinet Office.

The fact that this award – now less like a competition and more like a traditional accreditation scheme – has survived for ten years almost certainly demonstrates that it is valued by public sector providers, possibly because an important part of the assessment process is the feedback applicants receive. This is reported to have been very useful, with 92 per cent implementing some or all of their feedback (Cabinet Office 2000b). By the mid-1990s, public awareness of the Charter Mark was reported as growing, and this may have added credibility. It was also seen by some providers as a good alternative to the traditional accreditation schemes, which were not necessarily appropriate: Charter Marks were a way of recognizing and rewarding front-line effort, through a specifically public service scheme – the only one until recently (see below).

Obviously the question must be asked: were the award winners simply good at presentation, or has there been some real improvement in selected areas of public service? The Charter Mark is awarded to budget-holding service delivery units, and it would be unusual for a whole organization to be involved. So the issues of organizational culture and purpose discussed in the last three chapters are not tackled by this award. Nevertheless, as one trigger for improvement, it appears to have won its place among service providers and possibly the public.

Service First

It may be that the popularity of the Charter Mark was what induced the Labour Government, after it took office in 1997, to retain the award. After public consultation (Cabinet Office 1998a), the Charter Mark was relaunched through the 1998 White Paper 'Service First' (Cabinet Office 1998b). This, preceding the major central government modernization programme by some months, was the first sign that the new government was serious about improving public services across the board.

Taking into account the weaknesses of the Charter programme (apart from the Charter Mark element), Service First aimed to put much greater emphasis on the active involvement of users – 'putting users first' – and involving front-line staff. New ways of spreading 'best practice', of stimulating innovation and encouraging 'working together' were all part of the new philosophy.

One of the first acts was to set up a 'People's Panel' of 5000 randomly selected people from across the UK (this was abolished in February 2002, on the grounds that public bodies were now much better at carrying out their own consultation). This was used for some important and interesting research on access to services, and on what matters to different groups of people.

It was at this stage that the phrase 'continuous improvement' began to dominate central thinking about quality: this may have influenced some of the later developments to be described in the next two sections.

The main problem with Service First, as with the Citizen's Charter before it, was the lack of political commitment or involvement.

In the United States, Vice-President Al Gore was an enthusiastic, committed and widely respected champion of public service improvement throughout his eight years of office. In the UK, although the Prime Minister has a general interest in the issue, at each stage of development there has been in practice only one more or less enthusiastic, fairly junior Cabinet Office minister in charge, often for only a short time and generally with little influence either within their own party or within the government machine. Far from influencing or penetrating the inner workings of Whitehall, the main effects appear to have been on work at the local level. Meanwhile the ministries have continued in much the same way they have always done, providing little evidence that any thinking about quality was going on at all. For a government that was introducing a huge number of new policies, the lack of leadership, of implementation plans and, specifically, of ways of ensuring that different services and departments worked together, was a major weakness.

Modernization, 1997–2001

In the life of the 1997–2001 Labour administration, the loudest political message was largely about 'failure'. Little faith seemed to exist that public services were either delivering good services (albeit patchily) or that they could do so, given the right support. Prime Ministerial speeches about the 'scars on my back' were not designed to boost the morale of public service workers, while the two-year moratorium on funding for public services (owing to a pre-1997 pledge not to change the previous government's spending plans) also sent a strong message to public services that their funding problems were not going to be tackled in the near future.

The situation began to change in 1998–99, when ideas about 'modernizing' government began to emerge. Under the rubric of Best Value (see next chapter), some work was already beginning in local government. With the publication of the White Paper *Modernising Government*, the whole of Whitehall and beyond was to be tackled (Cabinet Office 1999a).

The White Paper made five commitments:

1 To deliver policies that achieve outcomes that matter
2 To deliver responsive public services that meet the needs of citizens, not the convenience of the service provider
3 To deliver efficient, high-quality services and not tolerate mediocrity
4 To be proactive in the use of new technology to meet the needs of citizens and business and not trail behind technological developments
5 To value public service, not denigrate it.

The briefly fashionable language of 'joined up' services became widespread (within government and local government circles at least), and there were many ministerial exhortations to 'modernize'. A flurry of activity (within the Cabinet Office) followed, with lists of action points and invitations for further suggestions. All this is recorded on the 'Modernising Government' website (http://www.cabinet-office.gov.uk/moderngov).

A year later, in 2000, a 26-page progress report, linked to the contents of the White Paper's Executive Summary, was published (Cabinet Office 2000a). This reported on action, such as 24-hour access (the Passport Office was prominent here), on the new government website (www.ukonline.gov.uk) and electronic service delivery (E-government), and on studies that had been commissioned for the modernization programme from the Performance and Innovation Unit (set up in 1998 to contribute to 'joined-up and strategic policy making'). The current and past work of the Social Exclusion Unit was also reported here, as was the setting up (in June 1999) of yet another new unit within the Cabinet Office, the Centre for Management and Policy Studies (CMPS), whose 'core purpose' was to 'work with Departments and others in the drive to modernize government'. Working with the Civil Service College, the CMPS reviewed training for civil servants, leading to new programmes to support crosscutting approaches. They also devised induction programmes for new Ministers, starting in September 1999. In addition, the CMPS began to study and disseminate 'best practice' in policy making.

Other reported progress included the use of the People's Panel (operated through the Service First programme) to set a baseline of satisfaction with public services. 'Service Action Teams' were set up to work on particular aspects of public services – life episodes, change of address, longterm care, retirement and bereavement, access to services and extended hours services. Other actions now brought under the modernizing umbrella included the 'Invest to Save' budget, the TNT Modernizing Government Partnership Award, audit issues affected by the new agenda, the Better Government for Older People initiative, and the work of the Women's Unit in the Cabinet Office.

Towards the end of this very comprehensive report, a list of specifically quality-related activities appears. Service First and the Charter Mark were of course subsumed under the new policy (by 2000, there were 1700 holders of the award). The curiously titled 'Public Sector Benchmarking Project' (initiated in 1996 and still in existence) was absorbed into the 'Public Sector Excellence Programme', strongly promoting the EFQM Excellence Model (see Appendix and Figure 4.2, page 73). And a new Central Government Beacon Scheme would promote and reward good practice within central government (complementing the existing schemes for local government, health trusts and schools). The first Beacon awards – in the form of a certificate – were made in November 2000 to organizations already using one of the four favoured quality tools, whose chosen example of 'good practice' was then judged on suitability, transferability, wider appeal and ability to disseminate (Cabinet Office 2000b).

In addition, there was a Quality Schemes Task Force, composed of representatives of bodies like the British Quality Foundation and the British Standards Institute, together with the Cabinet Office, the Department of the Environment, Transport and the Regions, and the Department of

Trade and Industry. This group, which was set up by the Cabinet Office Parliamentary Secretary Peter Kilfoyle in January 1999, reported to ministers in December 1999. It found there was a great need for guidance on the four most prominent quality schemes, the first two of which were being promoted by the Cabinet Office: the Charter Mark, the EFQM Excellence model, Investors in People (IIP) and ISO 9000. Linking the schemes with Best Value was also to be the subject of published guidance. The possibility of integrating the different forms of accreditation was considered, but the fact that each scheme addresses a different facet of quality would make this difficult. Public sector workers needed training about the quality schemes – what they were for and how to be assessed. In addition, best practice needed to be better disseminated. It was suggested that these ideas should be taken forward through a 'Steering Group', chaired by the Cabinet Office and including representatives of the four quality schemes, together with people from key areas of government and practitioners, reporting to Ministers.

Most of the Task Force's recommendations were put into effect during 1999–2001. Guidance was published, road shows and training were on offer, existing best practice networks were maintained, and a new Steering Group began to meet (Cabinet Office 1999b, 1999c, 2000a). Within the Cabinet Office, the small group of people directly engaged with the 'excellence' work were clearly interested, committed and busy. The main problem was that they were only a small team, there was considerable staff turnover (PricewaterhouseCoopers 2000), and the different units within the Cabinet Office each had their own agenda, without a great deal of internal coordination.

Two reviews of this work have been published. In August 2000, PricewaterhouseCoopers completed an extensive review of the Excellence programme (originally the Benchmarking project mentioned above) (PricewaterhouseCoopers 2000). The research also examined the EFQM model as it was currently being used within the UK public sector. On this, it concluded that because it takes at least five years for such a programme to become organizationally embedded, it was not surprising that its effects could not generally be detected within the 52 per cent of public sector respondents (on a 27 per cent response rate) that had taken it up in some way. The efforts and impact of the Excellence Programme to promote this scheme were therefore not very visible either although, working from a zero base in 1996, some progress had been made. This report recommended a series of targeted actions to be undertaken by the Modernizing Public Services Group and by the Quality Division in the Cabinet Office. A key challenge would be to convince public sector organizations of the value of the Excellence model, mainly as a diagnostic tool on which to base plans for improvement.

Second, the role of the Cabinet Office in modernizing government was examined through a peer review (Cabinet Office 2001). The timing of this review is not clear from the report, but it seems to refer to the pre-election period of 2001, before the structural and policy changes within the Cabinet Office to be described in the next section. This review was carried out by a group of six high-powered individuals from outside the Cabinet Office, all except one from outside government. Their first comment was: 'Exposing the centre of Government to a peer review process took courage and demonstrates that the Cabinet Office is willing to take risks and become a learning organisation' (para 1.1).

Second, they saw 'modernizing government' not as a project, but as a journey. It was not a crisis-driven event, but a long-term effort to change government's role, institutions and services to serve the public interest and the collective good, and to enable public services to respond better to citizens' needs. They note that the *Modernising Government* White Paper was a vehicle to bring together a range of initiatives, existing and new, shifting the emphasis from providers to users, and bringing policy development and service delivery closer together. The efforts of the Cabinet Office to highlight the latter two points were seen as positive, but the peer review found that 'No-one seems to have a comprehensive view of the scope and scale of the reforms that are currently underway. The Cabinet Office should take time out to visit public sector organisations and document some of the most promising initiatives' (para 3.2.1).

This finding does not surprise this writer, who has also found it difficult to form a comprehensive view of what has been taking place, particularly since what was reported on above has changed again since autumn 2001.

It is tempting to quote this report in full, since it is full of insights into the problems of putting such a major programme of reform into action. A key message was that the public sector did *not* need instructions, cajoling or more guidance: they wanted leadership, and a role model of what 'modern government' should look like.

At its then stage of development, the Cabinet Office had a long way to go. It was not 'joined up' and was suffering from rivalry between the many units within it. Different elements of the programme were not therefore harnessing the knowledge available in other units, such as international comparisons, or the use of evidence-based research, or providing support for Departments to make the links between policy and delivery. It was also suggested that the Cabinet Office and the Treasury should work more closely together to develop a 'single team' approach to service delivery across Whitehall. The report ended with a strong plea to 'resist the traditional bureaucratic temptation to reorganise', but instead to concentrate on key tasks and to reduce the number of 'initiatives, reports, requests, plans, etc.' This would 'raise morale and help maintain the momentum' (para 6.3).

Unfortunately, in autumn 2001, reorganization is exactly what took place.

Improving public services, 2001–

During the May 2001 General Election, the Prime Minister, Tony Blair, repeatedly said that the main theme of his next administration was to be the 'improvement' and 'reform' of public services. At the time, there was no elaboration of detail, and it was difficult for anyone involved with public services to know what was intended. A major speech to the TUC was intended for early September 2001, but this was cancelled because of the September 11 events in New York. The speech was eventually published on the web on 16 October. This is a useful reference point for the rest of this section.

Emphasizing that public services should be mainly paid for collectively out of taxation – and suggesting that the public would now be willing to pay more in return for long-term benefits on their investment – the Prime Minister first reviewed some of the structural changes introduced in his first administration, then outlined the principles on which 'reform' should take place in the future.

These principles were:

- high national standards and full accountability
- devolution to the front line to encourage diversity and local creativity
- better and more flexible rewards and conditions of employment for front-line staff
- promotion of greater choice for consumers, with alternative providers if the existing one falls below acceptable standards (*Sources*: Prime Minister 2001, House of Commons 2001, Blair 2002).

All this was to be based on the fundamental aim of 'designing the system round the user' and 'the user comes first'.

In the Queen's Speech opening the 2001–2002 session of Parliament, four areas of public services were chosen for particular attention: health, education, crime reduction and transport.

In pursuit of these aims, both before and after the speech, structural changes were introduced within the Cabinet Office. In July 2001, under the heading of 'Improving public services', three new units were announced, all intended to 'strengthen the Government's ability to deliver change in the public services' (10 Downing Street Press Notice). These were:

1 The Delivery Unit, which would concentrate on achieving Government (and Treasury) objectives in the four service areas (based in the Cabinet Office and headed by Professor Michael Barber)
2 The Office of Public Services Reform (also based in the Cabinet Office and headed by Dr Wendy Thomson), to advise the Prime Minister on how to take the programme of 'radical reform' forward across the whole of the public sector
3 The Forward Strategy Unit (headed by Dr Geoff Mulgan, also director of the Performance and Innovation Unit – PIU), which was to do 'blue

skies policy thinking' for the Prime Minister, based in Downing Street (Grice 2002).

On 1 October 2001, there was a general reorganization of the Cabinet Office. The new Delivery Unit and the OPSR now accounted for two out of 19 policy groups and units within the Cabinet Office (source: December 2001 Organization chart of the Cabinet Office and Office of the Deputy Prime Minister). Some of the former units, such as Social Exclusion and the PIU continued in more or less their previous form. Others, including all those that had previously covered the quality programme, changed.

The Modernizing Public Service Group ceased to exist, and component parts were attached to the Centre for Management and Policy Studies (which was responsible for the Excellence programme), the Prime Minister's Delivery Unit or the Office for Public Service Reform. The task of the 12 staff in the CMPS working on the Excellence programme and Best Practice was to encourage the spread of good practice across the public sector through training, seminars and road-shows. The long-term aim was reported to be to change the public sector 'mind set', but whether this was achievable through exhortation alone, and with such a small staff, was a matter of concern for this unit. It was also trying to network between government departments, encouraging them to talk to each other and to develop commitment to quality improvement. It was noted that most work relating to quality depends on individuals within the ministries, and that there is a great need for leadership on quality issues (and that where this exists, as in some of the agencies, considerable progress has been made). Since October 2001, the 'Charter Mark and Beacon Scheme' unit has had responsibility for the promotion of government award-based programmes: the Charter Mark, the central government Beacon scheme, the TNT Partnership award, and 'Public servant of the year' (the Charter Mark assessment process is now contracted out).

'Learning Labs' to help front-line staff learn from each other, and the Service First quality networks, both initiated under the modernizing government regime, were located in the Centre for Management and Policy Studies. At the time of writing, it was reported that serious attempts were being made to develop better information and coordination between these units. Meanwhile, the Office of Public Sector Reform, with 30 staff, was developing its own programme. The approach here, as in many of the other units (PIU, SEU, the Delivery Unit) was to develop a series of short-term projects, largely arising from the Prime Minister's autumn speech. The work would mainly take the form of studies and reports, with one 'hands-on' programme targeted at government departments – a high-quality, intense (six-week) 'management consultancy' process designed to develop a holistic audit of departments compared with an 'ideal' type of management. The general focus of the first year's programme appeared to be mainly on management processes. This fits well with the analysis given in Chapter 2 that the organizational infrastructure is the necessary platform for quality improvement. The short-term nature of the work, and the lack of capacity for follow-through means that this work is entirely dependent on the will of others to take up the ideas and put them (assuming they are good ones) into practice.

Conclusion: where next?

Work to promote and build quality improvement in local government and the health service are examined in the next two chapters. As explained earlier, other central government work could not be analysed for this book. However, taking the Cabinet Office experience as a guide to government intentions, developments since the introduction of the Citizen's Charter in 1991 show some movement.

The main changes are, first, the increased recognition that citizens (and communities?) as well as users are concerned with public services (though much of the rhetoric still highlights users only). It now seems to be understood at the highest level that not only should users be encouraged to know their rights and to complain when things go wrong, they should also be more directly involved in the design of services, with services meeting *their* needs and not those of the providers.

Second, although the 'stick' of threatening 'special measures' in case of 'failure' still exists, and the possibility of 'alternative providers' could be interpreted as further privatization, there seems to be a genuine belief in the capacity of the public services to reform themselves from within. This, together with a much clearer recognition of the crucial role of front-line staff, must be helpful to those wishing to change but uncertain in the past whether this would be an innovation too far.

Whether the government, through its inspectorates, performance indicators and Best Value regime, will truly encourage innovation (and therefore the risk of failure) remains to be seen. It is not noted for its tolerance of 'mistakes', and there must always be the fear of heavy-handed centralism, even while espousing the cause of local 'autonomy'.

Finally, in relation to the specifics of programmes, systems and initiatives to improve quality, the success of the Charter Mark scheme seems to be well established. Other awards no doubt have their place, both as a way of encouraging change and as a source for learning. This needs to continue throughout the public services.

The 'sponsoring' of particular quality schemes, in particular the Excellence model, went much too far in the early days. Public services perceived it as being promoted as the 'answer to all your problems', for example in the development of Best Value (see Chapter 7). A couple of evaluations further on, the approach is now more realistic. It is recognized that different schemes have a part to play, but that they need to complement each other and be suited to the problem they are tackling. The educational role of informing public servants in all parts of the public sector about the variety of schemes and how they can help is important. It provides a useful antidote to the proselytizing approach of private consultants peddling their wares up and down the country.

However, the Government's approach to quality has been fragmented, both in its policy and in terms of responsibilities and implementation*. There has been no consistent message or drive from the centre. Also, the process suffers, like the rest of the Cabinet Office, from the fact that there is no permanent cadre of civil servants to do the work. Short-term appointments and high turnover of staff undermine what continuity exists in the content of the policies and programmes.

Other important weaknesses of the current approach are:

- it is not holistic: it does not cover all aspects of quality improvement (see Chapter 3)
- it is not integrated: different parts of the Cabinet Office are doing their own thing, separately from each other and with competing egos – there is no role model for 'modernized government' here
- it seems to be having limited impact, both within Whitehall (territorial and silo issues) and outside (capacity problems)
- it has not yet succeeded in really putting the user and the citizen at the heart of quality improvement – the 'values' question (see Chapter 2)
- political leadership is weak: it is not clear which minister, if any, is personally committed to and understanding of the issues of change within the public services or who will drove the programme forward in the long term.

Nevertheless, more is being done now than ever before. If internal integration and better links with ministries can be developed, there is a good chance that the synergy of different approaches can work to the benefit of all those who currently use public services, who may use them in the future, or who, as citizens, want UK public services to be among the best in the world.

---

* It is interesting to note that a programme for 'Civil Service Reform', personally introduced in 1999 and subsequently led by the Permanent Secretary, Sir David Wilson, and managed by the Civil Service Corporate Management and Reform Unit at the Cabinet Office, was not mentioned by any of those interviewed for this chapter. Nor were any cross-references found on any of the innumerable websites studied at the same time. Yet this programme's objectives are closely related to the modernizing government theme and there is a clear agenda for improving central government services. This omission reinforces the impression of fragmentation and lack of internal communication within the Cabinet Office.

7

Quality in local government

Lucy Gaster

Introduction

Many of the immediate issues affecting citizens' everyday life are the responsibility of local government. Roads, traffic, rubbish, street sweeping and lighting, crime and environmental health – all of these and many other services such as education and social services are a concern to local people. But too often residents have perceived and experienced local government as impenetrable, uninformative, unresponsive and patronizing. They have been passed from pillar to post – 'not my responsibility, sorry, you could try . . .' – and have felt helpless, angry and fobbed off. They wonder who is responsible for what, and what their Council Tax is paying for. Often they do not know who is their local elected councillor, and if they do know the name, they do not know the extent of their powers to intervene, either to put an individual case, or to develop new policy to meet new local needs.

This, of course, is a 'worst case' scenario, and many councils are no longer like that. However, it does reflect the real experience of far too many people in all parts of the UK, who cannot understand why their council tax and their votes should produce so few results, and whose main concern is that the council should deliver basic services at a reasonable standard, timely and appropriate, and suited to the people needing them.

This is a problem which local government, too, has recognized and, to some degree, has tried to respond to since the early 1980s. At that time 'quality' had not really been 'discovered' – but remoteness, unnecessary bureaucracy and unresponsiveness certainly had, at least in a few of the more radical councils. These wanted to do something about it – indeed they felt it was essential if local government and local democracy were to survive at all – but the purposes, mechanisms and potential outcomes were at that time obscure.

This was a period when local government was least popular, both with central government and with the electorate. Turn-out at elections was getting lower and lower – at 40 per cent, the lowest in the European Union (Stewart 1996b) – resources were increasingly squeezed through the 'rate-capping' mechanism, and directly provided services were under threat from privatization, removal from local government, or through contracting out. Local government was therefore compelled to fight on several fronts. It needed to show local people the value of local democracy and the special benefits of locally run services. And it needed to convince central government that it could provide services efficiently, effectively, economically and at an acceptable standard. New strategies and approaches were needed, perhaps with new people and certainly with new skills to carry the changes through.

This chapter is not a complete history of local government since 1980. But it is necessary to go back that far to understand the motivation for and direction of change, and to trace some of the trends, such as neighbourhood working, which are now becoming almost mainstream.

Following a brief and selective historical overview, the chapter concentrates on the recent policy framework and specifically on policies and practices most closely related to how local government services are delivered. The analysis mainly relates to the 410 councils in England and Wales. The different policies and practices of Scotland and Northern Ireland are not covered here.

Background

Local government has four distinctive characteristics:

1 It is a democratic institution, whose stakeholders include both elected councillors and the public at large – the citizens and communities of the locality.
2 It is highly complex, aiming to meet an extraordinarily diverse set of needs and delivering (or 'enabling') a huge range of functions.
3 It is in the process of rapid and fundamental change, partly stimulated from within, partly as a result of changes in the external environment. With central government hard on its heels, its very role and purpose now need to be redefined and its place in the wider world of 'local governance' has to be developed.
4 It has developed some bad habits, which will take a long time to eradicate. Departmentalism has created 'baronies' and 'fiefdoms'. Top-down

working and lack of delegation or trust in front-line staff is common. Attitudes based on 'we know best' and 'it's not my responsibility' are proving hard to change. There is a shortage of high-quality leadership.

Responsibilities: who's who, services, regeneration and local democracy

Local government is responsible for delivering a wide range of services, covering social services, education, housing, planning, environmental services (waste disposal, street cleaning and lighting) and others such as community development, youth service, environmental health and trading standards. Some services are required by statute and some are discretionary, meaning that the local council can decide whether and how to meet particular needs.

Who's who

These services are directed at the political level by locally elected councillors who are elected every four years, sometimes en bloc, sometimes a third at a time. This means that policy is formed by local political parties and, at a broad level, expressed in the manifestos published at election time. These policies both reflect the national policies of their particular party *and* the local situation, where more attention may be paid to issues such as parking, traffic and transport, recycling, and relations with other services such as police and health.

Detailed policies are developed during the period of office, formerly through an array of specialized committees, now (since 2000) through a 'Cabinet' system where individual councillors have 'portfolios' of responsibilities. A few authorities have, after local referenda, decided to opt for an elected mayor as the prime leader and figurehead for the council. By early 2002, only in London had such a mayor actually been elected (with very limited personal powers compared with mayors in France, some parts of the United States and many other countries).

Officers are accountable to the councillors for carrying out both the local policies and those required by central government. Directors may be responsible, as they always have been, for specific service areas such as education, housing or social services; or they may have wider, 'strategic' and 'corporate' responsibilities, such as 'the built environment', 'social care and community' and so on. They are responsible, through service units or traditional departments, for the day-to-day running of the services. It is often officers, both at the strategic, council-wide level and at the very local level, who engage in developing partnerships and new arrangements with other organizations – again, health, police and the voluntary sector come to mind – in order to provide services that meet local needs. Although in a few councils, councillors ('Members') have taken the lead in introducing policies and initiatives to improve service quality, on the whole it has also been officers who have taken the lead on this.

Service delivery and regeneration

As noted above, most services delivered through local government are based on statutory requirements. This does not mean that the precise amount, form or quality of these services is laid down, and these can vary enormously from place to place – the 'post-code lottery' as it is sometimes called. For basic services, local government has considerable discretion to decide on whether and how to 'improve' their services, and how to consult with or include their 'stakeholders' in this process (see Chapters 3–5). However, until the early 1980s, the way services were delivered was in practice largely in the hands of the professionals. Their protective attitude made it difficult to challenge the 'custom and practice' of 'how we've always done it', reinforcing the impenetrability and lack of flexibility experienced not only by members of the public but by councillors and other officers as well.

For many years, services were a 'given'. Relatively little attention was paid to whether they were good or bad, met real needs or did not, were equitably distributed or equally available to all sections of the community. This has profound implications for the development of 'quality' policies in local government.

In addition, local government has always had some discretion to introduce new and different services to meet specific local needs, and has had the power to raise small amounts of money to pay for them.

'Economic development' was one such 'discretionary' service in the past, growing in importance during the 1980s in response to structural change and loss of jobs in manufacturing industry. The whole notion of 'regeneration' (social, economic and environmental) began to dominate, partly because urban programme central government money was being made available specifically for this (often through national competitions) and more recently, following the Local Government Act 2000, because councillors must now have regard for the economic, social and environmental 'well-being' of their area. For many councils, especially but not exclusively in urban areas, regeneration became 'core business', often attracting more political and officer attention than the apparently mundane (and difficult) business of delivering day-to-day services. This has been much to the detriment of those services, and much to the disadvantage of the people living within the regeneration areas, where money from glamorous new projects could be obtained, but where the services were often as neglected as ever.

The damaging effects of this split between 'regeneration' and 'service delivery' is now being acknowledged through the introduction of programmes like the 'National Strategy for Neighbourhood Renewal'. This promotes 'neighbourhood management' as a multi-agency tool for bringing services and regeneration together at the very local level (Sullivan 2001b).

Local democracy

In addition to their service delivery and regeneration responsibilities, as the only directly elected body at local level, local authorities have particular responsibility for the health of local democracy. This can partly be achieved through councillors' own way of working: this is 'representative democracy' (Burns *et al*. 1994).

Councillors have a range of roles – representative, policy-making and strategic, and now 'executive' and 'scrutiny'. The latter two were introduced by the Local Government Act 2000. This aimed to streamline the 'political arrangements' and make decision making more accessible and transparent by reducing the number of committees and introducing executive and policy-making 'cabinets' and/or directly elected mayors. The effectiveness of these arrangements, which appear perversely to have produced a strong centralizing and exclusionary concentration of power within councils, has yet to be demonstrated.

It is also increasingly expected that councils will encourage 'participative democracy', through processes and structures for consultation and participation by local residents (citizens and communities) and by service users (DTLR 2001b). Some councils have pursued this issue for over 20 years. Others are very new at the game. There is huge variety in both the methods and the sincerity with which local people are becoming involved in local decisions (Lowndes *et al*. 1998). Local government may be at the forefront among public and voluntary services, but there is still a long way to go.

Structure

Local government structure is also complicated. Following the 1993–95 Local Government Review, 'unitary' or 'all/most-purpose' councils were established throughout Wales and Scotland, and in selected (and disputed) large urban areas in England not already served by metropolitan boroughs. Also in England, five counties – Avon, Berkshire, Cleveland, Humberside and the Isle of Wight – were reconstituted into unitary councils, and the former county councils were abolished (Stewart *et al*. 1997). In the rest of England, some smaller urban areas and most but not all rural areas retained the two-tier system established in 1974, with responsibilities divided between county councils and district councils. The review left a legacy of bitterness in many of these areas, and it has taken a long time for counties and districts in those areas both to recognize that they need to work together and to begin actually to do so.

To add to the confusion for the citizen wondering who is responsible for what, long-standing 'agency agreements' have meant that in many areas – but for different services, such as highways or some environmental services – district councils have acted as the 'agent' for the county. Similarly, some parish and town councils, the third tier in many areas, also operate agency agreements and are being encouraged to do more of this, to bring services nearer to local people (Rural White Paper, DETR/MAFF 2000). Parishes and town councils – which can now also be established in urban areas if local people vote for them – also have the right to raise a 'precept' to finance services such as community halls and more or less any local initiative, such as a one-stop shop, which they feel will be publicly supported.

Contracts, CCT and 'enabling'

Relationships between local government and residents and service users have long been complicated by the division of responsibilities for different services. Public surveys have shown time and again that most people do not know where to go for different services, and many people still believe that local government is responsible for health services (MORI polls, *passim*) (see also Chapter 8). However, although a few professional services such as architects have been regularly 'bought in' over the years, the use of contracts was not a major issue until the early 1980s. Indeed, in the 1960s and 1970s, the trend was rather the other way, with councils developing their own workforces, either directly or at 'arms length' through Direct Labour and Direct Service Organizations (DLOs and DSOs). The roles of 'client' (housing services for example, or the refuse collection department) and 'contractor' (housing repairs and refuse collection DLOs) thus existed in most authorities, but they were all under the same roof and ultimately accountable to the same people: the councillors.

However, there was no guarantee that services were being delivered efficiently, or that resources were being used economically. This had begun to concern central government in the late 1970s, but was a major issue for the incoming Conservative Government in 1979. This had no faith in or particular loyalty to local government, was intent on 'rolling back' the state, and conceived the idea of the 'enabling', minimal council as the way forward.

The idea behind 'enabling' was that councils would retain *responsibility* for services, which other, mainly private sector, organizations would now *deliver* through contracts. Councils therefore had to learn to specify exactly what needed to be done and then let, manage and monitor the resulting contracts. 'Contracting out' could be either compulsory or voluntary, and was in fact achieved by both methods, through government legislation and by government 'encouragement'.

Compulsory Competitive Tendering

Since 1980, there has thus been a major shift in the pattern of service delivery. At that time, a Local Government Planning and Land Act introduced the concept of 'Compulsory Competitive Tendering' (CCT) for selected blue-collar services: highways maintenance and construction, and building maintenance and construction. The 1988 Local Government Act extended CCT to refuse collection, street cleaning, schools and welfare catering, other catering, vehicle maintenance, building cleaning and grounds maintenance. It also allowed for CCT to be extended to the white-collar services in due course (Davis and Walker 1998; Watt 1998).

CCT meant that councils had to put the defined services out to open competitive tender, and to be able to show that the winning tender had been awarded through a proper process. If, as happened frequently in the early days, the contract was in fact awarded to the in-house DLO/DSO, they had to show a 5 per cent return on their finance (which private firms did not). As contracts came up for renewal, a larger proportion was let to private firms, which were now geared up to compete in this new market.

In 1990, the NHS and Community Care Act introduced the concept of the 'purchaser' (client) and 'provider' (contractor) in social services. A few years later, in 1996, government regulations based on the 1988 Local Government Act were used to define the 'white-collar' services to which CCT would apply. For most services, it was recognized that an in-house capacity would still be needed for policy development and statutory duties, so CCT only applied to defined proportions (40–45 per cent) of the total existing services such as legal, personnel, finance and information technology. However, for housing management the proportion was 95 per cent (Watt 1998: 202). It should be noted that neither blue-collar nor white-collar CCT applied to councils or services under a defined 'de minimis' budget level. Smaller district councils were therefore not affected, at least for some services.

Meanwhile, through 'externalization', 'outsourcing' and 'hosting' processes, some councils were voluntarily taking some internal services like payroll or information technology out of their systems. They were making deals with private firms to take over the staff and supply the services in 'partnership', at least in part as an attempt to pre-empt government legislation and do it 'on their own terms' (Martin *et al.* 1995: 27).

By the mid-1990s, the 'contract culture' was therefore well embedded in local government (Walsh *et al.* 1997). Unfortunately for the citizen, this did not bring much tangible benefit, certainly in terms of the quality of the services they experienced (Walsh 1991b; Walsh and Davis 1993). This is not the place to make a full analysis of the effects of the contract culture. Five major effects relating to quality can, however, be noted:

1 Contracts were extremely detailed and prescriptive, but largely focused on 'throughputs' – the frequency of rubbish collection or grass cutting, the number of repairs carried out within set times and so on – rather than results (were the streets clean after the refuse collection had taken place; could the children play on the grass or was it full of broken glass and dog excreta?).
2 Contracts and monitoring of contracts revolved mainly around cost, not quality. The temptation – and pressure from legislation – was to choose the cheapest company, not necessarily the best (and private contractors' use of cheap labour and corner-cutting working practices was liable to produce worse services than before).
3 The contract process was itself expensive, taking a lot of time and therefore incurring 'transaction costs' both for the client and the contractor. This, of course, reduced the amount of money available for actual services.
4 The use of contracts created (even more) a 'them and us' culture between different parts of the service delivery system. This created extremely weak links in the 'service chain' (see Chapter 4) and reduced accountability to the end-user – the local resident – to an absolute minimum: the whole process was very inward-looking.
5 The main 'positive' to emerge from this process was the need to be clear about what services were required and what could be delivered. This led to a great deal of interest in and expenditure on accreditation for ISO 9000, as a way of guaranteeing the quality of the *process* of service delivery (see Chapter 4 and Appendix). It did not, of course, guarantee the quality of the *product*, and created an expectation among clients and purchasers that contractors should possess an accredited system of some kind. For small voluntary organizations providing social or other services, the costs of this may be too high, thus excluding them from the market and reducing the possible range of provision.

'Enabling'

While the dominance of CCT and the 'contract culture' exercised the minds of local government councillors, officers and academics, the effects of the wider concept of 'enabling' should not be neglected. The original philosophy, as propounded by the Conservative government, was to maximize the use of the private sector in providing services, on the assumption that it is automatically cheaper and better (Deakin 1994). In this scenario, the role of local councils would be reduced to meeting once a year to open the contracts. This was an extreme vision of the 'enabling council', first propounded by Nicholas Ridley, one of several ministers responsible for local government in the 1980s. In practice, councils were adept at finding ways of making the new regime work to their advantage. When doing this, a much wider view of 'enabling' began to emerge in the mid-1990s, one that is remarkably consistent with what is now expected of local government. The three new 'enabling' roles that emerged for local government (Martin *et al.* 1995) were:

- *The client*: specifying, letting and managing contracts
- *The strategic purchaser* (or *'commissioner'*), influencing and developing the 'market' of provision and deciding priorities for local provision
- *'Community governance'*: developing the role of the local authority across the whole sphere of local provision, developing networks and partnerships with other service providers and 'enabling' local people to participate and take charge (see also Sullivan (2001a) for how this term has developed and acquired new meanings).

This interpretation locates local government as having a far wider role than in the past, more proactive and 'shaping' within the local area and the local community. 'Enabling' in practice has in fact laid the foundations for the new responsibilities of the early twenty-first century, when there has been far greater emphasis on delivering high-quality services, on partnership working, on seeing local councils as just one among equals at the local level, and on the central importance of relationships with local communities.

However, one major disadvantage has been that the relationship between provider and consumer has been weakened and confused. The lines of responsibility and accountability are, for the citizen, opaque and complex. In this stretched out 'service chain' (see Chapter 4), who is ultimately responsible for the quality of the service and where, if so inclined, can citizens put pressure and exercise influence? The dominance of the blame culture in local government, as in so much of the public sector, has sadly made it even more difficult for people to know and exercise their rights, and even more difficult, too, for front-line staff to make bold decisions, which might be appreciated by the member of the public but which may later be seen by management as 'risky' or even 'wrong'. The contract culture undoubtedly added to the 'watch your back' culture – and this is the opposite of the 'quality culture' put forward in Chapter 2 of this book.

Inspection and audit

Before looking at policies affecting local government since 1997, one further element of background data is needed. This concerns the way public services, and local government services in particular, are assessed.

Historically, the district auditor was the main actor in this field, together with specialized inspection bodies such as inspectors of education and social services. The district auditor's main concern was whether public money had been spent appropriately and according to legal requirements. This has always been an important safeguard for the public.

In 1982, the Conservative Government established an entirely new central body – a 'quango' reporting to the Department of the Environment

(DoE). This was the Audit Commission, which now incorporated the previously separate district audit function. The main purpose of the Commission was to examine and report on local authorities' 'economy, efficiency and effectiveness', known in shorthand as 'value for money', or 'VFM'. How was this to be done? The main methods used were, first, the development of a wide range of 'performance indicators', which would enable comparisons by time and place; and second, on-the-spot inspections.

The Audit Commission saw performance indicators as performing several different functions – demonstrating the achievement of objectives, identifying areas of practice for further investigation, helping make explicit the responsibilities of staff, as triggers for new policies and as the basis for resource allocation (Brokenshire 1987). However, the perception from within local government, at least at the start, was that central government would use them as the basis for yet another attack on local government. There was therefore great suspicion of the Audit Commission when it started work.

In practice, although local government and other public services are now drowning under audit and inspection regimes, as noted in earlier chapters, the Commission has concentrated largely on constructive criticism. Also, it has not hesitated to criticize the 'perverse effects' of government policies, and it has been continuously interested in 'good practice' and innovation. It has not turned into the 'big brother' initially feared.

However, the advent of Citizen's Charter league tables (see Chapter 6) has meant that selected statistics have, as local government feared, been used to identify successes and failures in different types of service. This is inevitably divisive and has led to defensive reactions from the public services. The new regime of Best Value, described below, appears to have reinforced the 'heavy-handed inspection' mode, compared with the 'how can we help you to improve' mode: this is frustrating both for local government and, it was reported (interview), for the Commission itself. It has also reinforced the 'watch your back' culture inside local government. Fulfilling the statistical requirements becomes more important than creative deviation from the norm, which will not show up positively in the returns to central government and the inspectorates (DETR 1999a, 1999b).

An important positive effect of this regime has been to make local authorities think about their services more clearly. Even the more reluctant councils began to be aware that careful comparisons between similar councils are valid and useful (Gaster 1997), while many councils, frustrated at the top-down and insensitive nature of government performance indicators, have begun to develop their own performance measures at the local level (DTLR 2001c).

From the point of view of quality improvement, which depends on monitoring and review for evidence of improvement, this is a positive development. The problem is that with the overload of measurements and inspections, local government councillors and officers do not always see it like this. Users and citizens, having hardly been involved in the process, and being dependent on annual reports or local publicity to tell them what has been happening locally, have scarcely been affected.

The role of the Audit Commission is one of the central features of the new policy framework within which local government now operates. This framework is described in the next section.

Local government under Labour: central control and 'initiativitis'

The policy framework

One of the first acts of the new Labour Government in May 1997 was to ratify the European Charter of Local Self-Government (Council of Europe 1985). This important document is the foundation stone of post-1989 efforts in Central and Eastern Europe to introduce democratic practice at the local level. It sets out some basic principles to which this country is now signed up. These include:

> Article 3: Concept of local self-government: (Paragraph 1): Local self-government denotes the right and the ability of local authorities, within the limits of the law, to regulate and manage a substantial share of public affairs under their own responsibility and in the interests of the local population.

> Article 4: Scope of local self-government: . . . Local authorities shall, within the limits of the law, have full discretion to exercise their initiative with regard to any matter which is not excluded from their competence nor assigned to any other authority. . . . Public responsibilities shall generally be exercised, in preference, by those authorities which are closest to the citizen . . .

> Article 6: Appropriate administrative structure and resources for the tasks of local authorities: Without prejudice to more general statutory provisions, local authorities shall be able to determine their own internal administrative structures in order to adapt them to local needs and ensure effective management. The conditions of service of local government employees shall be such as to permit the recruitment of high quality staff on the basis of merit and competence; to this end adequate training opportunities, remuneration and career prospects shall be provided.

These extracts from the Charter show that democracy at the local level is highly prized in the whole European community (it applies to all 44 members of the Council of Europe), based on the principles of autonomy, subsidiarity, closeness to the citizen and meeting local needs. Regrettably, the Charter is little known in the UK, even by people in the world of local government, and there have been few, if any mentions of it by the government when formulating its policy towards local government. Nevertheless, it is worth keeping these principles in mind when considering recent policy developments.

In the years following the advent of the 1997 Labour Government, two important White Papers on local government were published (DETR 1998; DTLR 2001b), and a good deal of legislation has been enacted in relation to the first. In addition, there have been numerous policies and initiatives from different parts of central government, as well, of course, as the Modernizing Government policies described in the previous chapter. It is neither possible nor appropriate to list all the recent policy developments affecting local government: the list would be too long and certainly too confusing. 'Initiativitis' is a disease from which local government is suffering badly (Wilson 2002), making it difficult to decide on priorities and *very* difficult to make sense of the whole (Performance and Innovation Unit 2000).

In practice, the policy most obviously relevant to the quality question is that developed to promote Best Value (see next section). However, other policies to promote joint working and to reach *all* people and communities are also extremely important, providing the opportunity to develop a culture and organizational framework capable of delivering the 'citizen-centred quality' advocated in this book (see Chapter 2). The work of the Social Exclusion Unit and more recently, the Department for Transport, Local Government and the Regions (DTLR) on social inclusion and 'neighbourhood working' is highly pertinent, as is the development of Local Public Service Agreements and Local Strategic Partnerships (see Office of Deputy Prime Minister website for details of all these). In parallel, several Government departments decided to carry out or pilot new policy initiatives through 'zones'. These were areas (usually 'deprived' according to various indices) where concentrated and joint efforts would be made to solve distinct problems: health, education, economic development or community safety. Some of these zones overlapped geographically, and it was easy for people living or working in them to become confused about who was doing what. Nevertheless, the underlying theme of joint working and citizen-led approaches were yet another indicator that public services were beginning to move in the same general direction. And in all of them, local government was expected to play a prominent part.

In addition, legislation (Health and Social Care Act 2001 and the Health Act 1999) enabling budgets to be pooled and authority to be delegated means that 'Care Trusts' can now be set up between local government and Primary Care Trusts (PCTs) and/or NHS Trusts (see also Chapter 8). The first of these was due to be in place by spring 2002. 'Care Trusts are being formed in order to ensure that services can be co-ordinated and

integrated locally to provide high quality, responsive care to local people'
(Department of Health 2001b).

The connections between many of these policy initiatives, together
with the new political arrangements introduced in the Local Government
Act 2000, are helpfully analysed by Helen Sullivan and colleagues, who
also review the possibilities for bringing them together through an area-
based or neighbourhood approach (Sullivan *et al.* 2001).

These policies are all attempts to encourage local government to
combine and implement its very wide-ranging responsibilities in both a
more strategic and a very local way. The overarching aim, if it can be so
described (it has never been spelt out, though the 2001 White Paper does try)
is to ensure that services are developed which meet the full range of needs.
These needs can be identified through close work with communities,
including the 'hard to reach' (that is, people who have been or who feel
excluded from mainstream society), by joint working with partners, and
by changing local policy and practice. This challenging agenda will be
difficult to put into practice, which may explain the Prime Minister's enthusiasm for elected mayors: charismatic leaders as change agents could be
thought to be the way forward. As noted earlier, however, local authorities
and, through local referenda, local citizens, have shown much less interest
in this idea, preferring the Cabinet model of collective responsibility.

The main problem, as ever, is the balance between, on the one hand,
central direction, control and punishment; and, on the other hand, local
decisions based on local autonomy. These tensions have always existed and
will always exist, and local government will continue to have to work
within them. However, the scales were definitely weighted towards central
control in the first Labour administration (1997–2001), as they had been
during the whole of the Conservative administration of 1979–97. In the
second Labour administration (2001–), at the time of writing, it seems best
to give the benefit of the doubt: there is evidence of a real intention to
encourage more local autonomy and diversity, but there is still a lot of
central control, partly exercised through the Audit Commission and other
inspectorates, partly from the fact that only 25 per cent of local government income is raised through local taxes (compared with 52 per cent in
1980, see Jackman 1985). This gives central government a great deal of
financial power. The question of how much local variation the government
will tolerate, bearing in mind considerations of equity, consistency, use of
resources, and possibly the views of citizens, has yet to be resolved.

At the end of the day the centre does have the power to insist upon
change. New Labour has not been slow to use that power but at
the same time it recognises the need to secure the co-operation of
key stakeholders at local level if the modernisation agenda is to be
successfully managed.

(Wilson 2002: 29)

The 1998 White Paper and Best Value

The Labour Government came into office in 1997 with a promise to abolish CCT. This, the party recognized, was extremely unpopular (at least among local government activists and trades unions) and had not produced noticeably better services. Nevertheless, the government did not want a return of the *laissez-faire* approach and it did want to encourage consistent and good quality service production. This was an early priority, and led in 1997 to the publication of a series of consultation documents, followed by a White Paper in 1998 (DETR 1998), which outlined its new approach to local government.

The White Paper was based on two important principles:

- the need for change, for local government to become more outward-looking and responsive to local people
- local choice and diversity.

Specific proposals – most of which were later incorporated in legislation – included:

- New internal political structures (options for cabinets, mayors, etc.) aiming to enhance democratic practice; and variations in arrangements for elections and other forms of local participation such as area forums to encourage higher voting turn-out.
- Improved financial accountability and a new ethical framework to enhance probity and develop codes of conduct and standards of behaviour for elected councillors and staff.
- Beacon councils – to encourage and reward 'best-performing' councils which would 'set the pace of change and encourage the rest to innovate and to modernise' (White Paper para 2.18)
- A new concept of 'scrutiny', to enable councillors to examine and 'call in' executive decisions and to review service delivery and other local issues.
- Promoting the economic, social and environmental 'well-being' of communities through the development of 'community leadership' and working in partnership with other agencies and local communities at the local level. Under the Local Government Act 2000, councils now have a specific power (but not a duty) to develop a joint 'community strategy' to address these issues.
- Improving local services through Best Value – the new arrangements designed to replace CCT.

'Best Value'

Mainly because of the urgent need to abolish CCT and put something in its place, Best Value was the first of the White Paper ideas to be put into practice, first through a pilot programme (DTLR 2001a) and then, in April 2000, across the board. Two activities are involved:

- all services must be reviewed every five years
- a 'best value performance plan' must be published annually.

Each of these may be audited (the plans) and inspected (the reviews) by the Audit Commission. By mid-2001, 3000 reviews had been completed and 600 reports published. This cost £50 million in 2000–01 (Audit Commission 2001).

The reviews must be based on four principles – the 'four C's'. These are:

1 *Challenge*: why and how is the service provided?
2 *Compare*: How does the service compare with others, including non-local government services?
3 *Compete*: Have the 'principles of fair competition' been embraced when deciding who should deliver the service?
4 *Consult*: What are the expectations of local service users and residents about the service?

(For more information, see the Audit Commission's website (Audit Commission 2001–02).)

In order to put Best Value into practice, local authorities were strongly encouraged by the DETR and the Cabinet Office to use the EFQM Excellence Model (see Chapter 4), or to try the other quality schemes being promoted by the Cabinet Office (Investors in People, Charter Mark and ISO 9000 – see Chapter 6) (Cabinet Office/DETR 2000).

Best Value appeared to offer great possibilities for re-thinking services and working on their quality and it was generally welcomed by local government. Unfortunately, this opportunity for innovative thinking was not widely taken up either in the pilot programme or in the first full year of operation (Audit Commission 2001). Most authorities concentrated on reviewing existing services; they were unimaginative about considering the needs of citizens or areas (but some did undertake citizen-centred, cross-cutting and area-based reviews); they were cautious about challenging past practice; they were inhibited by their departmental 'fiefdoms' and by the different rules and legislation affecting different services; and they became bogged down in the time-consuming *process* of review rather than thinking enough about how the service could be changed (DTLR 2001a).

> Reviews are complex and often very expensive projects and many councils have reported 'getting lost in the process', either because reviews were not well scoped to start with or were not managed efficiently.
>
> (Audit Commission 2001: para 58)

These difficulties were reinforced by the inspection process, by the fear of punishment for 'failure' and by the prevailing organizational culture.

In some pilots efforts to improve services are also being dogged by a 'culture of compliance'. Two decades of detailed prescription and tight control of local authority spending imposed from the centre, has [sic] produced a generation of service managers and committee chairs who are accustomed to focusing on 'micro-management' and operational issues. . . . (They are) unused to addressing major policy issues or taking a proactive role in shaping new models of service delivery.

(Martin 1999: 59)

A good deal of learning has emerged from Steve Martin and colleagues' evaluation of the pilot authorities and from the Audit Commission's reviews (DTLR 2001a; Audit Commission 2001, 2002). However, it is not yet lclear whether local government now sees Best Value as an 'opportunity' (to improve services in innovative ways) or a 'threat' (to local autonomy). It seems to be widely recognized that changes to the Best Value process are needed, both internally and in the inspection regime, if the policy is to achieve the service improvement originally envisaged, but local commitment to radical and long-lasting action has yet to emerge.

The role of the Audit Commission

As noted above, the Audit Commission has played and continues to play an extremely important role in local government developments. It is not, of course, the only inspectorate (local government currently has to submit 60 different plans to different parts of Whitehall, all of which have to be inspected and approved) but it is the most wide-ranging. Like other regulators, it recognizes the burden of inspection on local government, and sees the need for better coordinated or even, for cross-cutting issues like safeguarding children, merged inspections (Platt 2002; Audit Commission 2001).

The Commission's consultation for its 2001–04 strategy highlighted three aspects of service improvement on which local authorities now wished to focus. These were:

1 focusing clearly on what matters to service users
2 making joint working deliver real benefits
3 stimulating innovation

A less burdensome inspection regime, together with better information about 'what works' in other authorities, was identified by local authorities as likely to help. The Commission has taken this to heart and expressed an intention in its published strategy to develop its work along these lines, reflecting this in how it does its own work (Audit Commission 2002).

User and citizen involvement is now to be a major theme in all the Commission's work and particularly in the audit and inspection process (which would now be merged). Rather than focusing on particular services or groups of services, pilots were being developed for 'comprehensive performance assessments', where councils would be scored across a range of criteria and categorized as:

- top performing
- striving
- coasting
- under-performing

These categories are identified as a key feature in the 2001 White Paper on local government (DTLR 2001b), with the idea that the top-performing and striving councils will be rewarded for their efforts. However, it is difficult to see what is the incentive for the lower two categories, which will simply find themselves being labelled as 'poor' and receiving no help to get out of the rut.

Other Audit Commission pilots will look at how to carry out cross-cutting 'citizen-focused audit' reviews (based on the needs of particular population groups), and 'user-focused best value inspections' (based on the direct involvement of users in the review process). As well as resolving the problem of how decentralized local authorities, like South Somerset District Council or Coventry City Council, could knit their own area-based approach with the mainly service-led approach of Best Value, these new kinds of review fit well with the citizen-centred concept of quality put forward in this book.

Quality improvements in local government

Policies to link with citizens and improve services: decentralization and participation

Best Value has undoubtedly dominated local government thinking about service quality since 1998. However, although a good deal of work has been carried out under the Best Value banner, this is not the first time that local government has considered quality improvement and other policies to improve services for the public. As noted earlier, the growing unpopularity of local government, together with the actions of the previous government, concentrated the minds of many councillors and officers in the previous two decades.

A more public-oriented and accessible approach was increasingly seen as an essential part of good local government practice. The work of the many councils during the 1980s to decentralize service delivery (Burns *et al.* 1994), and subsequent moves towards area-based planning and delivery of services during the 1990s (Gaster 1995b) constituted real 'bottom-up' attempts to improve service quality. This was not always a conscious process, since the objectives of many decentralization initiatives were never made explicit (Sullivan *et al.* 2001), but retrospective evaluations help to show that some aspects of service quality, couched in terms of 'access', 'integration' and 'responsiveness', were generally at the heart of the programme.

Decentralization and related initiatives – one-stop shops, call centres, 'kiosks' for IT access – illustrate local government's ability to change and improve the experience of the public when they first come into contact with their council. The weakness of many of these efforts has been in their implementation: front-line staff, in a marginal and undervalued position within most organizations, have had great difficulty in persuading the rest of the Council that what they are doing is important and significant for the *whole* Council's work (Gaster 1991b; Gregory 1998; Sullivan 2001b).

The current central government exhortations (and sometimes requirements) to 'consult' the public are also nothing new for local authorities. They have in practice long led the field, sometimes in the context of decentralization policies (neighbourhood forums, area committees and the like), sometimes as a distinct and separate policy (Stoker 1997). However, analysis shows that it takes a long time for the new approach to become credible with local people (Gaster and Taylor 1993), and that while a wide range of techniques has evolved (Gaster 1995b, 1996a, 1999a), any one council is unlikely to use more than a very few (Lowndes *et al.* 1998).

The use of quality systems

In the early 1990s, when 'quality' was beginning to be discussed within local government, the then Local Government Management Board and the several local authority associations (representing different types of council) were enthusiastic. A working group was established, a certain amount of networking took place, and two directories of 'quality initiatives' were published. These listed the initiatives being undertaken by different services (housing, trading standards, etc.) within councils to involve the public and to adopt a range of ready-made quality systems, of which ISO 9000 was much the most common. Some councils, such as Braintree District Council and Bradford Metropolitan Council, developed council-wide approaches. In Braintree's case, this was based largely on ISO 9000; in Bradford's case, it was based on a 'learning organization' approach, which encouraged the use of different systems (ready-made and home-grown) to solve different problems.

These councils, together with the London Borough of Islington and the Metropolitan Borough of Tameside, were the only four that could be identified in 1996 as taking a corporate approach to quality (Gaster 1997). Elsewhere, each service unit tended to adopt its own method. Progress was often helped by councillors and senior officers who championed the work – but their support was too easily diverted to other matters.

There was, then, some kind of foundation for the Best Value policy in 1999. Unfortunately, a major problem was that 'quality' had been associated in staff minds either with the double standards of 'customer care' noted in Chapter 4, or – rightly or wrongly – with cuts in resources and staff. This naturally affected morale, and although the commitment and enthusiasm of front-line staff for their work and often for their 'customers' is well-known, this did not necessarily extend to specific 'quality' initiatives, especially as an 'add-on' to their 'normal' work.

A lot of persuasion was – and is – therefore needed to convince staff and councillors that 'quality' can be meaningful and even helpful, and that it should be integral, not extra, to everyday work. Analysis of the use of the Excellence model (promoted by DETR and the Cabinet Office but not by the Audit Commission), both as a general tool (PricewaterhouseCoopers 2000) and specifically in the context of Best Value (IDEA 2001) found that although many councils were reported as using the model, very many of them had not found it useful. As many as 37 per cent of the 65 IDEA respondents (not all of whom were using it) said that it was not useful for the 'challenge' element of Best Value, though 56 per cent thought it was useful for the formation of performance plans. One problem was that managers were being 'told' to use it, without a great deal of faith or understanding:

> I didn't choose to use this model but had to because of a corporate decision to use it for all Best Value Reviews. We hadn't any real experience of using the model previously and spent a lot of time and scarce resources getting nowhere really, which was very frustrating. I feel those who influenced the policy decision really didn't understand what it was all about in the first place. They saw it as the answer to everything.
>
> (Service review leader, district council, quoted in IDEA 2001: 7)

Conclusion

The current picture of quality in local government is thus rather mixed. Achievements in taking government and services closer to citizens through decentralization and public participation, and improvement in some services in some places show what can be done if there is commitment and support to do so. On the other hand, the forces working against change, both within the local government culture and from the outside world, can undermine or negate those very achievements, which have often gone unrecognized and undervalued either by government or the public at large. Table 7.1 sums up the discussion.

If 'quality' has not progressed across the board as far as might have been expected since it came to the fore in local government in the early

Table 7.1 Achievements and tensions affecting quality in local government

Achievements	Tensions
Increased clarity of specification, process and service objectives (CCT, service planning, quality systems and Best Value reviews)	Focus on process at expense of outcomes; focus on standardization at expense of flexibility; incremental 'improvements' in existing services – lack of radical thinking about service design
Decentralization policies: getting closer to consumers, citizens and communities	Lack of clear objectives; failure of back line to support front line; marginalization of front line
Consultation and participation policies for public involvement	Honesty and clarity needed about the power to be transferred or shared; need for clear objectives; timescales and timetables often too short; need for variety of methods; need to demonstrate impact
Innovation and development of needs-led and cross-cutting approaches	Major cultural change needed, with involvement of front-line and other staff, unions and the public; complex and difficult; appropriate performance indicators and coordinated inspections needed; danger of being judged (as 'failed' or 'successful') too soon; challenge of 'partnership' working
Leadership and commitment from politicians and senior management	Need for commitment to be sustained over long periods; need for management style which facilitates trust, innovation and risk
Central government commitment to improving public services (Best Value and Modernization)	Ambivalence about whether to trust local government to succeed on its own; divisive culture of 'success', 'failure', intervention and punishment; insufficient attention to 'quality' per se

Source: Gaster 1999b

1990s, why is that? Is there something special about local government that makes it particularly difficult to achieve a coherent and effective approach?

There is probably enough evidence to suggest that many of the problems experienced in local government are in fact common to most public sector organizations aiming to implement a quality programme. In the current policy climate, two of the most important are:

1 'Initiativitis': the disease affecting most of the public sector, deriving from the large number of policies and requirements emanating from central government, especially since 1997.

2 Organizational culture: despite the efforts of leading councillors and officers to develop outward-looking, cross-cutting and public-oriented cultures in local councils, local residents in far too many areas are still experiencing the old problems: failure to respond to questions and complaints; being passed round the system; lack of knowledge of front-line staff; protectionism about working practices and fiefdoms.

Nevertheless, there has in practice been an enormous amount of change during the 1990s, much of it generated from within. In the 1980s and first half of the 1990s, when central government's only interest in local government was to demonstrate its distrust and remove as many of its powers as possible, councillors and officers put many of the building blocks in place – patchily rather than comprehensively – to develop clarity of purpose, a public-oriented style and culture, and practical improvements in their services.

With the publication of the 2001 White Paper, which promotes local autonomy, experiment, citizen involvement and quality standards, the signs are hopeful for the future. There is a lot of 'good practice' to learn from and build on, given the will, the capacity and the necessary encouragement and support to do so. The spirit of the European Charter lives on.

8

Quality in health

Amanda Squires

Introduction

Health and its care have become a universal political priority as a result of
their impact on national economy, the risks to health shared by the community, and a moral responsibility for equity of care within societies regarded as
developed. The welfare-style National Health Service (NHS), created in 1948
to meet these economic, social and moral requirements, typified the expectations of the British post-war culture. By 1990, changing influences, especially
raised public expectations, resulted in political focus on welfare services and
the subsequent introduction of market-style provision. The aim was to enable
provision of care to become customer, rather than service led and to reduce
public expenditure: the reality was a debate between cost and activity. It
quickly became apparent that competition within a public service was counter-
productive, and in 1998 further reform was implemented whereby provision
would be funded on the basis of evidence of clinical governance (quality
improvement), ensuring that quality would be considered equally alongside
cost and activity. This chapter considers quality in NHS healthcare provision
in general, with ambulance services as a particular example.

The British health service, 1946–90

To understand the changes in the NHS since 1990 it is necessary to look
briefly at its history. Before the Second World War, healthcare provision

in the UK was provided through a mix of compulsory insurance for workers, charity for the poor, and payment by others through voluntary insurance, subscription or direct payment. Access, particularly for women and children, required careful financial consideration. The main causes of ill health were accidents and infections; and care, rather than cure, was the main solution (McKeown 1986). All occurred within a culture of professional (medical) power, gained through both public recognition and an agreement between the medical profession and the state to limit demand to the supply available (Salter 1998).

The need to improve the delivery of healthcare after the Second World War was based on the frustration of the public and some professionals with the pre-war fragmentation of services and inequity of provision and post-war concepts of efficiency, rationality, collectivism and citizenship rights (Ranade 1994).

The key features of the service – the National Health Service – were that it should be (Allsop 1984):

- comprehensive: from 'cradle to grave'
- collective: tax funded and free at the point of delivery
- universal: coverage of the whole population
- equal: geographical uniformity.

The Minister of Health now had direct responsibility for hospital and specialist services and indirect responsibility for family practitioner and local authority health services. The local authorities provided community and environmental services, maternal and child welfare, health visiting, home nurses, chiropody, vaccination and immunization, aftercare for mental illness and learning disabilities, and maintenance of health centres (Levitt *et al.* 1995). Some of these responsibilities had been held before the 1946 NHS Act, and some had been provided by a variety of voluntary and statutory as well as private agencies. Boards of Governors (for teaching hospitals) and Management Committees, appointed by central government, administered the hospitals. The multi-party conception and wide public support for the NHS gave the service 'sacrosanct' status.

Strong and Robinson (1990: 10) reflected that:

> The NHS as created in 1948 was brilliant but partially flawed: brilliant because it offered real and politically viable solutions to many of the key problems in paid health care delivery; flawed because, faced with the rampant power of the medical profession, it failed for nearly 40 years to establish a proper management structure and an integrated corporate culture.

Legislation to develop organization and management in the NHS occurred in the 1970s and early 1980s. Community Health Councils were established under the 1973 NHS Reorganisation Act. They were independent, though centrally funded, and would act as 'the patient's watchdog' and represent consumers' views. At the same time health services provided by county and borough councils were transferred to the NHS – accounting for the fact that the public still regard some healthcare provision as the responsibility of 'the council' (see Chapter 7). The ambulance service was a relative latecomer to the NHS family. Although a statutory provision under the 1946 National Health Service Act, it was not until 1974 that responsibility for the service passed from local authorities to the NHS.

This period of reorganization culminated in 1983 in the introduction by the Conservative Government of 'general management'. Tacit collusion between managers and clinicians enabled the continuation of 'we know best' clinical autonomy, which protected existing services and evaded any possible challenge from patients or the general public.

By the late 1980s, political consensus about the NHS was crumbling. In 1988, a relatively small miscalculation in the NHS budget produced a massive financial crisis. Thousands of beds were closed before a particularly harsh winter (Appleby *et al.* 1990), ending 40 years of all-party support for the service (Levitt *et al.* 1995) and bringing policy, rather than just resources, into the political arena.

Expectations, satisfaction and stakeholders

By the 1990s, changing expectations, epidemiology, technology, demography and economics were driving governments across the developed world to review their health services. Rising public expectations have been shown to be the main influence, exceeding the even more publicized impact of ageing (Abel-Smith 1994).

The UK ambulance service provides a good example of this process, with rapidly growing demand and expectations over the years. By 2002, about 4 million patients were being carried for emergency or urgent medical need each year. Inappropriate use of the 999 service was a problem. Information campaigns were being used to educate the public about criteria for calling ambulances and suggesting other alternatives (especially that of contacting NHS Direct – a nurse-led health advice line), while ambulance assessment software was being refined to enable control staff to identify those calls for which an alternative would be more appropriate for the patient.

As has been described in Chapter 1, the gap between expectations and perception or experience produces high, medium or low levels of satisfaction with service quality. Quality in public health care has been described as:

> fully meeting the needs of those who need the service most, at the lowest cost to the organisation, within limits and directives set by higher authorities.
>
> (Ovretveit 1992: 2)

This definition implies that a number of stakeholders have an interest in the health service, principally users, providers and funders. The change in their expectations has accelerated from a slow start, is largely unexpressed and not only differing but largely misunderstood by and between them. This is because they are based on different assumptions:

- Users are pursuing a 'social' model with emphasis on interpersonal and organizational aspects. There is an assumption of infallibility of clinical care, as expected of quality assured and quality controlled consumer goods (Chapter 4). When health or healthcare fail *the provider is generally blamed for the failure*.
- Providers are pursuing a 'scientific' model, increasingly basing their care on interpretation of technical results, for example from pathology laboratories. Lack of evidence to support a universal scientific approach is shown by the fact that only 20 per cent of medical care is supported by evidence (20 per cent being actually harmful (Chatham 1998)), with an even lower evidence base in other disciplines (Firth-Cozens 1996), with notable exceptions. This reliance on interpretation of data results in *failure being blamed on the idiosyncratic user* who presents with a mix of unique conditions.
- Funders are pursuing a 'business' model, as they are measured on patient throughput and financial solvency. They do not generally have clinical experience and their central drive is for business success factors such as economy, efficiency and effectiveness (value for money). However, the lack of evidence about 'what works' makes it difficult to challenge existing clinical practice, leaving the *funder reliant on provider knowledge and autonomy* – already shown to be largely flawed.

Funders, called 'commissioners' in 1990 (subsequently re-named 'planners' in 1999 to avoid being identified with the former 'healthcare market'), are the new players. They are appointed on the basis of skills such as knowledge of health policy, analytical skills, management experience and, particularly, the ability to make objective decisions based on the often poor evidence provided (Herzlinger 1997). Funders are more likely to pursue targets of safety, effectiveness and efficiency (Vuori and Roger 1989; Stebbing and Dixon 1992; Wilkes 1993; Debrah 1994) – a business model.

However, unlike a private sector business model, this approach was constrained by the principles of equity and public accountability: improved services might attract more patients but, because the NHS is funded through capitation (number of people served in the community) rather than actual use of the services, they do not bring additional income and of course they put extra demand on the services.

The three main stakeholders – users, providers and funders – therefore operate within a potential blame culture but remain interdependent. These different perspectives provide the ammunition both for healthy collaboration and for unhealthy conflict.

The 1990 reforms

Since the 1988 funding crisis, the non-technical aspects of the NHS – that is, its organizational infrastructure – have no longer been sacrosanct or immune from public criticism. There was simmering public anger and concern about the way the NHS was being handled, for example were staff being properly supervised and held accountable for their actions? Public questioning was bolstered by increased knowledge of alternative models of healthcare delivery through travel, improved communication and media coverage. Experience and expectations of responsive services was growing, partly as a result of increased access (through employment packages) to the private healthcare sector, giving experience of what *customer* care, as a proxy for *clinical* care, could be provided. The fact that the scope of non-NHS care was relatively limited, being highly selective and excluding emergencies and, frequently, intensive care, was often unknown and therefore unconsidered by the private sector user. Overall satisfaction with the running of the NHS went down from 49 per cent in 1983 to 33 per cent in 1994, and by the end of the 1990s, interest in the service was top of the public's agenda (King 1998).

A confidential review of the NHS by the Conservative Government resulted in two White Papers: *Working for Patients* (Department of Health 1989a) and *Caring for People* (Department of Health 1989b). Both were enacted in 1990.

Working for Patients aimed to lead to a more responsive culture through a 'managed' or 'quasi'-market, limited to internal competition, using contracts. *Caring for People* addressed the implications of moving people from long-stay nursing (NHS) and local government residential institutions into social service funded care within the community.

'Responsiveness' was to be achieved by identifying and meeting the assumed needs of users through competition between providers. In practice, the criteria used were the more easily quantified components of cost and volume. 'Quality' was only used as a bargaining tool, rather than being an equal component in decision making (Figure 8.1).

Figure 8.1   The fulcrum of quality in commissioning.

The reforms were seen as a two pronged attack to raise both quality of care and its efficiency, first, through competition and second, through informing and empowering users (McSweeney 1994). However, there was no evidence that NHS users felt that their interests would be met through a market. The Conservative Government thought that, in the changing climate of public opinion, the availability of choice through a market culture would be welcomed. In fact, they underestimated public (and professional) suspicion of the Government's motives and their fears that it would lead to rationing. They also failed to comprehend the continuing appeal of the existing NHS – with all its known weaknesses – to most of the British public.

The overt aims of the 1990 NHS reforms were:

- to retain the advantages of the NHS (universal coverage, effective central cost control)
- to achieve quantifiable health gain
- to expand consumer choice and improve efficiency by competition through an internal market and formation of provider Health Trusts and GPs as fundholders.
- to replace custodial hospital care of people with mental health and learning difficulties with smaller, more homely community-based accommodation.

Within the Department of Health, the NHS Policy Board was set up to deal with strategy, while the NHS Management Executive (NHSME), later the NHS Executive, was responsible for implementation.

The objective was to change the culture of the NHS, to shift from being provider-led to being customer-led. The more business-like approach was to use the health authority commissioner or GP fundholder as a proxy for the user's needs. The fundamental difference between public and commercial services, where the relationship between satisfaction and efficiency is reversed, was to be met by money following the patient. There was, however, no evidence that commissioners could truly reflect users' needs (Propper and Le Grand 1997), and no advice was forthcoming on how to deal with the fact that the values of efficiency, competition and user choice are potentially contradictory: users might wish to choose a service that happens to be inefficient (Clarke and Newman 1997).

Although the overt government message of the 1990 reforms was 'user responsiveness', a more covert theme was detected by some authors. This was to break the power of the professionals, through focusing on the popular and attractive theme of 'quality'. Professionals had built their power base on the politically convenient concept of 'technical' quality (that is, *clinical* fitness for purpose). In practice, this had acted as a powerful obstacle to improving the 'non-technical' quality (interface/ambience – how people are treated), which the public needed and desired (Sutherland and Dawson 1998). A powerful clinical, predominantly medical, lobby still exists. The internal market has probably weakened it to some extent, though it could be argued that the power has now shifted to managers and funders, rather than to patients and citizens.

Problems of the 'market' approach to healthcare

The market approach to public healthcare is controversial and proved to be inappropriate because of the following issues:

- Monopoly of provision exists: there is limited entry and exit of providers, little information, and transaction costs result from setting up contracts and the need for public accountability.
- Resources (income) are not directly linked to consumption (expenditure). Frequently those in most need (children, disabled, unemployed and elderly) are paying the least into the system (this is equitable but not commercial).
- Incentives (e.g. to keep costs down) may be controversial, for example, the identifier, purchaser and provider of services necessary to meet a need may be one and the same, such as the GP.
- Profit to private providers is from public funds.

In this 'managed' market, the government role is to raise the funds (through taxation) for third-party commissioning, to regulate spending, and to facilitate the fair allocation of scarce resources. The advantages of economies of scale, the requirement for comprehensive scope, the political risk of spare capacity and bankruptcy, and the existence of monopoly provision led Propper and Le Grand (1997) to conclude that competition in the NHS was inappropriate.

The market concept was, in principle, rescinded with the 1997 change in government. The Labour Party manifesto stated that 'Labour will cut costs by removing the bureaucratic process of the internal market', and 'planning and provision of care are necessary and distinct functions and will remain so'. 'Commissioning' therefore became 'planning'.

The Patient's Charter

Almost in parallel with the 1990 NHS reform, the Citizen's Charter initiative was introduced (see Chapter 6). This was a potentially useful way to reinforce the message of user-led services. The Patient's Charter (Department of Health 1991) contribution to this initiative listed, for the first time, citizens' rights and the national and local standards that could be expected from the service. However, these standards were selected by managers and largely limited to conformance to visible and superficial organizational goals rather than ongoing clinical and organizational improvement. For example, reward was for short waiting lists rather than user-led criteria for inclusion on the list, sensible prioritization of waiting lists or effectiveness of the resulting intervention. The emphasis was on throughputs, not outcomes. Nevertheless, a more 'critical customer' began to emerge, more willing to complain and to bring health purchasers and providers to account in relation to the published standards.

A major review of the Patient's Charter was undertaken by the King's Fund in 1997 (Farrell *et al.* 1998). This concluded that the advantages of the existing charter were that it had:

- raised staff awareness of patient needs, issue and rights
- helped set standards and identify priorities for action
- set comparable standards for reviews of performance
- helped to move the NHS culture towards a 'user perspective'

The disadvantages were:

- lack of clarity about its aim – this engendered wide scepticism
- insufficient user or staff involvement in creating the charter
- too much emphasis on quantitative standards
- ignoring clinical standards and outcomes
- some standards irrelevant to patients' real needs – especially the vulnerable
- difficulty in monitoring – data costly to collect, sometimes fudged and/or ignored
- hospital services dominating at the expense of primary care
- low patient awareness of the Charter
- patients' expectations unrealistically raised
- little emphasis on patients' responsibilities

The 1991 Charter was revised and eventually overtaken by other initiatives. Farrell *et al.* (1998) suggest that despite its shortcomings, the principles of a charter are useful, provided it works from the patient's perspective in setting, providing and monitoring services.

Culture change and Total Quality Management

Managing change and achieving 'continuous quality improvement'

Success in developing a responsive culture centres on understanding and meeting not only the changing quality perspectives of each stakeholder, which have been outlined above, but also, in such a highly interactive service, their requirements for how the service is delivered.

The impact of change on the culture of an organization is proportional to the closeness of values between the individual (and the groups they form) and the culture expected to result from the change (Womack *et al.* 1990). The primary values held by the main 'change targets' in public healthcare, the providers, were largely those held when they entered the service: altruism and autonomy. Both of these public sector values were perceived as threatened by the change from 'welfare' to 'market'. Healthcare providers received support from the public, the *minor* change targets, who also felt threatened by the loss of the response they had become used to.

The concept of a comprehensive approach to quality was not explicit at this stage.

The principles of change management (see Chapter 2) include the need to understand the organization, the reason for change and the process of change; the existence of leadership and communication; measurement of progress; and reinforcement of the achievement (Clarke 1994). Because of the strength of the traditional culture, combined with public fear of change, a largely inexperienced leadership and the absence of quality measures of progress, the history of organizational change in the public sector shows that, once the immediate political pressures are relaxed, old-style behaviour emerges and long-term and unconsolidated change often fails (Goddard *et al.* 1997). This is certainly the case with the NHS.

The NHS QA and TQM initiatives

Although the superficial message of the 1990 reforms was user responsiveness, a more coercive theme is detected by some authors. It was known that Mrs Thatcher had a deep distrust of the professions, particularly those with autonomy, public support and detail she did not understand (Gladstone and Goldsmith 1995). A focus on 'quality' would therefore gain public support, at the same time attempting to break the power of professional cohesion (Sutherland and Dawson 1998) and improve efficiency. A letter in June 1989 from Duncan Nichol, then Chief Executive of the NHS Executive, had required District Health Authorities (DHAs) to have quality assurance (QA) in place by the end of that year. This was subsequently revised so as to focus on the implementation of the NHS Total Quality Management (TQM) project: this emphasized the need for a comprehensive quality improvement culture, with funding available for successful bids. Although these initiatives were government-led, improvement in clinical practice had always existed for the majority and there was considerable anger at quality being introduced by 'management' as a new concept.

TQM in the public sector faces particular problems. Fluctuating political influence affects clarity of goals, which compromises the long-term perspective necessary for success (Osborne and Gaebler 1993). In addition, existing bureaucracy can act as a brake or a filter, making it difficult for changes to reach the front line, while it is always difficult to measure the results of social goals as opposed to the manufacturing goals required from traditional TQM systems (Redman *et al.* 1995).

As we saw in Chapter 4, in its ideal form, TQM encourages autonomy, challenges the status quo, facilitates team-working and is intended to empower all, including junior staff and service users. These characteristics necessarily threaten the established order to varying degrees. In the NHS there was the additional problem of 'white coat' staff, whose allegiances were at least partly to other reference groups (professional associations) and who did not give wholehearted support to the initiative (Hart 1996).

These problems are likely to have contributed to the fact that the NHS TQM initiative was not regarded as a success, although there were notable exceptions. Ovretveit (1994) ascribes the failure to the short term-ism of government, lack of investment in the initiative, lack of clarity of client needs and satisfaction measures, and failure to involve powerful players. Other lessons were that existing strengths and existing, but hidden, good quality practice must be acknowledged and built on. There is also a need for sophisticated mutual understanding of the total organization and for consistency of policy (Southon and McDonald 1997). Policy was in fact unclear, with on the one hand, expectations of 'conformance' to specifications and standards (QA) within contracts, and on the other, 'empowerment' and 'responsiveness' (TQM). These are not mutually exclusive, but they do represent different priorities and processes, which was confusing for managers, staff and users.

The 1998 NHS reforms

In 1998, 50 years of the NHS were celebrated – with reservations. The review sponsored by the King's Fund records that:

> Something has got to give . . . we are in an era of uncertainty and a clash between social obligation and personal autonomy . . . It is arguable whether the present system in this country can contain the pressures for increased expenditure much longer. We may have to face the unpleasant possibility that in the second 50 years of the NHS, the ever growing opportunities and costs will make it impossible for health services to maintain themselves outside the laws of cost, supply and demand that influence the distribution of services and products elsewhere in society.
>
> (Rivett 1998: 484)

The acceptability of this view can be gauged from the fact that the author, a GP, became an official at the Department of Health, and that the foreword to the book was written by Prime Minister Tony Blair.

As well as concern about the cost of the service, and following the non-technical concerns (how patients were treated), technical (mainly medical) mismanagement surfaced in the courts and registration bodies during the 1990s. These were widely publicized, and another sacrosanct NHS pillar – that even if it was badly organized, the NHS was providing top-class medical care – was demolished.

As noted earlier, the Labour Government was already committed to change, producing a White Paper, *The NHS: Modern and Dependable*, in its first year of office (NHS Executive 1997) based on the following principles:

- National policy: keep what worked; discard what failed; improve quality and performance through promotion of clinical governance.

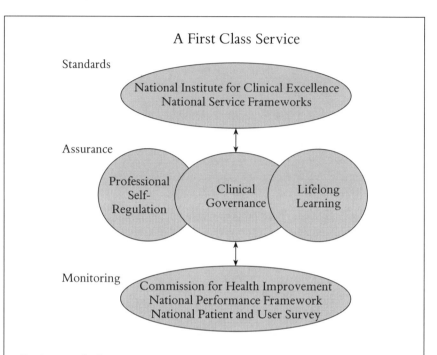

Standards

Assurance

Monitoring

Setting standards

National Institute for Clinical Excellence (NICE): wide membership to produce cost-effective *clinical* practice guidelines.

National Service Frameworks: for best *organization* of services.

Assurance

Clinical governance: process to assure *clinical* decisions.

Lifelong learning: tools for effective, high-quality care.

Professional self-regulation: sets, enforces and ensures professional and clinical standards.

Monitoring

Commission for Health Improvement (CHI): rolling programme of independent reviews, focused reviews, with power to intervene.

National framework for assessing performance: to monitor *delivery*.

National survey of patient and user experience: monitor *experiences*; results could trigger reviews.

Figure 8.2   Setting, delivering and monitoring standards.
Source: adapted from *A First Class Service*, Department of Health, 1998.

- Primary care groups: to promote health and cooperation with social services and to commission (plan) through contestability (the *potential* of competition) rather than frank competition. They were encouraged to become Primary Care Trusts with greater autonomy and responsibility.

'Clinical governance' was eventually defined six months later in *A First Class Service: Quality in the New NHS* as:

> a framework through which NHS organisations are accountable for continuously improving the quality of their services and safeguarding high standards of care by creating an environment in which excellence in clinical care will flourish.
>
> (Department of Health 1998: 33)

Statutory responsibility for *clinical* performance was, for the first time, allocated to chief executives of NHS Trusts, while three linked stages of standards, assurance and monitoring were envisaged at the national level so as to reduce geographical and clinical variation. The aim was to achieve this through a change in thinking, rather than by ticking checklists, as shown in Figure 8.2 (Department of Health 1998).

The National Institute of Clinical Excellence (NICE)

As part of the national policy framework described above, NICE was established in 1999 to take responsibility for setting technical standards, initially for drugs included on the NHS schedule, after intensive and comprehensive research on cost effectiveness. The results so far have not pleased some prescribers and users who retain their faith in experience of use or reports of use by others.

National Service and Performance Frameworks

A number of National Service Frameworks, with the emphasis on 'service' and therefore on multi-agency working, have now been published as part of standard setting. For example, the National Service Framework for older people (Department of Health 2001a) requires local consultation with older people and their carers, together with a shared vision and partnership working appropriate to the diverse needs of the local population. It also underlines the need for leadership, inclusive planning and good communication between stakeholders (see Chapter 10, Figure 10.1).

A national performance framework will be used to monitor quality (NHS Executive 1998). Key features of this approach are that service quality should be defined in terms of:

- health improvement: social and environmental, across agencies, influence behaviour affecting health of population

- fair access: geographical, socio-economic, demographic and care group equity
- effective: evidence-based, appropriate, timely provision, compliant with standards, by competent staff following best practice
- efficient: cost per unit of care/outcome, productivity of estate and labour
- user experience: responsive to needs and preferences; skilled care, continuity, waiting times and access; involvement, information and choice; environment and courtesy
- health outcome: reduce risk, meet need, avoid complications and premature deaths; improve quality of life.

The tone of the document is largely prescriptive and top-down. It is likely to fail to capture the hearts of those clinicians and managers who have relished their own empowerment to respond to users' needs since 1990. The NHS Executive did, however, suggest some frameworks for evaluation – rectifying an omission in the 1990 reforms.

Reviewing progress on quality improvement: the CHI

The Commission for Health Improvement (CHI) was set up in 1999 to monitor and improve the quality of patient care throughout the NHS across England and Wales. Like the Audit Commission (see Chapter 7), it uses a rolling programme of reviews (rather than inspections) to judge the effectiveness of clinical governance arrangements in all trusts (acute, primary care, mental health and ambulance/NHS Direct). This is a key task. 'Areas of concern' are noted and used as a focus for action by the health agency. A review considers the organization's systems and processes for monitoring and improving services, including:

- consultation and patient involvement
- clinical risk management
- clinical audit
- clinical effectiveness
- staffing and staff management
- education, training and continuing personal and professional development
- the use of information about the patient's experience, outcomes and processes.

Sources of information include information from patients and interviews with local stakeholders. The review team includes lay and multidisciplinary professional members. Reviews document notable practice as well as areas of concern and are published along with an action plan by the trust; these are already being used actively by the press and some patients to press for improvement. (Further information is available from the CHI website (www.chi.nhs.uk).)

Next steps for the NHS – 2000 and beyond

The legislation set out in 1998 risks a return to fragmentation due to the commissioning process, which, through seeking cost effectiveness and user responsiveness, is pursuing NHS funded provision of services both outside the local area as well as outside the NHS. Implementation a cross-agency quality approach as suggested in this text should avoid the risks of fragmentation but retain the advantages of competition/contestability. The eventual political direction has yet to evolve, and public reaction, from a cultural base which has changed hugely since 1948, will largely decide the future of the service.

The NHS Plan

In the year 2000, the latest publication to stimulate modernization of the NHS was published. This was the NHS Plan (Department of Health 2000). This was a plan for *investment* (more staff, more beds, new buildings, less waiting) and *reform* (national standards, incentives for performance improvement, modern matrons and opportunities to extend clinical roles through consultant nurses and therapists, health improvement).

A Modernisation Agency has been created. This supports local, patient-centred service redesign, working with local Modernisation Teams representing local stakeholders, and implementing policy locally. Of most interest to readers of this text will be the proposed integration of health and social services to pool resources and to set up joint Care Trusts. These will commission health and social care (including community care) in a single organization – of particular benefit to older people. The management of such change involving two distinct cultures (see also Chapter 7) will challenge all the staff involved, but, if successful, provide huge benefits to service users.

NHS trusts are rated on their activity (waiting lists), clinical focus (readmissions), patient focus (cancelled operations) and information governance, with three stars for the highest level of perfomance, two stars for performing well but not consistently, one star for showing concern and no stars for the poorest level of performance. In addition, trusts are monitored separately on their environment on a scale of 1–4, by CHI on a different scale of 1–4 for clinical governance, and separately again on their preparations for fluctuations in demand during the winter. All these scores are published for public consumption, and some are contradictory, being assessed at different times or against different criteria.

PALS and Patient Forums

Under the NHS Plan, another government initiative is to establish a national Patient Advice and Liaison Service (PALS). A local branch of PALS is to be established in every trust to respond to patients' concerns. It would replace the more independent but variable and little known Community Health Councils (CHCs) established in 1973 to represent patients' concerns. Considerable public debate and concern, particularly about the lack of independence of the new organization, has failed to prevent central government from going ahead with this initiative, which was implemented in 2002. There is also the requirement to develop Patient Forums on particular areas of local healthcare interest. A national Commission for Public and Patient Involvement is being developed to oversee standard setting and to support forums.

An example of how this might work is in the patient transport service. The statutory 999 emergency service is only provided by NHS ambulances, but in-house hospital services or contracted private sector companies sometimes provide other patient transport services. To ensure that they meet the local needs of patients, many of these services now have user groups. These assist in the development of services and monitor provision. They are also developing the anticipated statutory requirement for PALS.

Concordat

A further development under the NHS Plan was a 'concordat' with private health providers, working through a national framework. In theory this would use national standards to formalize local ad hoc arrangements to manage fluctuating capacity. Use of such facilities by NHS patients in Europe and the UK is already being made but the concordat had not been formally concluded at the time of writing.

The NHS Reform and Health Professions Act 2002 and associated reforms

This Act aims to progress work on quality improvement and professional accountability. As noted above recent high profile disciplinary and court cases (for example GP Dr Shipman, paediatric surgeons at Bristol and body parts retention at Alder Hey in Liverpool) have exposed the technical aspects of healthcare to public criticism as well as highlighting the numerous organizations involved in both professional accountability and organizational inspection.

The Act and associated reforms have a number of key components:

Coordination and inspection

The Act requires closer working between the various inspection organizations, and a subsequent ministerial statement indicated the creation of the Commission for Healthcare Audit and Inspection (CHAI). This will incorporate CHI's current responsibilities for clinical governance, investigations and monitoring progress on National Service Frameworks; its new responsibilities for inspection of management, provision, quality, access and availability; inspection of the private sector funded by the NHS; the power to recommend 'special measures' for poor outcomes, together with the responsibilities of the National Care Standards Commission for inspecting the private sector; and the Audit Commission's value for money studies in health. CHI already undertakes reviews of primary care with the Social Services Inspectorate.

Office for information on healthcare performance

Under the Act, CHAI is to combine the expertise available and become a central source of robust information on quality of care in the NHS. It will publish clear indicators; take over the star rating system; manage national staff and patient surveys; manage a national programme of clinical audits; and publish consultant performance.

Greater independence

CHAI will publish an annual report on the state of the NHS. The Chief Inspector of Health Care will be appointed to CHAI by its commissioners rather than by ministers.

Restructuring

The current Regional Office and Health Authority layers of management are being abolished and replaced by Strategic Health Authorities (in England, while Wales retains Health Authorities). Primary Care Trusts will cover the whole country (Local Health Boards in Wales) and be accountable for GPs.

Regulation accountability and integration

A new Council for Health Care Regulation is to be set up which will be the overarching body for professional regulation organizations including the General Medical Council (GMC), Nursing and Midwifery Council (NMC) and Health Professions Council (HPC).

A Council for Quality of Healthcare will include CHAI, NICE and the Patient Safety Authority.

Conclusion

Both external and the internal policy environments influence change. With regard to the external environment, the post-war era in the NHS has been influenced by technical and commercial innovations, political values and the tentative introduction of a self-regulating market economy. The main stakeholders – users, purchasers and providers – are uncertain about the government's current vision for the NHS, though it seems probable the future will provide opportunities for innovators. But there continues to be a lack of clarity about NHS values and strategic direction, affecting the whole cycle of quality (see Chapter 3 and Figure 3.1), although the clinical governance framework should provide a baseline for accountability and continuous improvement whatever route is ultimately pursued. If managers are unclear about what business they are in, they cannot identify appropriate stakeholders or define, develop, implement or assess service quality. If stakeholders are unclear, their expectations will be inconsistent with their perceptions and experience, and it will be difficult to develop clear roles and responsibilities. Only the mutual education of stakeholders and open and informed debate will clarify the situation.

The main political parties in the UK have agreed on the *principles* of healthcare. The disputes have been over *process*. If real debate is to take place between the nominally collaborating key stakeholders (government and their agents – managers, providers and users), the true division of views will eventually be revealed. This is likely to expose a conflict of values and will perhaps lead to greater clarity about the role of the NHS in public services – and its 'customers' – in the twenty-first century. Only when expected and acceptable quality is defined and agreed can the question of quality improvement really be tackled.

9

Quality issues in partnership working

Carol Hayden

Introduction

For some time partnership working has been the expected organizational context for securing regeneration funding and agreeing statutory service plans. Now, as an integral part of the current Government's modernization agenda, it is becoming not only a legislative requirement for the development of inter-agency community strategies but a prerequisite for 'joined-up' and, thus, improved public services. But does working in partnership make a real difference in terms of outcomes? Might it still feel like 'just another hoop to go through', a government 'flavour of the term', or a cosy way of working for those involved? Or can partnership have a role in improving service quality for users and citizens? And if so – how?

This chapter draws on the evaluation of the partnership-based Better Government for Older People (BGOP) programme to illustrate how partnership working can improve service quality. It looks at how partnerships can generate a common, citizen-centred perspective by which quality can be defined and assessed, what types of quality improvements are most likely to be responsive to a partnership approach, how such improvements themselves require 'quality partnerships', and what this means for the individual organizations involved.

Better Government for Older People

Better Government for Older People was established in 1998 as a national, Cabinet Office-led, action-research programme with partnership at its heart. The aim of BGOP was: 'To improve public services for older people by better meeting their needs, listening to their views, and encouraging their contribution' (Hayden and Boaz 2000: 2). Twenty-eight pilots were established across the UK, which drew together public, private and voluntary agencies to work with older people in order to 'make a difference'.

The proportion of the population aged 50 and over has doubled this century, from nearly one in seven in 1901 to one in three as we enter the new millennium (Office of National Statistics 2000). This trend is set to continue with around 25 million people – 40 per cent of the population – likely to be over 50 by 2021, of whom around half will be pensioners.

The language of a 'demographic time-bomb' focuses on the increasing number of older people as a growing burden on (the existing level and nature of) public services. This tends to assume that the nature of ageing, and the attitudes and aspirations of older people, are relatively constant. It thus takes an essentially pessimistic view about improving the quality of public sector provision, concentrating instead on how public services can be rationed to 'cope with' ever increasing needs, and how personal and corporate incentives to encourage more private provision can be enhanced.

In contrast, the BGOP programme was developed within a rather different ageing discourse, one that is concerned with the quality of increased longevity. As Tom Kirkwood put it in the Reith Lectures, the challenge is that of looking in radically new ways at the maintenance of health and the quality of life of older people (Kirkwood 2001). BGOP also reflected some of the thinking behind the government's modernization agenda, particularly in relation to the importance of a user-focus and the community leadership role of local authorities.

BGOP therefore encouraged older people to be seen as active citizens with a role in contributing to communities and local democracy, and entitled to public services that meet their needs. The evaluation of the two-year pilot programme showed that real achievements were made in the quality of service provision, which, to a large extent, reflected the development of local partnerships comprised of older people as well as a range of different agencies (Hayden and Boaz 2000).

Improving service quality through partnership

The most important quality indicator is in terms of outcomes – how services meet the needs of users. However, any underlying theory of service improvement will seek to explain the relationships between the catalysts for

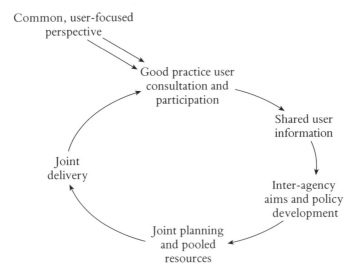

Figure 9.1 Service improvement through partnership.

change, the inputs or resources available, the change processes employed, and the resulting outputs and outcomes.

In understanding how partnership can improve service quality, it is therefore useful to disaggregate the different contributions that partnership can make at different points of the service improvement chain (see Figure 4.4, page 80). As shown in Figure 9.1, partnership working can contribute to the quality and understanding of user information; inter-agency communication, policy and planning; and better coordinated services at the point of delivery.

Partnerships for a user perspective

Real people don't think in organizational boxes. It may be a well-worn adage, but it's true and very relevant to why partnerships can improve service quality. The local government modernization agenda has emphasized the link between people-centred government and quality services (DETR 1998). However, if service quality is defined in terms of meeting people's expectations, then there has to be a common understanding of these expectations between the various different service providers that will collectively affect people's quality of life.

At the beginning of the BGOP programme, data on the 28 pilots' baseline positions showed that previous consultations had invariably been carried out by an *individual* agency or local authority department about a *specific* issue in relation to a *particular* service (e.g. changes to meal-on-wheels charges). A reluctance to ask older people open questions about the bigger picture (e.g. support for independent living) meant that a holistic perspective was seldom available, let alone shared between different providers. However, when older people were asked open questions about their needs from public services they frequently emphasized the importance of a joined-up approach.

> Older people have presented issues so that inter-departmental divisions seem so stupid. I'm embarrassed by our lack of ability to liaise with transport, planning, etc.
>
> (Health Partner)

The original Newcastle BGOP bid was informed by research undertaken by an older people's Action for Health group which, following one of their member's negative experience when her husband was discharged from hospital, highlighted the need for coordination between services over hospital discharge. Similarly, one of the key findings emerging from consultation with older people in Wolverhampton was the need to bring together bereavement services, then provided by at least half-a-dozen different agencies.

> Without partnership mechanisms for hearing what people have to say it [the bereavement centre] just wouldn't have come about.
>
> (Chief Executive)

Recent UK-wide research with older people confirms these priorities (see also Chapter 10, page 177). A study on the attitudes and aspirations of older people, undertaken for the Department of Social Security, found that the participants in the study 'made clear links between services so transport, safety and learning were all seen as providing access to other services and opportunities as well as being important in their own right' (Hayden *et al.* 1999).

So partnership working, through joint listening to an acknowledged 'common voice' improves service providers' understanding of users' needs and views in four key ways:

1 By appreciating that a 'service' in users' terms (e.g. discharge from hospital) actually means a number of different agencies each providing a component of the end service.
2 By recognizing that the quality of some services affects access to others – so, for example, transport affects older people's ability to benefit from health and care services.
3 By realizing that findings from consultations undertaken by one agency, such as older people wanting to remain active and independent for as long as possible, have implications across a range of services as part of a preventative agenda.
4 By discovering that adopting a 'user focus' as a way of thinking within a partnership is inconsistent with 'professional silos' and thus underpins a cross-cutting approach.

Partnerships for improved communication

Clearly it is important that an improved understanding of users' perspectives is used to improve service quality. An important stage in this process was through the BGOP partners improving their practice in relation to communicating with each other and with older people. This invariably included using the local partnership as an opportunity to conduct more innovative, inclusive consultations with older people than hitherto, which could actively feed into service development and enable providers to 'get it right first time'.

> Better Government for Older People's an opportunity and a structure when we are required to engage with the community . . . and it's public involvement – citizens, not just users.
>
> (Health Partner)

A number of pilots held joint consultation events between residents and staff from all the agencies involved. The outcomes of these were seen as invaluable, albeit somewhat challenging. In Middlesbrough, for example, a Community Futures day found that older residents on a local estate did not see information provision *per se* as a priority for action, in contrast to the views of representatives from agencies at the same event. The residents saw isolation and access difficulties as the real problem and wanted better transport to the town centre as well as improvements to the local shops to address this.

Many BGOP partnerships also provided a useful conduit for direct contact between services and older people that previously had not been perceived as available or appropriate.

> The [Older People's] Forums have now talked to the Health Trust, Road Safety, and Planning as well as Social Care.
>
> (Council Officer)

This direct communication with users was invariably seen as useful to the agencies in improving service quality. The experience helped reduce some of the fears and scepticism that had been associated with consultation. For example, the Harrow pilot had uncovered concerns about low benefit take-up and the stigmatizing image of existing claims information. This led the local Benefits Agency to use the partnership to consult with a wide range of older people's groups in order to redesign their leaflets.

> We've had to ask older people first – that's unusual for us – but we end up with a product [user-friendly leaflets] that's well received because people have asked for it in the first place.
>
> (Benefits Agency Partner)

The formation of BGOP partnerships, with a common focus of older people, thus enabled agencies that had had little previous contact to start considering how they could work together to improve service quality.

We now have a chance to work with Education and Leisure, where we struggled before, and also with the less traditional parts of Social Services.

(Health Partner)

Partnership working can thus improve the quality of communication in four key ways:

1 By developing a good practice consultation culture, through sharing ideas, resources, positive results and contact information about older people's organizations
2 By using users' views on what constitutes quality generally to inform a range of different provision (e.g. information in plain English and minority languages, customized services)
3 By using users' feedback and knowledge to improve specific services (e.g. designing sheltered housing, locating pedestrian crossings, delivering adult learning)
4 By providing a network of relationships in which to develop joint action planning for coordinated and integrated services based on users' perspectives and priorities.

Partnerships for quality services

In the views of the older people questioned as part of the BGOP evaluation, it was the increased responsiveness of services to their needs that made the most difference to them as end-users. This improvement in quality was usually related to enhanced inter-agency coordination through the partnership working that had been at the centre of each BGOP pilot.

This coordination took place at different stages in the service delivery chain. Although it was probably most noticeable to the users through joint working at the point of delivery, coordination at the policy development and planning stages was equally important for effecting change at the front line.

Joined-up delivery

One-stop shops are an oft-quoted example of joined-up delivery but improving quality is more complex than physically bringing services under one roof. Consultation had shown that the question of 'which roof' was important: older people dislike the image and atmosphere of Benefit Offices. These findings led to the introduction of a number of outreach initiatives involving the local authority, the Benefits Agency and local voluntary organizations that had contacts and credibility with some of the most isolated groups of older people.

For example, in Rhondda Cynon Taff, a series of information sessions have been held at day centres and luncheon clubs. At these, staff from a number of local authority departments (including Housing and Social Services), the Benefits Agency and Age Concern gave short presentations and were also available to talk to older people individually. A 'Benefits Bus' now visits local village centres, and the home library service has extended its information role in its contact with housebound people. New, user-friendly claims procedures have been introduced with peer volunteers helping other older people obtain initial guidance on their likely benefit eligibility (e.g. for income support or attendance allowance).

> We worked with Council officers who were already visiting excluded, housebound older people – the library service, home care supervisors, chiropodists – they're trusted people and haven't got the Benefits Agency image.
>
> (Benefits Agency Partner)

Through the 'Fair Shares for Us' initiative, Stirling Council and the Benefits Agency jointly run benefits advice roadshows across the large, rural authority. Publicity is designed to reduce possible feelings of stigma, transport is offered, and a complementary telephone helpline provides one-to-one follow-up. The new approach has resulted in an average extra benefit entitlement of around £8 per person per week for its several hundred users.

> We've done the statistical analysis which shows increased take-up . . . and our image is much improved – if BA staff wear Better Government for Older People badges (rather than BA ones) it improves our relationship with the public.
>
> (Benefits Agency Partner)

BGOP consultations showed that a lack of coordination between service providers can make older people feel dependent and vulnerable, rather than being supported in making decisions, in relation to life events such as care assessment or hospital discharge.

The establishment of local area primary care liaison groups on Ynys Mon provided a focus and a process for joint assessment of older people. The Community Home Care Organizers, who are responsible for home-care, play an essential front-line role as a link between older people and this group of providers. The system also includes the GPs, which other pilots have found a notoriously difficult group of professionals to involve in joint working. The project is now being extended to joint commissioning to target pooled finance from health and social services on older people who would otherwise be unlikely to stay at home.

In Hackney, social workers in the community resource team are now working from GPs' surgeries to forge connections between health and social care. Older people in Newcastle have commented favourably on the new coordinated 'going home from hospital' service following the introduction of a whole systems approach involving local managers and front-line staff from all the relevant agencies.

Older people in North Down (Northern Ireland) have welcomed closer working between the police, fire service, housing executive and health board, which has resulted in joint community safety events (covering accidents and crime prevention) and the introduction of jointly funded, enhanced Estate Warden posts. The inclusion of the shopping centre manager on the Hartlepool BGOP partnership has resulted in the development of a 'shopping access award scheme' led by older people, as well as improved coordination between retailers.

> The Shopping Centre manager has acted as a champion and brought in his sector (the retailers) into the partnership – they're now looking at combining resources for home delivery [to older people].
>
> (Project Director)

Joint policy and planning

Joint ownership of the ageing agenda and older people's needs has been a necessary prerequisite for improved service quality on the ground. One of the major achievements of BGOP has been the move away from the traditional view of older people as solely a social care responsibility. The pilots agree that the key to doing this has been through working in partnership around themes or 'people groups' to overcome narrow professionalism and departmentalism and take a strategic view of how to address cross-cutting service issues.

> BGOP can help provide homes for issues like transport and health that are not all Social Work's responsibility.
>
> (Chief Officer)

The development of a joint policy and/or strategy on ageing and older people has been an important message to service providers in a number of areas. In Coventry 'Meeting the Needs and Aspirations of Older People' is one of six sections in the Community Plan. In Hartlepool the inter-agency policy has shaped other partnership initiatives, including the Joint Investment plan (JIP), the Health Action Zone (HAZ), the Single Regeneration Budget (SRB), the Integrated Transport Plan and the New Deal for Communities (NDC).

> We wanted to do something . . . saw the need for joint action . . . there was a coming together of ideas . . . we agreed a vision and aims . . . joint funding means we can get things moving.
>
> (Education Partner)

Agencies are working together in Stirling to improve primary care for isolated and less mobile older people as part of their Rural Strategy. Space in residential homes has been utilized for day care and NHS clinics. Community care assessment is now undertaken jointly, and funding and premises are being sought for community resource centres for health, social care, information provision and leisure facilities. This degree of progress would not have been possible without joint commitment at a senior policy level in the many organizations involved.

> BGOP has given impetus to joint working – a lot of people have to be involved in the rural health and social care project – the Acute Trust, the Primary Care Trust, the Health Care Co-op, three group GP practices – and that's just the health side.
>
> (Health Partner)

Detailed joint *planning* through partnership working is an essential stage in translating a policy commitment to a coordinated, user-focused approach into improved quality 'on the ground'. To take another example, BGOP consultations showed that older people find home-care packages too restrictive. The main concern is that the options available concentrate on personal care rather than practical assistance to enable them to live in their own homes. In many areas, however, local authority home-care services have actually become more specific and less flexible in recent years so this type of assistance is now extremely rare.

Tackling this problem first required a shift in *policy* towards acknowledging the importance of a holistic, preventative approach with the aim of promoting independence and choice. Using this as a 'peg', pilots were then able to develop initiatives in response to these concerns. Hammersmith and Fulham, and Hartlepool used winter pressures and joint finance monies respectively to introduce home repairs schemes in conjunction with local voluntary and housing associations.

The formal involvement of users in joint policy development and planning processes has been crucial to ensuring they result in improved service quality. The Hammersmith and Fulham Older People's Consultative Committee meets quarterly with a panel of senior Councillors and, through this mechanism, has influenced home-care charges and the design of very sheltered accommodation. The older people's forums in North Yorkshire feed into coordination and development of preventative services at a strategic level through the local HIMP (Health Improvement Plan) planning structures.

> The District Planning Groups, part of the Joint Strategic Framework for Older People, value older people's creative, constructive dialogue – some now have older people as joint chairs.
>
> (Health Partner)

Critical factors for quality partnerships

The course of true partnership . . .

The quality of a partnership will affect its ability to improve the quality of services through the different stages outlined above (see also Figure 9.1). However, as noted in Chapter 2, developing effective and sustainable partnerships is not an easy task. Evaluation of the BGOP partnerships found that among the various difficulties of building any new set of working relationships, two main problems stood out during the early part of the programme.

The most common initial problem was that, for many of those involved, the partnership did not feel like a partnership, but rather a local authority reference group. Council 'leadership' of BGOP was perceived as directional management of a non-negotiable agenda. This not only affected the priorities and content of the BGOP action plan, but also the partnership process itself. For example, some partners felt that they would always be 'junior members' of a team while meetings were always held in Council premises and task-groups always chaired by local authority officers in typically bureaucratic local authority style. This problem affected other members' motivation and confidence to both attend and take an active part in partnership meetings.

The second main problem concerned the remit, role and responsibility of the partnership representatives. In a number of BGOP partnerships, the individual members developed good working relationships based on mutual trust and respect, around a common interest (i.e. older people). However, if the individuals concerned had difficulty using partnership decisions to influence the way their organization worked (either because they were fairly junior, rather specialist or, ironically, marginalized as 'the partnership person') frustration soon occurred. In these instances, the partnership felt like the proverbial 'talking shop'.

Although the BGOP partnerships did experience problems, the two-year commitment, the expectations of older people, and the formative action research approach were all helpful in creating a culture where these problems had to be addressed rather than allowing them to undermine, or even destroy, partnership working. This meant that a significant number of the pilots made changes to the way their partnerships worked, which resulted in tangible improvements.

> We now have access to decision makers – officials are listening. We don't have to be aggressive – we can debate issues.
>
> (Older person)

The variation between the partnerships, both across the 28 pilots and over the two years, enabled the BGOP evaluation to identify four key elements, which, if in place, are likely to greatly improve the chances of partnership success in achieving desired change. These are:

1 Integration – through 'nested' partnerships at different organizational levels
2 Inclusivity – by ensuring all relevant stakeholders are actively involved in a partnership
3 Role clarity – through a decision-making remit with delegated responsibilities

4 Leadership – of the partnership and within the constituent organizations to achieve change.

Integration

Although we talk of 'partnership', effective partnership working requires a nest of integrated partnerships at different levels of governance, within and between organizations, to cover a range of purposes and functions. Even taking, by way of example, the fairly specific issue of improving the quality of services to support older people in living independently, there are a number of relevant partnerships, as shown in Table 9.1.

Table 9.1 Partnerships for different purposes

Area remit	Strategic remit	Service remit
Authority-wide	Local Strategic Partnership BGOP Steering Group	Community care planning partnership HIMP partnership
Neighbourhood/ Locality	Neighbourhood management team/forum NDC partnership	Integrated local primary care team Joint assessment team Local task group (older people)

A strategic partnership, whether at an authority-wide level or more locally, is concerned with agreeing an overall vision and objectives and putting in place a comprehensive action plan to make these a reality. For most of the BGOP pilots, the inter-agency Steering Group operated at this level. For those pilots concentrating on a locality, like North Down, Middlesbrough and Nottinghamshire, this strategic partnership was still required but in a smaller geographic area. Moving away from the specific example of older people for a moment, equivalent strategic partnerships can be identified in the new Local Strategic Partnerships (LSPs) and the New Deal for Communities (NDC) Partnership Boards at the authority-wide and neighbourhood levels respectively.

However, a strategic level partnership is unlikely to be able to implement the action plan 'on the ground'. The BGOP pilots found that more specific, service delivery partnerships had to take responsibility for this activity. Sometimes this would be a case of using existing grouping like the Health Improvement Partnership (HIMP) and sometimes it would require a new partnership, such as a local older people's task group, which would organize, for example, a programme of accessible healthy living events using peer educators. Again, analogies to these can be found for other service areas and more general regeneration initiatives.

Although some of these individual partnerships might include the same people meeting with a different remit, it is more likely that they will involve different people so that, in effect, partnership becomes a sustainable way of working at all stages of the service improvement chain (see Chapter 4).

The cultural shift to working through a 'nest' of partnerships is vital to performance management within, as well as between, the organizations involved. Without such a shift, individuals in partnerships invariably feel they have to work against their own organization's silos, often with little impact, resulting in the 'talking-shop' frustration mentioned above. Therefore, unless front-line staff working in 'joined-up' ways have support from their senior managers through a 'joined-up' policy framework, and policy makers can have confidence that their joint decisions will result in changed practice 'on the ground', the chain is likely to break for want of a missing link.

Given the importance of partnership working at all levels of governance, the BGOP pilots reported the lack of 'joined-up central government' as a major barrier to local coordination between, for example, health and social care. Government departments and targets tend to relate to single services and individual agencies. This makes pooling mainstream budgets difficult because there is no mechanism to measure joint outputs or acknowledge joint accountability (Hayden and Benington 2000).

> There is a risk to 'joining up' budgets by not being able to meet Audit Commission specific targets – we will only ever be able to 'pool the spare [resources]' if we each have to separately account for inputs and outputs.
>
> (Health Partner)

However, there are some signs that progress is starting to be made. The development of local public service agreements (LPSAs), the Audit Commission's emphasis on strategic, cross-cutting Best Value inspections and the introduction of the National Service Frameworks are all helpful and hopeful.

Inclusivity

The BGOP programme required local authorities to establish a Steering Group to bring together different agencies – from the public, private and voluntary sectors – and older people to jointly shape and steer each pilot.

Not infrequently, partnerships between the local authority and health services were already in place and could be built on to widen the existing, often statutory, remit. The results of working more closely with government agencies such as the Benefits Agency and Inland Revenue have already been discussed. Many pilots appreciated the opportunity to develop closer relationships between the statutory and voluntary sectors. As well as strengthening existing partnerships with charities such as Age Concern and Help the Aged, this enabled new links to be forged with other relevant organizations, such as churches, refugee organizations and Voluntary Services Councils.

The BGOP evaluation showed how the engagement of users and citizens is essential for partnerships to result in improved quality. Agency representatives and older people alike reported positively on their new relationship as an important outcome in itself.

> Better Government for Older People is a chance to work alongside Council officers – we now have more understanding of problems, budgets, who's involved with what and so on – we can sit down together and raise ideas for internal change.
>
> (Older person)

The BGOP evaluation showed that members of partnerships need not only to be formally involved, but also to *feel* fully involved. This can make the difference between a genuine partnership in which value is added and acknowledged through the range of different contributions, and a glorified local authority reference group, as discussed above, where other organizations question what difference they are making to decision making beyond apparently providing additional legitimacy.

Many of the BGOP pilots commented on the 'quality time' that has to be invested in building inclusive partnerships if these are to be effective in joint decision making and prove sustainable over time. Time is important to building trust between partners so they feel listened to and thus able to share information, expectations and their own organization's objectives. In turn this openness seems to assist in the vital task of developing collective ownership of, and responsibility to, a common agenda, with joint priorities and a written action plan and timescale.

> There were lots of organisational/cultural differences – our shared values statement took much longer than expected – differences in jargon, definitions.
>
> (Project Director)

Facilitated, away-day type events for 'team-building' were found to be particularly useful for building trust and openness at the initial agenda-setting stage of the partnership. A number of the pilots also valued their contribution to ensuring 'time-out' for monitoring and review, and to develop and sustain creative working relationships between people who were otherwise unlikely to work alongside each other.

An enabling style of chairing also emerged as an important factor in all partners feeling 'equal round the table' (a description used by South Lanarkshire), despite obvious disparities in resources and responsibilities. As a partner in another pilot put it:

> The Chair (of the BGOP Steering Group) is very good. His style's not local authority – more an inclusive community development approach.
>
> (Partner)

In other areas specific arrangements were made to ensure that meetings and events felt inclusive for all partners. These included the adoption of a 'good practice meetings' guide developed by voluntary sector partners in Rhondda Cynon Taff, and the working groups in Harrow being chaired by older people and a range of partner organizations, rather than automatically by Council officers.

Role clarity

The BGOP evaluation found that for any partnership to be effective and sustainable, there had to be clarity on the role and responsibilities of a partnership, *and* of all the representatives on it. This requires member organizations to collectively agree the remit of their partnership and how they are to be represented as part of the 'terms of engagement' of the partnership.

Different partnerships will be established for different reasons. We have already discussed the usefulness of a set of integrated partnerships to cover strategic and service delivery remits at authority-wide and smaller geographical levels. A recent research report by Gaster *at al.* (1999) suggested a 'ladder of partnership' ranging from an 'information exchange' to 'collaboration and full partnership' (see Chapter 2). This framework was designed to help local authorities and voluntary organizations analyse what sort of partnership they were in and what they would aim for in the future. This degree of clarity, however arrived at, is crucial to avoid the frustration and fragmentation that can arise due to differing expectations and misconceptions.

Notwithstanding the potential usefulness of 'information exchange' type partnerships in some situations, the BGOP evaluation found that for the pilots' partnerships to be effective in improving public services for older people, it was essential for them to have a decision-making remit that led to action and tangible change. Moreover, agency representatives need to have sufficient delegated responsibility or mandate (with backing from their managers) to participate in joint decision making and be able to commit resources for action.

> There's lots of enthusiasm – people are willing to take risks and experiment with high level support behind them.
>
> (Partner)

Without this delegation it is easy for partnerships to be frustrated through 'all talk and no action'. Likewise, representatives require sufficient status or authority to influence the sort of change in their own organizations that is required to contribute to a joint response to a user group's needs. This ability underpins the likelihood of being able to sustain partnerships through 'bending' and drawing in mainstream resources after, or instead of, the time-limited, project funding that partnerships are often initially set up to manage (although not in the case of BGOP).

Citizen and user representatives must reflect different local groups and communities. Typically, the effectiveness of older people in BGOP partnerships relied on the strength of older people's engagement more generally in local forums and other organizations so that representatives have support from, and communication channels into, the wider community of older people. This in turn has implications for local authority investment in community capacity-building to ensure effective resident participation in partnerships.

Experience has shown how important it is for the local authority to sort out its 'partnership' working within the council to be able to lead, and engage in, external partnerships. This requires organizational development and human resource strategies to enable local authority staff to work across internal and external boundaries. As for other organizations, a fundamental key to achieving this cultural change is to delegate decision making to the lowest appropriate level within clear policy and operational frameworks – the tight-loose framework suggested in Chapter 4.

> I can get on with things and make decisions and can commit our department to things, as I'm quite clear about the overall remit and the service plans.
>
> (Council Officer)

It also helps if all partners are clear on the potential benefits of working jointly to their own organizations in terms of meeting internal priorities and government expectations. The Benefit Agency's input to the local BGOP partnerships was actively encouraged by its Chief Executive who publicly stressed the need for new approaches to 'modern service delivery'. In effect local staff became accountable to their employing organization for the outcomes (e.g. increased take-up of pensioner benefits) and to the local BGOP partnership for the process.

> The steer that came down was that we should be working together.
>
> (BA Partner)

As well as influencing their constituent organizations, partnerships invariably have to be able to take some action themselves, with some 'quick wins' to achieve credibility and show what can be achieved through pooling resources. A number of BGOP pilots therefore secured a joint budget for this purpose, using contributions from the different partners and bidding jointly for external resources.

Leadership

Despite the high profile of partnerships and a wealth of literature on factors for effective partnerships (see for example, Audit Commission 1998; Gregory 1998; Holman 1999), there is relatively little debate on *how* to manage partnerships compared with hierarchical organizations.

Recent leadership research distinguishes between transactional leadership (creating the procedures and systems for efficient organizations) and transformational leadership (the strategic and motivational qualities for effecting change). While stressing the increasing importance of transformational leadership due to 'the increased demands on organisations to deal with a far greater complexity, turbulence, ambiguity and unpredictability' (Alimo-Metcalfe 1998: 35), most academic research on public sector development remains primarily concerned with leadership within organizations rather than across them. Research carried out through the Warwick University Local Authorities Research Consortium concluded that 'inter-organisational leadership is complex and requires developmental and influence skills, as well as traditional hierarchical skills'. Moreover the research showed that 'the modernisation debate has taken insufficient account of this complexity' (Hartley and Allison 2000: 39).

As a key example of its community leadership role, the effectiveness of the local authority in enabling, but not running, the partnership is seen as crucial in encouraging active participation and inclusiveness.

> [The BGOP partnership is] a coming together of ideas – the local authority supports and enables but doesn't do everything.
>
> (Voluntary Sector Partner)

However, within two- or three-tier local authority areas, partnership working can expose a lack of clarity around the community leadership role. Who represents (in this case) older people, who should respond to their views and needs, and who is responsible for coordinating partnership working and community planning? In pilots such as Devon, progress has been made on resolving these tensions through the establishment of partnership committees in each district which, as part of their wider role, take the lead in coordinating the specific district-based BGOP projects, while the County Council oversees the whole pilot at the strategic level. This allows flexibility between districts for innovation in response to local needs.

As well as implications for community leadership by an organization (that is, the local authority) as outlined above, effective partnerships require political and managerial leadership from individuals. However, this requires very different skills and behaviours from those required to manage individual services or single organizations. The BGOP evaluation found that senior managers who were responsible for leading partnerships had to be able to combine the two roles of corporate change agent and community leader, which requires the following capacities:

- understanding of older people and an ageing population as strategic and corporate issues
- integrity as a 'corporate' player (i.e. not competitive or possessive about one service area)
- influence within the corporate management team

- credibility with inter-agency and community partners
- ability to secure staff resources and funding packages for an integrated approach
- a visionary, enabling, inclusive interpersonal style.

Part of partnership leadership is to ensure that the more integrated, 'joined-up' way of working reaches all parts of all partner organizations. One of the strands of the Scottish Borders' pilot was to measure the effectiveness of improved partnership working in providing simpler access to community care services across health and social work, and to test the need for more formal integration of these services. The local evaluation produced evidence of the success of the new approach in terms of avoiding duplication and delay, reducing bureaucracy and resulting in a higher level of satisfaction expressed by users and carers. The evaluation also identified three key components of the change management process necessary to further improve and develop the partnership approach. These were: maintaining multi-agency commitment to the new arrangements; creating and reinforcing the new culture; and providing the appropriate practical support and training for staff (Scottish Executive 2001; see also Chapter 2).

Other pilots found that part of the leadership role is to 'champion' the training and development necessary to bring about sustainable, whole-organizational change. To this end Kensington and Chelsea undertook a programme of awareness raising with their Executive Board and Departmental Management Teams, and South Lanarkshire held a seminar for managers from leisure, education and health promotion.

> Senior managers had a useful course looking across services to take the departmental blinkers off.
>
> (Chief Officer)

The BGOP evaluation found that the local partnerships required leadership at an operational, as well as a senior managerial, level. Moreover, this was needed on a full-time basis and required a specific set of skills and behaviours. Those capabilities that the pilots found to be most important were:

- vision and imagination – to promote and pursue a change strategy
- enabling skills – to engage older people and develop open, inclusive partnership working
- project management – to ensure the action plan is coordinated and implemented
- commitment and enthusiasm – to motivate and support others to achieve change

This mixture of transformational and transactional leadership at middle-management levels in local authorities is likely to become increasingly important to address cross-cutting issues through partnership. The investment in such staffing capacity would seem to be an indication of local authorities' commitment to their community leadership role as part of modernizing government and an essential ingredient of putting partnership working into practice.

Conclusion: developing 'quality' partnerships

Partnership working can improve the quality of local service delivery, but only through quality partnerships. The most important contribution of a partnership approach is through the development of an understanding that the service user is the common frame of reference. This understanding can inform, and be informed by, the active participation of users and citizens in service design and delivery. The resulting customer perspective can then provide the motivation and trust to unlock innovation and creativity in pursuit of improved quality through cross-cutting service improvements.

As with services however, partnerships will be more effective in improving quality if they themselves are 'joined-up' to enable links between back-line decision making and front-line practice. This requires partnerships to operate at different levels within a whole systems framework, so they become the *modus operandi* for Gaster's models for improving service quality and for connecting service chains (see Chapter 3, Figure 3.1 and Chapter 4, Figure 4.4) and to ensure an effective interface between policy and action. A partnership approach thus has to inform joined-up thinking, policy, planning and delivery in improving public services.

To be effective, all partnerships also have to be well led and managed to ensure 'fitness for purpose'. This entails actively including all relevant stakeholders, establishing a common agenda with clear objectives, and being able to take decisions that ensure action within their particular remit.

This will be easier to achieve if there is an understanding of the necessary organizational development within the constituent agencies. This will invariably require an increase in delegated managerial and financial responsibility alongside concomitant mechanisms for joint accountability. It will also necessitate a reduction in rigid vertical hierarchies within organizations and a better understanding of the contribution that individual services can make to the wider, citizen-centred agenda. Both these changes will, in turn, depend on a commitment to, and investment in appropriate staff training and development for new capabilities at all levels of the partner organizations.

Part IV
Quality in practice

10

Quality from the citizen's perspective: campaigning, consultation and involvement

Tessa Harding

> Service users are . . . judging the quality of services in two ways: they are concerned that services will help them achieve the outcomes they aspire to; and they are concerned that services are delivered in ways which empower rather than disempower them and their peers as individuals. The motivation for getting involved with service agencies is primarily to achieve these two objectives. User involvement is not an end in itself but a means of effecting change both in the outcome of services and in the behaviour of staff.
>
> (Beresford *et al.* 1997: 78)

How do older people judge quality in health and social care? This chapter reviews the evidence, and finds that older people, like other service users, have a very different perspective on quality from that of professionals. They have their own criteria, and this chapter reviews those and assesses the implications for the way services are currently provided. It argues that, for services to aim to meet their aspirations, older people themselves need to be directly involved in planning, shaping, evaluating and improving them, and discusses how far we have progressed down the road towards meaningful involvement.

Why older people's views matter

It would be a brave commissioner or provider of services these days who would seek to assess quality of health and social care services without drawing on the experience of those who use those services. Both Government policy and good practice require those who use services to be consulted and involved in their development.

It is the experience of those who use the services that is the ultimate test of their quality and suitability. Services, after all, exist *for them* – that is their prime purpose and function. If services are not meeting the needs of users or would-be users, then they are not doing their job, no matter how sophisticated the thinking or how smooth the system. At the most straightforward level, therefore, service users can be seen as the 'customers' or 'consumers' of services. Like all good providers, health and social services agencies and practitioners need systematic feedback from their customers as to the quality of the product, and that feedback needs to be used to improve quality.

However, older people and other service users are concerned not just about the nature of the services they receive today, but about what those services can help them achieve. Services are a means to an end, and that end is a better quality of life. Having a better quality of life means having choice and control over how one lives, and access to those services and facilities that enable one to have a full and active life, regardless of age or disability. As well as shaping health and care, therefore, older people want to ensure that wider mainstream services, such as transport and adult education, take account of and are responsive to their needs. What they are seeking to achieve are those wider outcomes of independence and inclusion in society and an acceptable quality of life to which most of us aspire.

Older people are articulating their own priorities and want to shape services in such a way as to achieve more satisfactory outcomes for themselves and others (HOPe 2000). Those aspirations are increasingly being recognized both in research (Boaz *et al.* 1999), and through initiatives such as the Better Government for Older People programme (BGOP 2000) (see Chapter 9), in which older people have been directly involved in local authority decision making, removing barriers to participation, ensuring that local services are responsive to their needs and finding solutions to local problems. This goes well beyond a simple consumerist approach; it is an example of older people claiming their rightful place as citizens, with a real and equal say in the decisions which affect their lives.

The Government is doing a great deal to encourage public involvement in developing local authority and health services, through Local Strategic Partnerships, Patient and Public Involvement in the NHS and a variety of other measures. As Qureshi and Henwood (2000) point out, a range of people have a legitimate interest in the quality of our public services, including service users, their carers and relatives, and citizens in general.

Consequently, 'accepted ideas of what constitutes quality per se, and the acceptable quality for public services, will be subject to negotiation and change over time'.

Older people's views of quality

What makes a good quality of service from the point of view of service users, particularly older people?

Until recently, there was little information from older people themselves on their views of what constitutes a good quality service (though there has been more from other groups of service users). However, that has begun to change. Increasingly, older people are playing a role in determining quality both directly, through their involvement with services, and indirectly, through research. It is crucially important that they should do so: however good the intentions of service providers, they cannot by definition provide that perspective, and users of services need to speak for themselves. There is a fundamental difference of perspective between service providers, who are asking 'Am I providing a good service?' and that of service users or patients, who are asking 'What needs to happen to improve my quality of life?' Both the user perspective, of desired outcomes, and the professional one, of ways to make those possible, are needed to form a joint and rounded view.

A number of studies have been undertaken to determine older people's views of the quality of the social services they receive, and their findings demonstrate a good deal of consistency. Research undertaken by Norma Raynes with residents in care homes asked how they assessed quality and how they wished to see quality improved. Residents, meeting in a focus group without staff present, were asked what made a good home, and for one thing they would change to improve the home they lived in. Participants said that a good home was one in which there was a variety of things to do, where interests and hobbies could be pursued, and where there were opportunities to take part in organized activities. They wanted responsibilities and jobs to do within the home, from watering the plants and feeding the birds to helping in the kitchen. They wanted to go out and have a change of scene, to meet people and do ordinary things outside the home. Food was important too – good quality and variety (Raynes 1998).

Another study by Susan Tester and her colleagues invited frail older people in care homes to define what the determining factors of quality of life were for them. Four key factors emerged: individual resident's activities; their relationships and interactions with other residents, staff and visitors; maintaining their individuality and autonomy; and the physical environment of the home (Tester *et al.* 2001).

The older people in Raynes's parallel study of domiciliary care valued the services they received, without which they could not have continued to live in their own homes. They defined a quality service as characterized by reliability, continuity and flexibility; cheerful staff; more help with house-work; clear information about the services they were entitled to, and staff who were competent. In addition, people under 80 wanted someone to do things with and opportunities to go out and meet people, while those over 80 emphasized good neighbours and something to keep their minds occupied. Both groups mentioned access to transport and to health care as requirements if they were to be able to remain in their own homes (Raynes *et al.* 2001).

These findings are echoed elsewhere:

> (Older) people wanted to be able to plan and organise their days, and enjoy a normal pattern of life. They wanted to maintain their own standards of cleanliness and tidiness in their own homes, to feel se-curely connected to the world, and to avoid boredom and isolation.
>
> (Qureshi *et al.* 1998: 9)

Clark and her colleagues point out that older people want 'help, not care', and that the very services described as 'low level' by professionals have a high value to older people. Particularly valued are help with housework, gardening, house repairs and maintenance, security, laundry and opportun-ities for social participation (Clark *et al.* 1998). Older people from ethnic minority communities knew little about home care, but felt that language and a knowledge of dietary requirements and favoured activities were important (Raynes *et al.* 2001). Older people also say that home care should be available earlier, to those who need just a bit of support to remain independent, and that

> simply leaving people without help until they become dependent is unacceptable and a thoroughly short-sighted policy . . . The whole concept of home care needs to be reviewed to ensure that it provides a properly supportive personal service with greater control in the hands of the user.
>
> (HOPe 2000: 10)

This perspective on the role that home care should be able to play in supporting older people echoes the ideals of the early days of the NHS and Community Care Act 1990, and the role of care managers as envisaged then. In practice, home care as currently provided is rarely able to offer the supportive, personalized help that older people are looking for. Home care has become tightly rationed, with eligibility criteria that limit its availabil-ity to those who are most disabled and restricts it to personal care tasks and the prevention of 'risk'. There is little scope for flexibility or responsiveness and little time for helping people to achieve the quality of life they are looking for. Services are simply too stretched, too thinly spread and too task orientated to provide the kind of service that older people say they want (Henwood 2001). Tony Blair's Government is firm in its declaration that it wishes to promote the independence of older people, and home care should be a cornerstone in that endeavour. It will, however, require a major review in the purpose and design of home care if it is to fulfil that role (see also Chapter 9 for examples of where the BGOP partnerships are having some impact on home care).

Older people's views on health care are no less firm. They want to see improved quality in the services that exist, but they also prioritize differently between services. The HOPe group, a group of 15 older people drawn from community organizations that contributed to developing the National Service Framework for Older People, had plenty to say about the need to combat ageism and age discrimination throughout the healthcare system. They were also emphatic about the need to respect people's dignity and individuality. Like their peers involved in the research on social care, they too argued strongly for greater investment in early intervention, in rehabilitation and in helping people to stay healthy and deal with the 'ordinary problems' of ageing, such as hearing loss or painful feet.

> Given early attention, such problems do not need to become a source of major difficulty – but left unaddressed they can all too easily lead to a downward spiral and the loss of independence and mobility.
>
> (HOPe 2000: 8)

Older people clearly attach great importance to community health services – audiology, chiropody, continence services, bereavement counselling, aids and equipment and so on.

There has been a great deal of concern about the quality of medical and nursing care that many older people receive, particularly in some hospital wards and in accident and emergency departments. Health Advisory Service (HAS) 2000, an independent research organization, undertook a study at the request of the then Secretary of State for Health Frank Dobson in 1998/99. They identified a range of factors that contributed to poor care, from the state of the hospital environment and the availability of basic equipment, to food being placed out of reach of patients and rude or neglectful behaviour by members of staff (HAS 1999). Their findings were echoed in the mass of anecdotal evidence collected by Help the Aged's Dignity on the Ward campaign over the following two years. A research study commissioned for the campaign used the experience of older patients as well as staff interviews and independent observation to analyse the subjective perceptions which appear to underpin the receipt and delivery of good care (Davies *et al.* 2000). The researchers conclude that services need to foster 'the six senses': 'a sense of security, a sense of significance, a sense of belonging, a sense of purpose, a sense of continuity and a sense of achievement'. They distil those elements of good practice that are likely to result in a positive culture of care and emphasize the importance of ward leadership in requiring and demonstrating good practice and attention to the individual, now being seriously pursued through the NHS Plan (Chapter 8). Significantly, the

Theme 1: Respecting the individual

Standard 1: Rooting out age discrimination
NHS services will be provided, regardless of age, on the basis of clinical need alone. Social care services will not use age in their eligibility criteria or policies to restrict access to available services.

Standard 2: Person-centred care
NHS and social care services treat older people as individuals and enable them to make choices about their own care. This is achieved through the single assessment process, integrated commissioning arrangements and integrated provision of services, including community equipment and continence services.

Theme 2: Intermediate care

Standard 3: Intermediate care
Older people will have access to a new range of intermediate care services at home or in designated care settings, to promote their independence by providing enhanced services from the NHS and councils to prevent unnecessary hospital admissions and effective rehabilitation services to enable early discharge from hospital and prevent premature or unnecessary admission to long-term residential care.

Theme 3: Providing evidence-based specialist care

Standard 4: General hospital services
Older people's care in hospital is delivered through appropriate specialist care and by hospital staff who have the right set of skills to meet their needs.

Standard 5: Stroke
The NHS will take action to prevent strokes, working in partnership with other agencies where appropriate. People who are thought to have had a stroke have access to diagnostic services, are treated appropriately by a specialist stroke service, and subsequently, with their carers, participate in a multidisciplinary programme of secondary prevention and rehabilitation.

Standard 6: Falls
The NHS, working in partnership with councils, takes action to prevent falls and reduce resultant fractures or other injuries in their populations of older people. Older people who have fallen receive effective treatment and rehabilitation, and with their carers, receive advice on prevention through a specialist falls service.

Standard 7: Mental health and older people
Older people who have mental health problems have access to integrated mental health services, provided by the NHS and councils to ensure effective diagnosis, treatment and support, for them and for their carers.

Theme 4: Promoting an active, health life

Standard 8: The promotion of health and active life in old age
The health and well-being of older people is promoted through a coordinated programme of action led by the NHS with support from councils.

Figure 10.1 Themes and standards in the National Service Framework for Older People.

researchers found that these elements were as likely to benefit staff as they were patients.

The National Service Framework for Older People, published in March 2001, sets out clear themes and standards (Figure 10.1) for improving the quality of the healthcare that older people receive and sets ambitious targets for change (Department of Health 2001a).

The standards reflect much of the learning described above, as well as many of the issues raised by the group of older people which advised the Department of Health on its development. It remains to be seen how effectively they are implemented, given the pressure of other priorities on the healthcare system. The development of Primary Care Trusts and Care Trusts (Chapter 8), and the extent to which they take on the challenge of providing a quality service for older people, will hold the key.

Key themes

It is clear from these examples that quality according to older people depends on a number of factors, all of which need to be in play for quality to be realized. A number of consistent themes emerge.

'Staying in control of one's life' is a strong and repeated theme across the research.

> The key to independence and inclusion for older people is to stay in control of their own lives – to be able to make their own choices, choose their own way of life, and access those services and facilities that enable them to do so on their own terms.
>
> (Harding 1997: 39)

In their research on the expectations of three age groups concerning long-term care, Henwood and Waddington (1998) found that the older participants had indeed experienced services that took control away from them and undermined their dignity and self-respect, while younger participants felt that future generations of older people would not stand for that.

Herzlinger (1997) draws attention to these future elders who are also knowledgeable and resource rich (Chapter 1) and who can actively contribute if given the chance – but equally could cause much waste of organizational energy if disregarded. How services proactively incorporate such views will affect their ultimate success.

A second key theme is the importance of recognizing and accommodating the individuality of service users – a 'one size fits all' approach is definitely not acceptable. What people want are services which are responsive to their particular needs and circumstances and that are able to accommodate personal preferences and priorities. 'Person-centred services' are seen as important by all older people but they have a particular significance for older people from ethnic minorities who need such services to reflect their own cultural norms and expectations – without that sensibility and adapt-ability, services are simply not 'usable'.

> The phrase 'putting the person first' emerged as a way of summing up virtually all of the comments about the positive ways services treat users and how users want to be treated . . . it is to be hoped that the principle of putting the person first will prove to be a core element, if not *the* core element, of the codes (of practice for social care workers).
>
> (SOL 2001: 3)

The principle that services should be responsive on an individual basis is now firmly embedded in national policy: the National Service Framework for Older People makes person-centred services its second standard, and proposes that the single assessment process for all older people accessing health and social care should reflect this principle. Because of the effect of existing organizational cultures, changing practice is, however, more difficult than changing policy (see Chapter 2).

A third theme is that quality is dependent on *how* help is given as well as *what* is given. '*Does he take sugar?*' is a phrase that neatly captures how people can be diminished and disempowered by the very services that are intended to support them. There is a mass of anecdotal evidence about poor attitudes towards older people, from overfamiliarity and patronizing behaviour to downright neglect and abuse. The nature of the relationship between the individual staff member and the individual service user is central to quality.

One study asked a wide range of service users what they expected and wanted of workers. They identified the quality of relationships with staff (respect, courtesy, honesty, reliability), the quality of the skills staff have (listening and communicating, knowledge about services, negotiating skills), and the way services were managed (flexibility to enable people to have some choice and control in their daily lives, services which take account of cultural and dietary needs, enough time for workers to do the job).

> The things that stand out about the workers we identify as empowering are such things as being treated as individuals and real people. They engage with us as equals rather than distancing themselves and seeing us as dependent clients.
>
> (Wiltshire Users' Network, quoted in Harding and Beresford 1996: 7)

Interaction is, of course a two-way process and *mutually* conducive rela-tionships, skills and understanding of constraints will further enhance the experience for both parties.

Interestingly, the three key themes above are mainly about the culture of services rather than a lack of resources per se – though overworked staff and tightly rationed services clearly don't help. Nonetheless, it would seem that a significant amount could be done to move towards services that approximate more closely to what older people want at relatively small cost.

The fourth theme would need new investment: older people don't think that the current balance of services is right. They want to see health and care services which help people stay active and independent given much greater priority and made more widely available. There is an important message here for Government and for service planners in local authorities and in Primary Care Trusts, about investing in the good health and mobility of older people. Attention and resources are heavily concentrated on meeting the needs of those who need high levels of support at present, to the virtual exclusion of other priorities. Older people see that as short-sighted and a recipe for creating dependency.

There is scope for much more creative thinking. Standard 8 of the National Service Framework makes a move in the right direction regarding health promotion for older people, but Health Improvement Plans offer perhaps a more comprehensive vehicle for such a change in emphasis, as does action by local Councils to improve older people's access to all mainstream services, under the Better Government for Older People programme. A key driver for moving thinking forward, as exemplified in BGOP, is the direct involvement of older people themselves in planning and decision making (see Chapters 9 and 11).

Approaches to involvement

There is no substitute for first hand experience. Services planned for older people without their direct involvement are unlikely to meet their needs most effectively or efficiently.

(HOPe 2000: 7)

Government policy has placed increasing emphasis on the involvement of service users and the public in planning, evaluating and monitoring health and social care services since 1998. *The New NHS: Modern and Dependable* (NHS Executive 1997) emphasized the need for openness and public involvement. Detailed guidance published in 1999, reinforced this message:

Health Organisations now need to work with patients, service users, their carers and local communities to develop ways of improving health and making services and care responsive to individuals' and local communities' needs.

(Department of Health 1999: 2)

Subsequent Government publications have elaborated on the theme and provided examples of good practice (Cabinet Office 1998b); and the National Service Framework for Older People has provided for the involvement of older people through formal participation in governance arrangements for health and social care and in a variety of other ways. Furthermore,

> age, culture, access to economic resources, ethnicity, physical and mental disability and sensory impairment are among the factors which can lead to social exclusion and need to be taken into account in engaging all sections of the community. . . . NHS and health organisations should make special efforts to involve under-represented individuals, groups and communities.
>
> (Department of Health 1999: 5)

Public bodies have without question been put on their mettle to involve older people. So where and how can such involvement happen?

Examples of involvement

User involvement in social care has nearly a ten-year history, although older people's involvement is more recent. Many lessons have been and continue to be learned. Patient involvement in healthcare is much more recent and still in its early days.

Carter and Beresford identify a number of areas where older people could be directly involved in planning and developing the services that support them. They mention monitoring and evaluating services; professional education and training; funding allocation and the setting of budgets; defining and measuring standards and outcomes; commissioning and undertaking research; and shaping, regulating and reviewing professional practice (Carter and Beresford 2000). Many examples of involvement in these and other fields exist, though relatively few have been written up, and more such information would be valuable. Of course, the fields above are not mutually exclusive. In Wiltshire and Swindon, the User Network has been in existence for some ten years and user involvement has become more the norm than the exception. Older and disabled people and other service users are involved in a wide variety of ways with health and social services while also running their own independent projects on advocacy, on support for those using Direct Payments and on transport (Wiltshire and Swindon Users' Network 1999).

Three brief examples of involvement are given below.

Developing national policy

When the Department of Health was planning the National Service Framework for Older People in 1998, it invited Help the Aged to convene a group of older people to advise it, along with a group of Carers convened by the (then) Carers National Association. Fifteen older people from diverse backgrounds across England were invited to participate in the Older People's

Reference Group. They started by defining their own concerns and priorities for change and put these to the Department. Throughout the process of developing the Framework, there was dialogue between the reference group and those leading the initiative, sometimes through an intermediary and sometimes face-to-face. The process was not always straightforward or exemplary, but sufficient trust was built between the various parties to make it workable. The National Service Framework when it was published showed clear signs that the Department and Ministers had taken note of many (though not all) of the views expressed by the Older People's Reference Group. Once its work for the Department of Health was complete, the group reconstituted itself as the independent Health and Older People group (HOPe), published its own agenda for change (HOPe 2000) and members set about talking to older people's groups and health professionals across the country about older people's own priorities for health and care. Their views were well received and confirmed by local experience.

Influencing the commissioning of services

The studies undertaken by Norma Raynes (referred to above) were commissioned by Manchester Social Services Department to bring user views about quality into the contract specifications for the purchase of residential and nursing home care and domiciliary care respectively. As a result of this research, some aspects of the existing quality standards were validated and new elements were added when local authority contracts were reviewed. The report on residential homes was sent to all homes within the city, and some spontaneous changes resulted, with homes making greater efforts to provide activities and opportunities for older people. The researchers felt that those who participated in the research had been empowered by the process and gained from being listened to and knowing that their views had resulted in change.

Older people evaluating services alongside professionals

Blunden (1998) describes an approach on Merseyside, where involvement went beyond traditional forms of consultation to 'enabling older people to play an active part in evaluating current provision and influencing future service development'. Initially the project involved just two older people from a local day-centre among a large group of health and social service professionals. However, it soon became clear that the professionals were dominating the discussions and the process was becoming disempowering for the older people involved. Seven more older people were recruited from local pensioners' organizations. Pairs made up of one older representative and one professional visited local care settings to talk to older people, the representative taking the lead, the professional taking notes. Information was collected and brought back to the group to identify what had been learnt and what lessons could be put into practice. The process was seen to be stimulating for all involved and effective in providing key information on service needs and preferences.

In each of the examples above, older people were brought in to advise on developing services. They had influence, but there was no shift of power from the professionals into the hands of older people themselves. Even on an individual level, Direct Payments have only recently been extended to older people, so there is little experience of how older people will choose to use them. On a collective level, there are examples of day centres and resource centres controlled and run by older people themselves, and of advice centres run by older people for older people. Older people also, of course, work extensively as volunteers on local projects such as befriending schemes, voluntary transport schemes and so on. Most voluntary and community organizations depend heavily on their work.

Involvement is not an end in itself but a means to an end. As Carter and Beresford point out, there is no one right approach to involvement, and each approach has its strengths and weaknesses. There are numerous accounts about methods of involvement: Thornton (2000) and Carter and Beresford (2000) both give examples and illustrations, though Thornton suggests that 'we still know little about which methods older people prefer for different purposes'. It does seem clear, however, that for most purposes, face-to-face methods yield richer results than more abstract approaches such as questionnaires. These also seem to be preferred by many older people, especially if it is an opportunity for them to talk face-to-face with someone who is really in a position to make change. The older people in Patmore's study thought that senior managers should themselves be in regular contact with those who use services, so they had 'direct eyewitness education in older people's everyday realities to be able to influence and act on policy' (Patmore *et al.* 1999).

Care has to be taken, however, to ensure that older people feel safe enough to give their honest opinions. Those who are literally dependent on health or care services cannot afford to alienate those on whom they depend and may be reluctant to voice criticisms for fear that the service will be withdrawn or that they will face retribution. The Dignity on the Ward campaign found that most complaints about hospital care came not from the older people themselves but from their relatives, and then only after the older person had died (see also Chapter 8). Confidentiality and trust are essential if people who feel vulnerable are to say what they really think.

Some principles

Experience has shown that older people are often keen to be involved in developing services – but only if they believe their involvement will make a difference. Many people have experienced forms of 'consultation', which happen in a vacuum and do not lead to visible change, which is discouraging to all concerned. Carter and Beresford (2000), two very experienced actors and commentators in the field of participation, say that people go through a process of cost-benefit analysis in deciding whether to participate:

- What are we likely to get out of this?
- What will it actually cost us (in energy, time, skill, money)?
- Could we get further doing it differently?
- Should we be putting our efforts into other things?

If older people are satisfied that they will be listened to as equals, that their issues will be taken seriously, and that solutions will be sought to the issues they raise, they are more likely to wish to be involved than if a health or social care agency is simply 'using' them to solve its own problems, or worse, for window dressing (see discussion of the 'manipulation' level on Arnstein's (1969) 'Ladder of Participation' in Chapter 2).

Older people are not the only ones who may have anxieties about involvement. Health and care professionals are likely to have their own concerns too. They may worry about not knowing whom to involve; about not knowing how to go about involving them; or about raising expectations and not being able to satisfy demands. In an action research study of six London GP practices, some GPs worried that older people would not be able to contribute to discussions or would be over-critical of services (Sheppard 2000).

Where active efforts have been made, however, and those involved have been willing to learn and adapt, many of these fears prove groundless. The UK-wide Better Government for Older People programme (see Chapter 9), which encourages local authorities to engage with older people locally to develop broad-based strategies for an ageing population, aims 'to improve public services for older people by better meeting their needs, listening to their views and encouraging and recognising their contribution' (Hayden and Boaz 2000: 2). Evaluation of the experience of the 28 pilot areas highlights many examples where older people, working together with local authorities and other local agencies, have brought about changes in services and in their own environments, which have brought considerable benefits. Older people have often been instrumental not only in identifying problems but in developing solutions and there is a real sense of shared endeavour in some of the pilot areas.

Similarly, primary care staff taking part in the London GP study referred to above noted that they had gained significantly from the participation of older people. They had become increasingly aware of the needs of older people and were able to direct what they had learnt purposefully into discussions about possible changes to their services. Nicholls's examination of community involvement across London Health Authorities noted that many had made efforts to involve local communities and a range of benefits had emerged, particularly from projects with high levels of community involvement. These included the development of more user-sensitive services and the establishment of longer-term mechanisms for involvement (Nicholls 1999).

Whose agenda?

Nonetheless a key question remains, 'Who is setting the agenda for involvement?' Thornton identifies two approaches to involvement, which she calls 'top-down' and 'bottom-up' (Thornton 2000). Top-down involvement is initiated by public authorities on themes of their choosing. Older people are increasingly being invited to become involved in health and care issues, though social services agencies have been quicker off the mark than their health colleagues. (Thornton points out that only a small minority of activities within Health Action Zones are focused on older people and none of the 12 research projects on user involvement in the NHS commissioned in 1999 focuses on older people.) However, their stake in other fields of public interest such as regeneration, transport or leisure often goes unrecognized. Older people still seem to be invisible to many significant fields of public policy.

When older people organize themselves through Senior Citizens Forums or similar local action groups, their agenda for change is very wide (Help the Aged 2002). Although it varies according to local circumstances, that agenda is likely to include transport, access to information, the closure of shops and post offices, the state of pavements and lack of public toilets, the level of the pension, the quality of community care services, getting to the hospital, hospital discharge arrangements, housing and a variety of other issues (see the 'citizen's question' discussed in Chapter 3). Senior Citizens Forums are run by and for older people and are independent representative bodies.

Many areas now have active Senior Citizens or Older People's Forums, whose role it is to establish older people's own priorities and seek to influence health bodies, local authorities, transport providers and others. These also provide an opportunity to learn about the legal, financial and organizational constraints within which these services work. In Brighton, the Forum has acquired a formal status and relationship with the local authority and is moving towards the model of the Senior Councils that exist in the Netherlands, Denmark and other European countries. At national level, older people are represented by the National Pensioners' Convention, to which many local Forums are affiliated, and by other networks such as the Older Women's Network UK and the Older People's Advisory Group to the Better Government for Older People programme. A 'partnership body' that establishes a formal link between organizations representing the interests of older people and Government has recently been set up, though there is as yet limited representation from older people themselves.

Local Forums represent the growing presence of an older people's movement, which is the means by which older people can have a voice and a say in local developments. Some Forums receive support from their local authority, the local Age Concern and other local agencies, but many do not. Help the Aged has a programme of support to Forums, called Speaking Up for Our Age, which has a strictly 'hands off' enabling approach. It is designed to support the empowerment of older people through Forums by offering grants, policy information, opportunities to extend expertise and a Forum to Forum newsletter; it does not seek to influence the content of their work.

Senior Citizens Forums are not the only means by which older people may be involved in developing services, as has been seen above, but they are the main route through which older people can express and work collectively on those issues that are of greatest significance *to them*. They are therefore central to the citizenship of older people, as well as a key reference point for those who are charged with improving services and the quality of older people's lives.

The future

The past few years have seen considerable efforts by older people themselves and by service providers to ensure that older people play a real role in influencing both the services they use and the communities in which they live. The BGOP programme has begun to explore what that could look like in practice and the Government's emphasis on public participation looks set to ensure that efforts will continue and multiply. The NHS is developing a formal structure for Patient and Public Involvement, with patient (including older people) representatives involved in key positions. Many older people are becoming involved in the Local Implementation Teams being established to take forward the National Service Framework for Older People, and are actively engaged in helping local health services to root out age discrimination and make services more patient centred. But there is still a very long way to go. Older people's interests and their participation are still overlooked in many arenas of public policy making. Older people are still seen as 'recipients' rather than citizens, as 'takers' rather than 'givers', as consumers of health and care rather than partners and full members of society with the wide panoply of interests that that implies.

If that is to change, and the deep-rooted ageism in our society is to be overcome, determination will be needed on all sides. Public policy across the spectrum will need to take account of older people's interests, and older people themselves will need to be present in decision making.

The mechanisms through which older people make their views and priorities felt – Senior Citizens Forums and the like – will need acknowledgement of their role and proper support and resources to carry it out effectively.

There is really no alternative: the population is ageing and older people make up an increasing proportion of our society. They can no longer be set aside as an overlooked minority. But equally, and crucially, to overlook older people is to overlook the contribution they make to the well-being of society as a whole. This is an area we have hardly begun to recognize and explore. Until we do, we deny ourselves the benefits that older people and an ageing society can bring, to families, to communities, to decision making and to the wider world.

11

Partnership and participation: better government for older people in South Lanarkshire

Pat Scrutton

In the beginning . . .

Ageing of the population raises long-term strategic issues for society, the economy, the polity, and the community as a whole, not just old people themselves. . . . It therefore requires a strategic response across public, private and voluntary sectors, not just more social work and community care.

(Benington 1998: Section 14)

The seeds of the Better Government for Older People programme were sown by the Warwick University Local Authorities Research Consortium in 1997. They were aware of what Sir Stewart Sutherland calls 'the silver tide' – the huge growth in the proportion of the population who are 50 and over. And they were conscious that neither local or national policy agendas nor resource priorities reflected this demographic shift (see Chapter 9).

The Consortium undertook research into the challenges posed by this ageing population and reached the conclusion that fundamental change in the way public, private, voluntary and grass-roots sectors work was needed:

Older people, like other citizens, deserve to have services that are carefully co-ordinated and integrated to meet their needs. At present, services are too often fragmented and unco-ordinated, even at times of greatest need. For example, it has been estimated that a person suffering a bereavement may have to deal with up to 17 different agencies to handle all their affairs.

(Benington 1998: Section 15)

Alongside this need for an integrated strategic approach, the research emphasized the importance of recognizing older people as active citizens with a major role to play in their local communities and not, as they were frequently portrayed in the media, as a burden on the public purse.

The government's modernization agenda provided an opportunity to test out this approach in practice. A national Steering Committee, with representation from central and local government, the academic community and the voluntary sector, was established to oversee a two-year action research programme, Better Government for Older People (BGOP), and a national core team was appointed, based in Wolverhampton. No funding was made available from central government for the local pilots, who paid a subscription fee to the national programme as well as funding the local work.

As noted in Chapter 9, the aim of the BGOP programme was 'to improve public services for older people by better meeting their needs, listening to their views and encouraging and recognising their contribution' (BGOP 1999: 6).

The programme was launched in June 1998. Twenty-eight pilot sites were chosen across the UK, of which 22 were in England, two in Wales, one in Northern Ireland and three in Scotland: Scottish Borders, Stirling and South Lanarkshire. They varied greatly in type and size of geographical area and in the breadth or narrowness of their focus.

South Lanarkshire, the focus of this chapter, is very large and geographically mixed. It encompasses part of Greater Glasgow and a new town (East Kilbride) as well as towns, villages and an extensive rural area. Its population of 307,420 is spread over 177,116 hectares.

The original bid from South Lanarkshire was couched in deliberately general terms:

1 To develop and implement, in partnership with older people, a strategy for tackling the issues and needs prioritized by older people, the council and partner agencies, the aim of the strategy being to ensure that more responsive and innovative policies and services are developed and implemented that meet the interests and needs of older people in South Lanarkshire.
2 To provide clear, accurate and accessible information for older people, on both their rights and the types of services available to them; to develop the skills of older people and interactive forms of information using various mechanisms including imaginative uses of new technology.

In South Lanarkshire the local project was funded jointly by South Lanarkshire Council, Lanarkshire Health Board and Greater Glasgow Health Board.

The funding covered a full-time project manager post and administrative support, and a budget to ensure that participants would not be out of pocket.

Looking back, it is interesting to muse on the extent to which we have fulfilled or are fulfilling the original aims, though not necessarily in the ways we would have predicted at the time.

Building the partnership

On hearing that the bid had been successful, the Project Director (a senior social work manager and the author of the bid) established a Steering Committee. This met for the first time on 2 June 1998, with an initial membership of:

- South Lanarkshire Council
- Lanarkshire Health Board (now NHS Lanarkshire Board)
- Greater Glasgow Health Board (now NHS Greater Glasgow Board)
- Lanarkshire Healthcare NHS Trust (now Lanarkshire Primary Care Trust)
- Greater Glasgow Community and Mental Health Services NHS Trust (now Greater Glasgow Primary Care Trust)
- Strathclyde Police
- Scottish Homes
- Age Concern Scotland
- Lanarkshire Community Care Forum
- Lanarkshire Elderly Forum

The bid was based in part on an existing action research project, the Disability Strategy Project, funded by the Joseph Rowntree Foundation and supported by the Scottish Community Development Centre between 1997 and 2000. Several lessons had been learned from the experience. One was the need for a dedicated project manager post to coordinate the work and to drive it forward. Another was the question of 'balance' on the Steering Committee between service users and officers. At the beginning of the Disability Strategy Project there had been an assumption that service users should be in the majority. They themselves were, however, quick to realize that this was less important than two other factors: having 'the right people' round the table, that is, those whom they wanted to influence; and keeping the group itself to a workable size.

When the Better Government for Older People Steering Committee was established, the same principle was adopted. This led to invitations to the Lanarkshire Elderly Forum to nominate four representatives and to the Lanarkshire Community Care Forum to nominate two. (We were particularly fortunate in South Lanarkshire in that we benefited from the legacy of a well-established network of Elderly Forums established under the aegis of the former Strathclyde Regional Council.) The six older people's representatives were all relatively fit and active people, some with a history of activism, for instance through trade unions. It could be argued that they were 'unrepresentative', but they also had experience of participating in a range of groups and committees whose views they were able to bring forward. Geographically they covered most, but not all, of South Lanarkshire.

The first action of the new Steering Committee was to hold a seminar, which was attended both by members of the Steering Committee and by additional older people and staff from partner agencies. The main purpose of this event was to put flesh on the bare bones of the aims in the original bid by identifying the themes which would form the basis of an action plan. These were identified as:

- finance
- independence
- involvement
- information
- isolation
- seamless services

We will return to some of these in the next section.

The day also had a secondary purpose, which was to give people who would be involved in the project an opportunity to begin to get to know one another, and to break down some of the barriers – real or perceived. A partnership is a working relationship: good working relationships are based on trust; and trust to build relationships takes time to develop. This investment of time at the beginning of the process turned out to be thoroughly worthwhile.

Potential barriers to real partnership are manifold. For older people, scepticism was initially the most prominent: *'We've been here before; why is this time different?'* Other potential barriers include physical frailty, mental frailty, isolation, lack of confidence, finance, culture and language. For professionals, the potential barriers include bureaucracy and rules, fear, lack of experience, defensiveness, constraints of time and resources, and negative attitudes towards older people.

Steering Committee meetings are scheduled a year in advance. This gets them into people's diaries and improves the consistency of attendance. Refreshments are provided at all meetings, and before the December meeting, the Steering Committee throws a lunch to which anyone who has contributed in any way to BGOP over the previous year is invited. These lunches are seen as very valuable networking opportunities, networking being the natural extension of partnership.

The corollary of this is that, while Steering Committee meetings are formal in the sense that there are agendas and minutes and large quantities of papers both circulated and tabled, the meetings themselves are relatively informal and laughter is frequent. Taking something seriously does not need to mean sitting around a table for an hour and a half with frowns and long faces.

In our partnership, we recognize that everyone brings something to the table. What they bring varies greatly. They might have responsibility for substantial resources. They might have responsibility for major decisions. They might have access to a great deal of information or relevant knowledge. They might bring a rich experience of life. Or they might bring more than one of these. Once everyone's feet are under the table, however, every voice in the debate is equal. This is not achieved overnight. It depends on many of the factors touched on above, especially on access to information and on everyone being honest. It also depends on the chair.

John Benington's assertion that the strategic approach should not just be about 'more social work and community care' is pertinent. Although, as mentioned above, the project director was a senior manager in the Council's social work department, he was always clear that when he was 'wearing his BGOP hat' he carried a corporate responsibility. The Council also decided that there should be corporate responsibility at Executive Director level. The chosen director, who chaired the Steering Committee, was not the Executive Director of Social Work but that for Community Resources, with responsibility for sport and leisure, internal transport and cleansing. When he retired, he was replaced as chair by the Executive Director of Corporate Resources, whose responsibilities include equal opportunities. The locus of the project within the Council has now moved into this department. This has meant that the service perspective brought by the local authority was much wider than just social work, very much in the BGOP spirit.

The Steering Committee has undergone surprisingly few changes. The Scottish Homes representative withdrew, while, with finance as one of the priorities, the Benefits Agency and Inland Revenue Scotland have been very welcome additions. They have both spoken of the value of the networking opportunities which membership offers them – not least with each other! As a direct result of BGOP, they developed a programme of joint surgeries.

In June 1999, when the South Lanarkshire pilot was 1 year old, a mid-term review brought about a major change in the working groups. All stakeholders, including members of working groups and staff of partner agencies, were invited to the event. This was run by an external facilitator, who also provided a full report.

The clear message from the day was that, while BGOP was undoubtedly 'a good thing' and markedly different from what had gone before, some changes were needed.

The most important change was twofold. 'Working groups' became 'task groups', with an implied change of focus to getting things done. And they were no longer to be chaired by officers, but by older people *supported* by officers from partner agencies.

Significantly, these changes happened around the time of a conference in Ruskin College, Oxford, which the national BGOP team organized for older people from all the pilots (BGOP Conference 1999). The older people present very quickly recognized that, while they were very heavily involved in their local pilots, there was no equivalent participation at national level. By the end of the three-day event, the Older People's Advisory Group (OPAG) had not only been born, but was already growing its teeth, paralleling positive developments in local projects such as those just described.

Evaluation, evolutionary change and opportunism

Evaluation

Change is what BGOP is all about: changing policies, changing culture and changing practice.

As an action research project, BGOP was very closely evaluated. The national evaluation team was based at the University of Warwick, and each of the pilot sites was required to appoint a local evaluator. The roles adopted by local evaluators were as varied as the nature of the pilot sites themselves. One project was evaluated by local elected members; some sites commissioned external evaluators from academic institutions; and some local evaluators played very active roles in the local projects. In South Lanarkshire we were able to call on the expertise of an officer who had been appointed jointly by South Lanarkshire Council and Lanarkshire Health Board to evaluate the joint community care plan and related projects.

The national evaluators used 'process-tracking' methods. They visited the projects at the beginning and at intervals throughout the two years. The initial meeting was one element in the process of establishing a baseline. During subsequent visits, they attended local events or meetings as observers, as well as conducting interviews with a range of stakeholders. Results from the interviews and their observation of pilot activities and events were made available to pilots individually in anonymized form, and examples of good practice from all the sites were collected and disseminated.

Everyone involved in the project agreed that this feedback was invaluable. Positive messages about the effectiveness of working in partnership were reinforcing, confirming that we were working along the right lines. Because of the formative nature of the evaluation, constructive criticism never came as a shock, but tended to give renewed impetus to our attempts to address such issues as the wider involvement of older people, particularly those who were harder to reach.

Evolution: progressing the main themes

Finance had been identified by the older people present at the initial seminar as the most important topic. The *Finance* Working Group, aware that decision-making powers on the all-important issue of pensions lay in

Westminster, struggled to plan a work programme that would tackle local issues. The Project Manager chaired the group initially, and members were drawn from the Benefits Agency, the Inland Revenue, the War Pensions Agency and South Lanarkshire Council's 'Money Matters' service, as well as older people.

They quickly found that information was needed and organized a seminar for the Steering Committee on local government finance. The Executive Director of Finance was so interested in finding out what the older people's representatives wanted to know that he sent along a senior manager. The presentation was lively, topical and interactive and knowledge gained on the day remains in everyday use.

Recognizing, however, that the seminar had been of significant value only to those present, and wanting to engage more widely with older people, the group organized a conference, 'You and Your Money', which focused on personal finance. It was the first major local BGOP event, and 130 people squeezed into a conference planned for 75. An end-of-event evaluation questionnaire showed that the workshop sessions and the information stalls, which lined the walls, were very popular.

Later that year the *Information* Working Group ran a series of focus groups looking at the information needs of older people. One of the findings was a lack of information on personal finance, and particularly on independent financial advice. The Finance Working Group put together a booklet that included some basic information and, because such information gets quickly out of date, a large 'signposting' section with contact addresses and telephone numbers for further or more personal information. The booklet was printed with financial support from Inland Revenue Scotland. The initial print-run proved immensely popular and the booklet was reprinted. The Group now intends to revise the booklet annually, once budget information is bedded down.

The *Involvement* Working Group, in the meantime, was looking at ways of extending involvement in the project even more widely, to people who could not or would not want to attend a day-long event.

So three working/task groups were beginning to be concerned about different aspects of the same issue, with particular emphasis on reaching those who would not otherwise be included. As noted above, this growing local awareness was both confirmed and given urgency by the feedback from the national evaluators.

The Involvement group organized a roadshow, which went out to 12 different venues across South Lanarkshire where older people live or congregate: sheltered housing complexes; lunch clubs; social gatherings, etc. Each roadshow was hosted by a staff member from a partner agency, who spoke about BGOP and about any initiatives with which they themselves were involved locally, and encouraged those present to raise issues.

In parallel, a small group of older people had undertaken a course in video filming techniques. They went out with the roadshows and filmed them. The resulting video would be used in a further series of roadshows so as to continue the process of dialogue. The group of older people continued to collect footage for a second video, which they edited themselves, with the help of an editing course provided through BGOP.

Most of the issues raised during the roadshows were in line with the themes on which we were already working. One which came across strongly, however, was that of public and patient (ambulance) transport to hospitals, a clear case of lack of integrated working. The availability of information, the concentration of services in a few big hospitals, and the availability, timing and convenience of public transport are all part of this complex equation, which we are now beginning to tackle (see also Chapters 8 and 9). This set of problems is far from unique, and we plan to learn from experience elsewhere, as well as looking for local solutions.

Transport is, of course, one of the keys to 'promoting independence' and to 'preventing isolation', two of our original themes. Nevertheless, it was one of the hardest nuts to crack. It proved impossible to identify an officer who both had relevant service knowledge and experience and the skills to establish and support a working group. The success both of partnership and of resulting developments often relies on individuals to take things forward. The recipe will vary, but these are normally people whose own interest, energy and enthusiasm take them the extra mile. Such people are not thick on the ground, and this part of the project suffered accordingly. The Steering Committee tried to move things forward by inviting the Strathclyde Passenger Transport Authority to join, but they declined.

Eventually, in 1999 the Project Director himself established the Isolation Task Group. It took on two remits: transport and housebound people. This remit proved too broad to be manageable and when, in 2001, the Project Director moved on, two groups were established. The Transport Task Group and the Housebound People Task Group have therefore only recently embarked on their tasks. The latter is undertaking a survey of the views of housebound people, through the Local Healthcare Co-operative. The former is drawing up a bid for funding for a 'mystery traveller' scheme, based on projects undertaken in Kensington and Chelsea and Hammersmith and Fulham during the BGOP pilot phase.

The breadth and interconnectedness of the BGOP agenda also presented difficulties in tackling the vital issue of *independence*. We recognized that it was likely to have different meanings for people at different stages of their lives (Benington 1998):

- The first stage is the age of childhood and socialization.
- The second stage is the age of work and raising children.
- The third stage is the age after paid work and direct parental responsibilities.
- The fourth stage is the age of eventual dependence.

The BGOP aim is to make the third stage a period of active, healthy and independent living and contributing to society, so that the onset of the fourth stage can be postponed as long as possible, and involve as little suffering and loneliness as possible. Two sub-groups were therefore established, one called 'Independence and Opportunities', focusing on the third stage, or the 'Third Age' as it is generally called, and the other working on 'Independence in the Fourth Age'.

Unlike the other working groups, the latter group did not initially include any older members. Instead, the group met in residential or day care settings. After the formal business of the apologies, agreeing minutes, etc., the rest of the meetings were dedicated to listening to the opinions and concerns of the service users present. This gave the group the opportunity to hear from a significant number of older people using services across South Lanarkshire. The common issue which emerged most strongly from those sessions was the service users' lack of access to meaningful, interesting and stimulating activities – a major 'quality of life' issue highlighted by Tessa Harding in Chapter 10.

By 2001, this group had recruited a number of older members, and was working on two projects to address this deficit, including a funded pilot project taking arts activities into residential homes and day centres. This project, it is hoped, will become sustainable in the longer term by including an element of staff training. It will be evaluated, with a view to extending it across South Lanarkshire. At the time of writing, a second project was being developed, to introduce IT into care settings, probably using older volunteers.

Opportunism

The heading for this part of the chapter, 'evaluation, evolutionary change and opportunism' is, to me, the healthy mix on which BGOP has fed and prospered.

One opportunity that came our way was the International Year of Older People in 2000. South Lanarkshire Council had set aside a sum of money to mark the year, and we were able to use this to undertake two exciting projects. In January 2000, three older people and the Project Manager visited Ballerup in Denmark (the twin town to East Kilbride) to find out how the Danish model of 'Elder Councils' worked. And later that year we commissioned Gerry Cambridge, a published poet, to work with a local writers' group to produce scripts for short plays. We are now in the process of seeking funding for a touring production.

A second opportunity relates specifically to Scotland. BGOP happened at a perfect time, when the new Scottish Parliament was taking shape. With the advantage of (relative) geographic proximity, the three Scottish pilots worked together from the beginning. They were then in a strong position to influence the new Scottish Parliament.

In March 1999, 60 older people from the three pilots met at Murrayfield to talk about common areas of interest. They identified the first three issues about which they would want to talk to the Scottish Parliament: the voice of older people; transport; and community care. In the summer of 1999, they drew up an action plan, and in October 1999 they presented this to three Scottish ministers. Impressively, all three ministers stayed for the whole morning, and spent significantly more time listening than speaking.

All three areas began to be addressed. First, in 2001, the Scottish Executive established the Older People's Unit. One part of this small unit's remit is to develop an overarching strategy, linking issues of concern to older people right across the Scottish Executive. A second task is to develop mechanisms for the engagement of older people at national level. In February 2002, the Consultative Forum met for the first time. This is a group of representatives of older people's organizations, including three representatives from the Scotland Older People's Advisory Group. It is chaired by a Scottish minister and the Scottish Executive provides the secretariat.

Second, a free concessionary travel scheme (albeit limited in scope) is planned for October 2002.

Third, the Scottish Parliament and the Scottish Executive have agreed to implement the recommendations of the Royal Commission on Long Term Care ('The Sutherland report'), introducing free personal care in Scotland from July 2002.

Equally importantly, the three Scottish pilots established good day-to-day relationships with the Scottish Executive. This culminated in January 2001 in a conference funded by the Scottish Executive and a report, written by the national BGOP evaluators in collaboration with the pilots and the Scottish Executive, which drew out the learning points from the three Scottish pilots (BGOP Scotland 2001).

Maintaining the partnership

The partnership we have created in South Lanarkshire is a strong one. Shared values and goals, an atmosphere of openness, honesty and trust, and regular injections of humour provide an effective context for discussion and joint work.

Since 1998, the partners have put in funding, information, staff time, life experience, reports and presentations, and contributions to debate. Partner agencies have benefited from the opportunity to road-test ideas, policies and service developments over time with an informed audience. The older people's representatives have greatly valued the opportunity to 'have their feet under the table', to have their voices heard, and to be kept fully informed and up to date on local and national developments.

For every member of the Steering Committee, BGOP has been a learning experience. Planners and managers have learned that being honest with older people provokes not overwhelming demand, but a greater level of understanding. Older people have learned to understand the constraints under which planners and managers work. Both have learned that, beneath the job title or the label, older people, planners and managers are, after all, just people.

Right from the beginning of the pilot phase, the partners in South Lanarkshire acknowledged that the two years of the action research programme was too short a period to provide the necessary fundamental reorientation of strategies, structures, processes and cultures and the radical transformation in service design. They have recognized, however, that the process is now under way. Older people's issues have moved up the agenda; older people are directly influencing change; the culture within each partner organization is becoming more open, more prepared to listen and to respond.

With funding in place to March 2002, we are continuing to work in a way that both builds on the past and takes advantage of opportunities which arise.

In 2001, South Lanarkshire Council moved to a cabinet style of government (see Chapter 7). As part of this process, the Deputy Provost was named spokesperson for older people. The council also put forward a proposal for an Older People's Assembly, to be chaired by the spokesperson. The initial reaction of the older people representatives on the Steering Committee was to revert to their former scepticism. The proposal was (self-evidently) top-down. They feared that it was an attempt by the Council to 'take over' BGOP.

But after three years of BGOP, being older and wiser (and much better informed), they stood back and recognized that they were in fact being offered a number of opportunities. The active support and commitment of, and regular access to, elected members was one; the potential to bring on board new partners such as the Strathclyde Passenger Transport Authority, Scottish Enterprise Lanarkshire and Communities Scotland a second; the emphasis on the corporate nature of the Council's commitment to the project a third. In fact this last opportunity was in some ways the most important, as it is notoriously more difficult to work in a joined-up way across an agency than it is between agencies. Perhaps local authorities should follow the Scottish Executive's lead and establish older people's units!

The most important opportunity, however, was the impetus the Assembly gave to older people to develop a mechanism to give older people across South Lanarkshire a strong voice on this potentially powerful and influential body.

The Council has now also established the South Lanarkshire Older People's Advisory Group (SLOPAG). The 12 members of the group represent, and provide two-way communication with, their local areas. They all attend the Older People's Assembly, giving them and their constituents a very substantial voice.

Auspiciously, the Assembly was launched on St Andrew's Day, 2001, and had its first meeting on Burns's birthday 2002, complete with haggis lunch. The first meeting focused on partner agencies' budgets and on community planning (see Chapter 7). As a result of the latter discussion, SLOPAG will be represented directly on the community planning theme partnerships, which will be a very important platform for older people's issues in the next few years.

In parallel with the developments locally, the UK OPAG is undergoing a process of regionalization. There is now a Scottish Older People's Advisory Group (SOPAG), and therefore a structure whereby the voices of older people in South Lanarkshire, through SLOPAG and SOPAG and OPAG, can be heard at every political level.

The challenge

Much remains to be done. We live, in Scotland, in exciting times, times which are, indeed, a-changing. BGOP is not responsible for this change, but has been one of many catalysts along the way.

The challenge is to ensure that, both locally and nationally, the voice of older people is heard; that older people influence the process of change; that government is joined up in both horizontal and vertical dimensions; and that, as a result, all services become citizen-centred, seamlessly integrated at the point of use, and oriented towards keeping all citizens healthy, active, independent and involved for as long as possible.

Locally, our first challenge is to continue to develop robust and sustainable mechanisms that will enable the voices of all older people to be heard consistently and effectively. We have a strong base in the older people who are involved in the Steering Committee, the task groups and SLOPAG, most of whom are relatively fit and active. We have a wide network of 10,000 people who receive our newsletters. We are also working with the Users and Carers team in the Council's Social Work service to develop effective mechanisms for including older people who use social work services.

We need to break down the remaining barriers on both sides, so that real dialogue can take place between older people, the Older People's Assembly and its constituent partners.

For older people, as noted earlier, the barriers may include physical frailty, mental frailty, isolation, lack of confidence, finance, culture and language. The solutions will include individual and community capacity building, encouragement, practical support and, if wanted, training. SOPAG has already benefited from training in committee skills and in working with the media.

For professionals working in the partner organizations, the barriers may be real or apparent, constructed or intrinsic (see above). The solutions will be as varied as the barriers themselves, and will be political, strategic, financial, practical and personal.

The cost effectiveness of involving service users in the development of those services is – or should be – self-evident. By talking – and, more importantly, listening – to the people who know what is useful and effective, costly mistakes can readily be avoided, and better, more relevant services can be developed.

Attitudes, particularly those that have become entrenched over years, are always the hardest to tackle. Fear of change, and protection of long-standing territory, can mean that both institutions and individuals are reluctant to become involved. They can see that it could be a lot of hard work, and they are not sure of the benefits – or when they will arrive. A combination of personal experience, conversion by colleagues already involved, and good quality training seem to work. People and institutions do become involved, and partnership to develop better services for older people in South Lanarkshire is becoming a reality.

The South Lanarkshire Council appointment of the Deputy Provost as spokesperson for older people and the establishment of the Older People's Assembly will help raise older people's issues further up the policy agenda. Until now, in cross-cutting initiatives such as community planning, community learning strategies and social inclusion partnerships, children and young people have been given priority. Both for demographic reasons and for reasons of equity, this is a balance that now needs to be redressed.

Nationally, the prospects are bright. The Scottish Executive and the Scottish Parliament are both 'talking the talk' and 'walking the walk': establishing a strategic unit at the highest level, encouraging partnership, participation and more open and joined-up government through legislation and guidance, and even by example.

In 2000–01, national care standards were being developed. In South Lanarkshire, older people were invited to influence the first tranche of these, on the care of older people, at the stage where they were in a draft working document. They had a second bite of the cherry at the formal consultation stage which, as good practice dictates but has rarely been the case in the past, lasted for three months.

The challenge for the three Scottish pilots and for older people across Scotland is twofold. We need to ensure that the proposed Scottish Executive's 'overarching strategy' is effective in 'joining up' all services and areas of government, which affect older people's lives, but which have historically not talked to one another. And, reflecting local developments, both in the pilot areas and in other parts of Scotland, we need to ensure that robust, effective and sustainable mechanisms are in place for older people to enter into direct dialogue with the Scottish Executive and the Scottish Parliament.

Our vision is of a society in which the voice of older people will be heard loud and clear at all levels of government, and in which they will live full, active, interesting and valued lives according to their individual wishes, with ready access to social networks and services to enhance the quality of their lives until the day they die.

So, did it work?

My answer is an emphatic 'yes'. I was tempted to use the traditional analogy of turning round the oil tanker – that is, services for older people – or rather, the flotilla of oil tankers! Certainly, we are in for the long haul: think about services for people with learning disabilities or mental health problems in the early 1980s. Attitudes towards older people are only just beginning to undergo a similar sea change. People aged 50-plus now make up almost a third of our population. It is no longer appropriate – or even relevant – to think in terms of 'care or cure'.

A much better analogy than the oil tanker is a garden. Older people have been neglected for a very long time. But fallow soil is fertile soil. BGOP has very effectively tilled that fertile soil. Locally, in South Lanarkshire and more widely in Scotland, we have done more. We have planted seeds. Some have come to nothing; some are putting up sturdy shoots; others are just beginning to show.

Creating a garden, like every worthwhile process, takes time. There have been some relatively quick successes: our 'You and your money' booklet was one. Another example was a recent conference on age and employment, 'Age in employment: too costly to ignore', after which we received a message from a very senior executive from Scottish Enterprise Lanarkshire that he had, very unusually, not experienced a second's boredom during the four hours it lasted, and he was now significantly more alert to this crucial issue.

We are also in the process of developing a number of projects to develop volunteering opportunities for older people. A demonstration project in rural Clydesdale, for the Retired and Senior Volunteer Programme, is offering a range of opportunities in educational, care, health and environmental settings. A handyperson scheme will cover East Kilbride, and in Hamilton and Rutherglen and Cambuslang there will be projects to promote 'healthy living' and 'active ageing' to their peers.

However, while such 'outputs' are important, what will make the biggest difference in the longer run is the BGOP way of working: the process of developing a close partnership between older people, agencies, planners, managers and people delivering services on the ground. Not only does this ensure that the voice of older people is heard and listened to at all levels of government, it is also producing a cultural shift from the wilderness of 'cure if you can; care if you can't' to a richly colourful garden where older people's potential is recognized, their contribution valued, and where they can grow and blossom and thoroughly enjoy the second half of their lives. The sound of BGOP is *laughter*.

12

Making it work in health: a stakeholder model for quality management

Amanda Squires

Introduction

Changing needs, expectations and provision contributed to a major reform of the British National Health Service (NHS) in 1990 (see Chapter 8). The aim of the legislation was to create a more responsive and efficient NHS by 'commissioning' (later changed to 'planning') services, using contracts based on specifications of quality, cost and volume. These covered specialties such as acute and rehabilitation services for older people, mental health services and support services, for example chiropody.

The author was appointed to a Health Authority at the time of the reforms with the remit to develop and evaluate a model for quality management in healthcare suitable for the commissioning process. This chapter describes how the model was developed, and uses a practical case study to show how it was applied to the commissioning process for chiropody services.

'Quality' in healthcare: a stakeholder approach

'Quality' in healthcare is a common, but poorly understood, term (see Chapter 8). Each stakeholder (patient, provider and funder) has different, often contradictory but seldom shared expectations of quality. Unless these can be identified, understood and synthesized between the three main stakeholders, service quality that meets everyone's expectations is a myth.

The three key groups with a stake in the quality of the service are: purchasers responsible for the equitable allocation of funds; providers of healthcare delivering the service; and patients, carers and referrers, who are both users and (potentially) contributors to the service. For this research, a focus group representing patients, service providers and funders met to establish the nature of these different expectations.

Users' needs were defined as a combination of their own perceived health needs, the generic requirement that services should be convenient and responsive, plus any differences that might occur with different cohorts of users, for example people with particular disabilities or particular age groups. This is a *social* model.

For providers, expectations were rooted in professional and service values (see Chapter 1) increasingly based on research evidence of effectiveness. This is a *scientific* model.

For managers, expectations centred on cost-effectiveness, cost containment, equity and health gain of the population for whom they have responsibility. This is a *business* model.

The focus group developed a model to express these diverse expectations. This showed that to achieve continuous quality improvement, there needed to be agreement on expectations. This required mutual education, followed by the development of a clear, agreed specification. The trap to be avoided would be complacency with the expressed expectations (which might not be very high) and failure to appreciate that these change over time for each group.

Local development of a model for service quality

In the absence of an existing framework for the local management of quality within the commissioning framework, the stakeholder group agreed that future quality specifications should include three elements, in line with national developments at the time:

1 'Core' standards. These were developed for all providers, based on statutory requirements or central guidance such as the Patients' Charter.
2 'Care group' standards. These were drawn from national 'best practice' for all providers of specified services. This would also include national accreditation schemes.
3 'Service specific' standards. These were identified from the particular quality improvement required from individual providers in order to meet the requirements of local stakeholders such as users and purchasers.

Arising from this decision, the author developed a 'Quality Synthesis Model' (see Figure 12.1). The starting point is information (quality intelligence) from a number of stakeholder sources. Next, this data is synthesized in terms of the three core, care group or service standards. These standards,

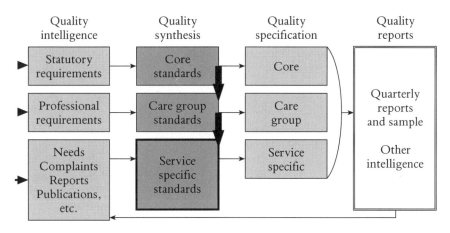

Quality intelligence	Quality synthesis	Quality specification	Quality reports
Statutory requirements	Core standards	Core	
Professional requirements	Care group standards	Care group	Quarterly reports and sample
Needs Complaints Reports Publications, etc.	Service specific standards	Service specific	Other intelligence

Figure 12.1 The Quality Synthesis Model.

or goals, form the basis of the specification agreed by the stakeholders for that service. Once agreed, the specification is then monitored, and the results are fed back into the system. This is added to any new information so as to progress towards further quality improvement in the next round of contracts. These would again be monitored, the results added to other quality intelligence and the process repeated. This is a practical example of the 'ratchet' process of improvement illustrated in Figure 5.1 (page 88). Figure 12.1 shows the connection between each stage of the model.

Using the model in practice

The Health Authority had chosen chiropody as the focus of this work due to the rise in demand and complaints, a history of poor recruitment, and lack of information about current service provision or its potential in the future. The first step was for a focus group representing patients (the Community Health Council and the local branch of Age Concern), service providers (chiropodists), and funders (Health Authority commissioning staff) to establish what their different expectations might be.

It was found that service users perceived chiropody as an 'on demand' nail-cutting service for all pensioners. Providers wanted to pursue higher level skills such as foot surgery as well as nail cutting for those at high risk of infection, such as diabetics. And commissioners were necessarily focused on the achievement of 'health gain' as well as numbers treated, which were the performance measures on which they would be judged. The result was that none of the groups had understood the expectations of the other two, and all parties were frustrated with the current service.

The next stage was mutual education by the three groups on how the perceptions had been established, and adjusting the specification accordingly. For example, the culture amongst older people was that production of the pension book resulted in nail cutting (this was subsequently denied by the Benefit Office). However, some chiropodists were happy to oblige, as nail cutting is a simple, quick task. The Health Authority activity data for chiropody was consequently impressive at a superficial level: numerous people were seen for quick, low-risk treatments, but the unmet needs of potential patients were unknown and unrecorded.

Purchasers, providers and user representatives then put into action the Quality Synthesis Model for quality specification for the chiropody service. They considered the relevant quality intelligence, which included statutory requirements from government legislation and guidance; the requirements of the Society of Chiropodists and Council for the Professions Supplementary to Medicine; and local assessments of health need, complaints, surveys and internal and external reports on the chiropody service. These included visits by the Health Advisory Service and publications, both by government and by others, identified through literature searches. The group synthesized the results to form objectives for the service specification. And they developed quantitative and qualitative monitoring requirements for the new contracts.

Initially, the 'core standards' were based on Patient Charter requirements regarding waiting time. 'Care group standards' were based on professional requirements such as giving priority to the needs of, for example, diabetics. The 'specific standards' were based on older people's expectations regarding assessment, explanation and choice.

The sharing of knowledge and mutual education resulted in agreement over which standards and goals were to be met, together with their order of priority. The result was that the criteria for access to the service were agreed; funding was provided for all current patients to be reassessed; staff would be trained in how to assess new referrals against the criteria and how to explain to patients who were disappointed that they were no longer eligible; a service was funded in conjunction with social services to provide 'social' nail cutting for patients not at risk; and a leaflet was developed to inform all current and new patients about changes in the service.

Changing practices

Considerable change by the chiropody service both to alter its way of working and to influence patient demand would be essential if the expectation of the Health Authority for a more responsive service was to be met. Throughout this book, we have emphasized that sustained quality improvement requires cultural change.

The discussion of change management theory (Chapter 2) showed that each component of the adapted Clarke model (Clarke 1994) should be pursued to maximize success:

- understand the organization
- appreciate the reasons for change
- know the process
- existence of visionary leadership
- established communication
- measure progress
- reinforce the change

The following paragraphs reflect how the model was used.

Understand the organization

To identify the existing culture, local purchaser and provider positions at the start of the project were self-audited, using the Crosby's Quality Management Maturity Grid (Table 12.1). This analysis showed that both organizations were at the most basic position of uncertainty, which meant that they both had a big opportunity to move to the right of the grid as responses to change management became more positive.

Table 12.1   Section of Crosby's Quality Management Maturity Grid (baseline)

Measurement categories	Stage 1: uncertainty	Stage 2: awakening	Stage 3: enlightenment	Stage 4: wisdom	Stage 5: certainty
Summation of quality posture	'We don't know why we have problems with quality'	'Is it absolutely necessary to always have problems with quality'	'Through management commitment and quality improvement we are identifying and resolving our problems'	'Defect prevention is a routine part of our operation'	'We know why we do not have problems with quality'

Source: Crosby 1980.

Appreciate the reasons for change

To address the deficit in knowledge about general quality issues, a local half-day rolling programme for quality awareness was developed and delivered by the author for staff at all levels. This covered the theory of quality and its application to health services. Analysis of participant evaluation sheets indicated that this was successful. For users, public meetings were organized to explain the NHS changes and invite comments on the development of chiropody.

Know the process of change, anticipate reactions and responses

The new task of commissioning had attracted people to the health authority who were committed to change. Providers' knowledge of the process of change management was enhanced by the quality seminars described above, although, in line with the general provider culture of the NHS, resistance and preference for the status quo could be anticipated. The original development of the Quality Synthesis Model (Figure 12.1) had involved some participants who also had an interest in the chiropody contract. However, so as to ensure that all the chiropody stakeholder participants were at the same level of understanding, a revision seminar on the model was undertaken by the author. The allocation of provider time for such activities had been a contract requirement.

It could also be anticipated that current users of the chiropody service would prefer the status quo (ongoing treatment) to reassessment, which would be followed either by discharge or by a period of treatment and then a further reassessment of need for the service. Non-users and new referrals also needed accurate and up-to-date information to counteract inaccurate hearsay. Explanatory leaflets, community presentations, and consistent messages from the service, Health Authority, Age Concern and the Community Health Council, were vital for success.

Existence of visionary leadership

Commissioners worked with service heads to help them move their service on from a very traditional 'cut and come again' culture. The effect of commissioning and potential competition under the new NHS internal market (Chapter 8) added reality to the need for change.

Establish communication

Communication between all parties was established through commissioning meetings between provider and funder and meetings between funder and Community Health Council. Direct information was also being received from users through direct dialogue and via the 'comments, compliments and complaints' policy.

Measure progress

It was agreed that the contract would be measured both through quantitative data on activity and cost and through quasi-experimental and qualitative information on perceived health gain and satisfaction.

A user satisfaction survey was developed to monitor progress on reducing the user expectation/satisfaction gap. Research into health needs would quantify current and future need. These data were used in the first pilot year to establish the baseline for future assessment of health gain, satisfaction and effectiveness. The findings informed the subsequent contracting process by contributing 'quality intelligence' to the synthesis process and at the same time facilitating continuous quality improvement.

The main differences between the first and second years were that information about footcare had improved, and the chiropodists' provision of the service itself had also quantitatively increased. There was also increased satisfaction with arrangements for follow-up appointments; increased expectation of domiciliary care; satisfaction with treatment venue; and increased satisfaction with clinic facilities. Areas for improvement were incorporated into the specification for the third annual contract, and so on.

The focus group re-assessed the service culture at the end of year three and agreed that progress had been made on the Crosby's Quality Management Maturity Grid from Stage 1 – 'uncertainty' – to Stage 3 – 'enlightenment' (Table 12.2).

Table 12.2   Section of Crosby's Quality Management Maturity Grid (after three years)

Measurement categories	Stage 1: uncertainty	Stage 2: awakening	Stage 3: enlightenment	Stage 4: wisdom	Stage 5: certainty
Summation of quality posture	'We don't know why we have problems with quality'	'Is it absolutely necessary to always have problems with quality'	'Through management commitment and quality improvement we are identifying and resolving our problems'	'Defect prevention is a routine part of our operation'	'We know why we do not have problems with quality'

Source: Crosby 1980.

Reinforce the change

The final stage of Clarke's model is 'reinforce the change'. This means that other organizational elements also need to change, to work with the grain of the new method of developing and implementing contract specifications.

Quality improvement is not a stand-alone process. It needs to be one component of a quality organization so that all its elements – for example, recruitment, reward, research, planning units – are pursuing the same principles (see Chapter 4). Not only will this attract staff with the same commitment, but each will help the others to reinforce this new culture. In this example, development of the service became a joint activity between the three stakeholder groups to ensure agreement and commitment.

Rolling out the model for *total* health

The model has now been repeated in a number of different healthcare contexts. These include user group specialties (for example, learning disabilities) and specialist services (for example, physiotherapy, occupational therapy). The supportive culture of the purchaser and provider organizations, the active involvement of users, and allowing the necessary time to introduce the new systems were keys to success.

The Quality Synthesis Model appears in principle and from experience so far to be suitable for wider use within healthcare, for example in Primary Care Trusts (PCTs). Even wider use of the model in other public sector settings would aid inter-agency work, supporting the government theme of 'joined-up working' and the new multi-agency Care Trusts (see Chapter 8).

Conclusion

In the NHS, local quality management through commissioning is viable so long as a systematic, participatory and cost-effective approach is pursued. The inclusive Quality Synthesis Model, which is based on stakeholder involvement, is offered as a structured yet flexible tool for wider use.

For implementation to be effective in complex environments such as the NHS, the approach must be one of quality improvement based on appropriate standards where they exist. This needs to be sustained long enough to establish the new behaviour and different professional practice. The tension for professional staff will continue to be that of simultaneously satisfying employer, profession and increasingly users (Johnson 1977). The Quality Synthesis Model has been shown to bring these expectations together effectively and to reduce the tensions in the service areas where it has so far been used.

The most likely barrier to achieving real change and improvement is the short-term political and financial timetable, which compromises the need for long-term consistency of vision to ensure that change is established. A flexible approach is needed, so that the principles of change management can be embedded. At the same time, responsiveness to changing goals and rising expectations needs to become the norm.

13

Making it work in housing: choice and need in social housing

John Crawley

Introduction

This chapter describes the work of a West Midlands social housing landlord – the charitable housing association called *fch* Housing and Care – to develop a better quality, user-focused lettings process.

As analysed in the first part of the chapter, social housing has inherited a legacy of values, practices and procedures which more or less excluded local people – the potential users and beneficiaries – from having any influence on decisions affecting allocation rules and procedures. It also excluded them as individuals from the allocation process. At the time of writing, the present system, being largely focused on physical need and immediate circumstances, takes no account of the holistic and user-centred approach to meeting housing 'need' in the broadest sense, which current public policy now advocates. In addition, it is inefficient and unfair. It needs to be changed.

In the second part of the chapter, the process of developing an alternative approach is described in some detail. This is 'work in progress', and the results are not yet known. Nevertheless, this attempt to improve quality in a very specific service, of great importance to citizens in need of housing, will be interesting to anyone trying to introduce improvements and change within their own service.

fch

fch Housing and Care (formerly Friendship Housing Association) is a 'medium-large' charitable association, founded in Birmingham in 1956 and now operating in the West and East Midlands. Its prime object is to provide 'housing and associated amenities for people in necessitous circumstances'. It provides around 3500 dwellings to rent, of which 80 per cent are purpose built and 20 per cent are renovated older housing. Of the stock, 44 per cent is in flats and 56 per cent is traditional family housing. There is no specialist sheltered accommodation and only a small amount of housing for people with disabilities. This is in inner city Birmingham, where 60 per cent of total *fch* stock is located. The association also runs a substantial and diverse range of care and support services, currently all located in the West Midlands. Locality offices serve Birmingham, Loughborough, Derby – the other two large concentrations of housing stock – and Nuneaton, all linked by modern, wide area and local information technology networks. The association employs around 400 part- and full-time staff. The Community Regeneration Department is responsible for the lettings service.

The context: history and politics in 'social housing'

One of the most significant trends in both service and manufacturing industries in advanced capitalist societies is the attempt to combine mass (volume) production and service delivery with individual choice, or at least the perception of such individuality. Hence the paradox of mass-produced aspirational designer labels. This is a result of increasing consumer affluence and the associated desire to reflect one's own personal style and individuality through your purchasing power in the marketplace. Those companies that have failed to spot and respond rapidly to this subtle but enormously significant shift in the mass-market end of retailing – Marks & Spencer, for example – have suffered dramatic reverses in fortune in an astonishingly short space of time. The experience has in some respects been paralleled by social housing, albeit in a different and complex context.

Increasingly, advanced digital technology is being relied on to deliver bespoke goods within a high volume and mass production process. This is even extending to traditional areas such as house-building, where off-site factory produced modules are coming back into fashion following the disastrous ventures into pre-fabrication during the 1950s and 1960s, led by council housing (part of what is now termed the social housing sector). The earlier quest was for speed and volume of production and assembly of standardized units. Unfortunately too many of them turned out to be defective structurally, or environmentally ill-conceived on bleak and anonymous estates. Today digital technology opens up the prospect of volume production of individually designed developments and units.

Service industries have tended to lag behind this secular trend. In some respects the sector has gone in the opposite direction. The huge growth in fast food outlets, for example, has been predicated on the big idea that the menu and product is identical across the globe, with quality equated with consistency of output as a standardized product, much like traditional manufacturing. There are signs even here however that change is afoot, in response to changed customer expectations. However, it is arguable that some of the trends, driven by the search for increased profit margins, have used digital technology to quite different ends. In financial services, for example, corporations have gone in the opposite direction, away from a local and identifiable presence (rural bank branches are the recent exemplar) toward anonymous – and not always accessible – delivery via remote call centres. Many customers argue that this pattern conflicts with consumer preference. The banks respond by reference to changed lifestyles and the demand for services to be accessible outside traditional office hours.

Social housing

What does this confusing picture imply for public services generally, and for one of the most problematic in particular, social housing? This chapter is based on the general experience of *fch* Housing and Care, and on a specific new customer initiative in letting its rented homes. It argues that change to improve services needs to be contextually based, not just mimicking ideas and initiatives from quite different private sector industries, but it must also challenge service providers' embedded assumptions about those services and their users.

Social housing's position within public sector housing is a recently coined omnibus term to cover council housing, housing provided by traditional housing associations and charitable trusts, and the new breed of local housing companies that have taken transfer of council housing stock in over 50 districts in England. It embraces one of the most problematic public services within an advanced consumerist society. Consider its predicament alongside the NHS. Much attention has been paid to the dilemmas facing the NHS as it seeks to 'put the patient at the centre of its activities' and provide faster, better services. These goals are set within a national debate where no one questions the good, only the efficacy and capacity of the NHS to deliver. The private alternative is seen as an unattractive as well as unaffordable alternative for the many.

The opposite is now the case for social housing. Provision of housing, unlike health and education, has never been seen as meeting a universal need, and in its public guises has only ever met the needs of barely half the population at its peak (with the exception of some districts, particularly in Scotland). Council housing originated in selective provision for the skilled working class. The poorest sections of the community, today identified strongly with social housing estates, were largely housed in the private sector, and on a very small scale by the early trusts from which today's voluntary housing association sector has sprung.

The post-war era saw huge growth in council housing, but this was never founded on a universalistic assumption about the role of the state in housing. In both policy and broader ideological grounds, council housing was conceived within a 'needs' rather than 'rights' culture. This led to the more or less explicit assertion that once the need was no longer paramount, the duty of the occupier was to vacate, freeing up the accommodation for those in greater need. Some of the rules besetting social housing to this day reflect this perspective, one of rationing a social good of which the beneficiary (supplicant) should be grateful to have temporary use.

For example, under-occupation is widespread in private housing and regarded as one of the first aspirational goals of a rising standard of living. Yet in social housing it is regarded as an offence against propriety (and is in fact an infringement of the Housing Benefit regulations).

Similarly, in the early 1980s, the Ministry decided that garaging was a 'frippery' that social housing tenants could manage without. Despite volumes of recent material concerning Best Value, the importance of the customer, the call for improved standards of construction, and the claim to devolve more responsibility to social landlords for setting their own standards and cost controls, no one has challenged this particular bizarre rule.

Pressures for change

There have been some legislative changes over the years to free up some of the occupancy rules, so that for example lodgers can now be taken in. The 1980 Housing Act introduced full legislative protection for 'secure tenants' of councils and housing associations. None of these legal changes have, however, been accompanied by a concerted drive to place the user at the centre of service delivery. Best Value (see also Chapter 7) promises to do so, but it is too early to know whether it will produce the essential sea change in underlying attitudes.

The impact of this deeply pervasive cultural inheritance on the housing sector, and on front-line housing managers and workers in particular, is significant in the context of quality initiatives and attempts to introduce a 'customer focus' into service delivery. The large majority of the population today aspires to the alternative, owner occupation. The 'needs based' inheritance of social housing has been challenged in recent years from two sources.

From within the profession there emerged increasing criticism of the concentration of poor and, above all, unemployed people and households on large estates where patterns of undesirable behaviour and inappropriate values were being replicated.

The debate in the USA about the existence and characteristics of an underclass was mirrored in social housing circles in Britain, a reaction to the economic and social polarization of the 1980s and 1990s under the Thatcher and Major administrations. The outcome was a series of attempts to produce 'balanced communities' by reference to employment, tenure and similar status considerations (Page 2000).

Second, the new Labour Government in 1997 imported the term 'social exclusion' from its largely European context to centre stage in British domestic social and economic policy. In 1998, the newly established Social Exclusion Unit defined one of its policy priorities in terms of the 'worst 1500 estates' in the country, establishing a close connection between social housing and social exclusion. Although empirically misleading in the many inner urban areas where private sector areas are more deprived, this correlation has been widely purveyed in public perception and in government promotion of its policy initiatives to combat exclusion.

The generalized shortages of all kinds of housing in the post-war period have been replaced by a pattern of acute local and sub-regional shortages, particularly in the South East and London, and particularly for family sized housing. But there are also emergent areas of low or collapsing demand for private and social housing, particularly in parts of northern towns and cities. The picture in the Midlands, where this pilot project is located, is patchy, with areas resembling both patterns. The more dramatic problems of market collapse, such as in parts of Salford, Greater Manchester, and the west end of Newcastle-on-Tyne go beyond the problems besetting social housing and are part of a much broader uncertainty over the viability of the communities involved and the unequal patterns of economic growth.

Housing associations have responded in two ways to these challenges. First, many have sought to broaden their overall purpose, moving from being 'merely' housing service providers to becoming social and community support and regeneration agencies. These associations now have a mission to work with local people to produce 'sustainable communities', defined as areas where people want to live. Second, the onset of demand shortfalls and sometimes competition for prospective tenants, combined with the pressure to improve financial performance, has generated a surge of interest in promoting 'choice based lettings', with a range of initiatives called for by the Government in its 2000 Housing Green Paper (DETR 2000). The project described in this chapter is *fch* Housing and Care's response to that invitation.

'Needs' versus 'choice'

Producer domination: eligibility rules

Brief mention was made earlier of the 'moral career' involved in the allocation of council housing to the deserving working class in both its pre-war and post-war guises. The underlying attitude that social housing is a public good which *officers* have a duty to allocate as a scarce resource, within eligibility rules defined by *politicians*, has remained largely untouched by the growth of consumer rights. Thus, the 1996 Housing Act (section 167(2)) defines the categories of housing need to which a local housing authority, and hence by extension a registered social landlord, must give 'reasonable priority'. In the course of the debate about rationing of healthcare in various ways, no one has suggested that it is necessary or appropriate for the Minister to specify within an Act of Parliament the categories of health need to be met by the NHS (although an 'evidence-based approach' is being introduced by the National Institute of Clinical Excellence (NICE) – see Chapter 8).

The history of the homelessness legislation since 1977 has, likewise, been dominated by shifting debates about how 'tough' it should be and who should be excluded, not by how it can be made more effective and inclusive as part of an integrated approach to meeting housing needs.

The universal appeal of health and education was founded on a value base that they are meeting fundamental human needs, that access to them is a right conferred by citizenship of an advanced democracy and that private sector provision is potentially divisive and detrimental to the 'public good'. All of this is in sharp contrast to housing, where the public good is to be served by achieving the sturdy yeoman goal of home ownership. This contrast has great significance for how the different professions have developed. In housing, management has been primarily about control, in terms of access to the stock of housing available, enforcement of the tenancy conditions (only relaxed somewhat in recent times in terms of permitting lifestyle variations) and latterly, on a broader front, through anti-social behaviour initiatives and powers. In today's talk of social exclusion, a new underclass, 'sink estates', 'neighbours from hell' and the correlation of drug abuse and crime with social housing, there is always an echo of the Victorian fascination with the alien dark forces of the slum-dwellers. How do we introduce a modern concept of consumer rights and customer choice here?

Defining 'need'

The traditional and still widely used basis for allocation of social housing tenancies is by selection of individual households on the basis of housing 'need'. This raises some obvious dilemmas:

1 How is need defined?
2 How is need measured?
3 What role does the applicant have in this process?
4 What does it achieve as an outcome?

Considering each of these questions briefly will help to identify why *fch* has launched a project to make fundamental changes.

How is need defined?

The official definition of 'need' is typically confined to physical conditions (such as overcrowding, lack of amenities, disrepair) and immediate occupancy problems (such as insecurity of tenure, home loss through harassment, violence or clearance, medical condition).

The social context (such as the need for support from family or other agencies, social isolation, other forms of vulnerability, a wish to live in a different neighbourhood) is either omitted altogether (this discussion does not cover specialist care and support accommodation and/or services) or treated as marginal. Yet these may be just the criteria that enable discharge from hospital (see Chapter 8) and illustrate the problems arising from lack of coordination *between* public services (see Chapters 2, 9 and 11).

Economic factors such as job mobility have been recognized, but they have not been extensively accommodated by the sector other than through a few government initiatives for 'key workers'.

How is need measured?

The result of using such eligibility criteria has been a widespread reliance (including at our own organization, *fch*) on assessment through measurable and quantifiable indicators. A points score is allocated for each indicator in relation to need (such as intensity of overcrowding). The prime justification for this approach is to produce an 'objective' assessment against which to prioritize applicants for a scarce resource where demand greatly exceeds supply. The applicant would then typically receive a limited number of offers of accommodation – judged to match the organization's assessment of the needs with appropriate accommodation within its control – at the moment where their need exceeds the needs of others. This might be several years after the initial application in areas of high demand and/or limited supply.

What role does the applicant have in this process?

The applicant's role is largely that of a supplicant, where one of the perverse consequences of this system is the clear incentive to 'enhance' one's housing predicament in describing it on the application form (a ten-page document for *fch*) to move up the housing register list. If one's need (or preference) is of the more intangible (social) variety, the likelihood is that you never reach the top of the list. Likewise, if you are an existing tenant wanting to transfer to another home, it is often very difficult to accumulate sufficient points. Some local authorities have been candid about the way a needs/points system works against existing tenants: they have introduced extra points where they want to gain access to a transferee's home (for example, because of under-occupation or to facilitate redevelopment).

What does this definition of 'need' achieve as an outcome?

This kind of system tends to produce the following effects:

- Many applicants, who have little understanding of the system or the basis of decision making, are disempowered. They are for the most part excluded from the process and given little scope to exercise choice over the accommodation they seek. They face the demand to make a quick decision to take the offer or be deemed not to be in 'real need' and lose out; and often have no idea when their opportunity will arise in this game of snakes and ladders.

- Decision making is justified by an artificially precise process of adjudication. This imposes a standardized judgement by the service provider about the assessment, calibration and weighting of the factors and degrees of need and living conditions to be taken into account. It is of course no more objective than any other person's set of measurements, a humble product of our post-Enlightenment infatuation with the supremacy of measurement and 'scientific' procedures as representing a superior, not just operationally efficacious, form of reasoning. The reality of course is that the capacity of individuals (and households) to cope with a given set of circumstances varies widely, just as our individual prejudices and tolerances vary.

- Individual choice and a sense of control over something as basic as your home and the immediate neighbourhood where you will live is minimized for the applicant, an unpromising foundation for any successful service relationship.

- The scope for the landlord to take into account a range of broader considerations when deciding what accommodation to offer, such as the mix of households and child density in a development, is equally inhibited, yet any allocation system needs to leave some discretion on individual lettings with the landlord if it is to be effective.

These then are the objections to such systems of determining 'need': they make the most of the elaboration of a bureaucratic rationing process in a situation – many more people seeking homes than are readily available – where the outcome perforce is that the majority go away disappointed. In an organization driven by a defined set of service values, the *system* exists to protect the office-holder when explaining that highly unsatisfactory outcome to the disappointed applicant, rather than being able to deliver a quality *service* that minimizes the adverse consequences for applicants. The system's claim is that it achieves accountability, fairness and targeting of scarce resources, by ensuring that individual whim or prejudice does not determine the allocation decision, by focusing on measurable and relevant housing need indicators, and by concentrating lettings to those with the severest needs.

The fch lettings project

Catalysts for change

The alternative system *fch* set out to devise was based on our service values, yet had to accommodate these public policy requirements. At *fch* the trigger for reviewing our allocation system was the feeling that the benefits of our 'needs' (points) system – in terms of demonstrably greater fairness of outcome – were only marginal, compared with the self-evident adverse and perverse outcomes outlined above.

However, the main catalyst for change in the sector has been neither the inherent inadequacies of such systems nor government exhortation, but the imperative of falling demand and unpopular housing. Marketing initiatives have become necessary for the first time, and projects based on European models, particularly in Holland, have proliferated. These tend to include advertising of vacancies and some liberalization of the allocation process, by enabling applicants to bid for available stock or increasing the number of offers.

In early 2001 the government released funding for a number of official pilot projects for local authorities and RSLs (Registered Social Landlords) to demonstrate 'choice based lettings systems'. Some initial research into 'new approaches to social housing allocation' by the Centre for Economic and Social Research at Sheffield Hallam University examined a number of projects falling into two groups. Some projects aimed at developing 'local lettings' policies based on a target profile for an estate or locality, intended to diversify the socio-economic profile of the area; others had a more explicit consumer and choice-based lettings orientation. Some reforms involved only marginal changes, while others had made a fundamental overhaul of their procedures and assumptions. Concern was expressed in the research that few systems for monitoring the impact of such initiatives were in place.

The research noted that these two approaches – both aimed at producing more 'sustainable communities', defined as places where people want to live – tended to overlap more than might appear from the initial contrast between tighter selection to match a profile and greater individual choice. Landlords 'were tending to introduce packages of measures rather than change a specific strand of policy'.

Analysing the problem

In the year ending on 31 March 2001, 1875 applications for housing were received by *fch*, of which 668 were added to the register. The number of properties let during the year was 292 (this excludes direct allocations from the local authority who, as with most housing associations, possess agreed nomination rights).

Lettings during the year therefore represented just 15 per cent of new applications received during the year; just over a third of applications resulted in people joining the register, with the remainder either being rejected, or not following up their application or withdrawing it. As a success ratio it is not very encouraging.

So a crucial management question is whether the control and account-ability achieved through the existing system is worth the adverse costs (financial and human) involved in achieving a letting. Or can and should the balance be changed?

From a quality perspective it is difficult to defend the current system. Even on the traditional territory of allocating scarce resources to those in greatest need, in one crucial respect – speed of access – the system already denies access to a group in potentially the highest need, those needing immediate housing for whatever reason. For the rest, the overall speed of response (offer of accommodation) depends partly on the type and location of the home you want – or are prepared to settle for – and partly on how high your score is. ('Type of home' is a generalization: if the customer is seeking flatted accommodation the supply, and hence the waiting time and points threshold, is favourable, whereas the demand for family housing is acute.) The most adversely affected people – who include long-term customers (existing tenants) seeking a change of housing through transfer – are of course those constantly displaced from the highest priority on the register by newcomers with greater 'need', that is, who have achieved higher points in the present system.

In addition, the lettings process was time-consuming and not very efficient. Substantial time and resources are devoted to the 'front end' filtering process, where initial enquirers (either directly or by referral from other agencies) by telephone, visit to a locality office or in writing are either advised that we cannot assist (generally because they seek housing in localit-ies where we have none) or are invited to complete an application form. The time from initial contact to completion of the process typically takes several weeks. It includes:

- despatch of the form and related information on stock location and availability
- receipt and processing of the completed form for assessment
- initial review of the form to ascertain whether it is fully and adequately completed with enclosures where required, and further checks as to whether the association can assist in relation to stated preferences for type and location of housing
- follow-up correspondence where needed and, exceptionally, a visit to investigate circumstances more fully

- associated enquiries to verify information – for example, a tenancy position or a medical condition
- detailed review of the form to assess the information and allocate points for all areas of need identified
- confirmation to the customer of their admission to the register, and the estimated time they will have to wait based on their needs score.

At *fch*, it was decided that a more efficient, higher quality and fairer system was needed. A 'lettings project' was established to develop the ideas.

Getting going

The project formally started in February 2001 with a workshop involving all the relevant service managers and other staff, together with the Chief Executive and Director, to set its scope. Following the workshop, a formal project team was established, led by the Assistant Director for Strategy and Planning, with the Chief Executive, two locality managers, the Communications Manager and two customer advisors who run the current housing register appointed to the project. The workshop, crucially building on earlier focus group work with tenants, identified four priorities for the *customers* – that is, people applying for housing:

- speed of response
- clarity of response
- minimal bureaucracy and form filling
- a letting of their choice.

In addition, six priorities for the *organization* were identified:

1 Avoiding inappropriate lettings, either letting to people who are not properly beneficiaries, or allocating lettings that leave the occupant discontented, with obvious potential adverse consequences for *fch*, the tenant or/and their neighbours.
2 Demonstrable fairness in the outcome of the new system, including the association's policy commitment and targets relating to equality and diversity.
3 Increased efficiency in providing the letting service, producing greater customer satisfaction by promoting clarity and certainty in the process and outcome.
4 For staff, reduced aggravation and distress from frustrated applicants wanting to know when they would be housed and why they had still not achieved 'poll position on the starting grid' to do so.
5 For customers, the greater satisfaction afforded by increased clarity and understanding of the system and certainty of outcome.
6 Sustaining performance on turnaround times to re-let homes on a sustainable basis.

These two lists cover between them most of the problems of the current system which prevent a good quality service being provided despite the dedication of the front-line staff administering it. These are the combined criteria by which we shall judge whether the changes we are introducing are successful or not, as perceived both by the applicants and by our organization and its staff.

Deciding new criteria is important, but even more so is developing an appropriate process to put them into practice.

The reforms

The reform therefore aims to change both the process (access) and the basis for allocation (outcome). The aim is to combine a more catholic approach to who can seek housing from *fch*, with continued adherence to priority social and physical housing needs.

This will be achieved by having two direct access channels for the association's own lettings rather than one as at present. (Local authority nominations will, as explained below, be largely unaffected.) One channel is open to anyone who wishes to be housed by us and is able to wait to secure the letting of their choice. There will be no formal income or other bars appertaining to their current housing circumstances other than the requirement that the tenancy would be the primary place of residence. The main requirement is that the person wants to live in an *fch* home and locality.

The summary details of the three channels are as follows.

Nomination by the local authority

This will remain largely unchanged from the current system because *fch* is bound by regulatory requirements to continue to provide this route. It includes the association's statutory obligation to assist the local authority in discharging its statutory duties to house people found to be in priority homeless need. This method is unsatisfactory in terms of both choice and selection. Nominees often have little knowledge of housing associations, let alone the particular one they are being nominated for, and generally started off seeking a council letting. The association often receives the barest information about the applicant and their overall suitability for the letting. However, planned changes to the risk and vulnerability assessment of direct applicants will be applied to applicants through this channel as well.

Fast track for immediate housing

The aim will be to offer housing within five to ten days of initial contact. The selection is as much the applicant's – their wish to move rapidly, to seize the opportunity – as it is the association's, through its assessment of their need. The first step in the process will be a *broad* assessment of the applicant's circumstances by interview, not pre-vetted through an application form. The main criterion for letting here will be the *immediacy* of the applicant's need, grouped under four *broad* headings for priority assessment:

1 Vulnerable because homeless: including potentially roofless, hidden homelessness, domestic violence and harassment.
2 Vulnerable because of personal support needs.
3 Re-locating to the area for employment or other reasons (including support to others).
4 Other immediate housing need: this could of course include other traditional indicators of physical need such as severe overcrowding or disrepair.

The association will be making a broad and inclusive assessment against these criteria, not 'pointing' up the detail on a severity scale to exclude applicants. Those presenting themselves will receive an offer based on the association's assessment of a suitable letting – based on both the applicant's stated preferences and the landlord's judgement on suitability – from the small number of available vacant dwellings. There will be no waiting list for future lettings. If the applicant turns down the offer they have the option of going on to the date order queue.

Date ordered housing register by choice

Applicants will receive offers (as many as they want) in their areas and by type of housing of their choice, once they have progressed to the top band of the register by date order of their original application. This will include all transfer requests that do not involve an immediate rehousing need. Information based on their choice(s) will provide guidance on the anticipated waiting time(s).

Each channel will receive an agreed proportion of the available lettings. In most instances for local authority nominations this is set at 50 per cent, but for some estates it is higher (up to 100 per cent for initial lettings) by individual agreement. For the two direct channels, targets will be set and reviewed regularly (at least annually) for each locality by reference to a range of factors, including pressure of demand for immediate housing and progress of the various 'waiting queues' on the date order register. Each locality manager will have delegated authority to direct new lettings to any of the three channels, subject only to achieving the quarterly lettings profile (plus or minus any agreed tolerance). The profile will include both the targets for the channels, and other service delivery objectives such as equality targets by ethnicity.

Crucial to the operation of both the new channels are the changes at the 'front end' in gaining access. Customer contact will be largely unchanged, with people identifying *fch* directly, or through press advertising, or through referral agencies including local authority advice centres, etc. A short interview based on a 'narrative' then replaces the present requirement to complete a ten-page application form.

This apparently minor change is intended to be the catalyst for deeper changes to the customer focus of the entire operation. The starting point of the 'narrative' is different from the current application form. It asks what are your housing aspirations, not what are your household details and current housing circumstances and the *fch* response must be: are we likely to be able to meet those aspirations, rather than can we and should we fit this household into our stock?

The project team assigned the task of drafting the narrative to the communications expert in the group, not the housing specialists. The information sought is confined to the minimum considered necessary to ascertain whether the association is likely to be able to meet the enquirer's expectations. The interview is completed 'on screen' on a computer, most commonly by telephone, but applicants can choose to be interviewed face to face in the locality office or by laptop in a remote venue, including an enquirer's home.

The script is linked to database information to enable the interviewer to provide up-to-date advice on projected waiting times for specific locality/ property queues, and to 'upload' the completed interview into the register. All of this can happen in one short event, rather than the current process stretching over weeks or months.

There are three possible outcomes to the interview:

1 The enquirer is advised that we cannot assist them and, if they wish, can be given advice on possible alternatives. This may be because we are not able to respond to their immediate housing need and they agree there is no sense in their joining a lengthy date queue; or because we do not have the right kind of property to meet their wishes.

2 The enquirer is advised that they may proceed, if they wish to, through the fast track and will receive an offer of housing that matches their wishes so far as practicable to address their need for immediate housing within the next two weeks. This is subject to two conditions. (a) A face-to-face interview to complete the assessment of their circumstances, including brief details of their current housing (landlord or other) to enable references to be taken up where applicable (for example, the status of their tenancy: have they just been deemed intentionally homeless by a local authority?). It will also enable a fuller picture of their circumstances to be completed, for the offer to be detailed and a visit to the home arranged, and will include signing the printed edition of the narrative interview to confirm its accuracy and truthfulness. A risk and vulnerability assessment will be completed (to ascertain whether the involvement of other agencies to provide necessary additional support should be investigated) and specific advice and support on welfare benefits, completion

of an application for Housing Benefit and advice on payment of rent is provided. The tenancy can be signed at that meeting or subsequently, depending on the individual position of the letting. (b) The applicant's willingness to move immediately (normally within two weeks) must be confirmed during the initial interview. Alternatively they may join the date register.

3 The enquirer is advised that they have been added to the date register. The narrative is printed and given/sent to them for signing. They will receive offers of lettings as part of a cohort of applicants when they are near the top of the date queue(s) for which they have applied. Information on lettings will be conveyed initially by phone or e-mail for speed at this stage. Procedures will then follow (2) above. People on the date register will receive six-monthly updates (or more frequent where the projected wait is short), confirming the current anticipated waiting time and requiring positive confirmation that they wish to remain on the list. While rapid decisions on individual offers will be required, there will be no limit to the number of offers an applicant may receive.

Implementation: the next stages

In September 2001, these policy proposals were presented to and approved by the Board of Management. The report set out the remaining critical tasks for the project to ensure that implementation at the front line actually delivers management aspiration:

- formal consultation with partner local authorities
- mapping of critical risks and drafting of detailed new operational procedures and policy guidelines for staff for the three access routes
- drafting of new 'vulnerability and risk assessment' procedures
- specification, production and testing of the IT programmes, system links and new suite of management performance reports
- review of the current management control environment and drafting of a new management lettings protocol
- staff training on all aspects of the changes for customer advisors, tenancy management workers and other staff with a direct involvement
- introduction of a three-month pilot in one locality from spring 2002, to include structured consultation with customers and local authority partners on their experience of using the new system and its outcomes
- review of the lessons from the pilot and necessary policy, procedural and system changes, and any additional training needed
- consultation with and migration of existing people on the register to the new system
- introduction of the new system across the association.

Too often management and front line are not adequately connected when 'management' becomes enthused by a radical change agenda. Front-line staff then become the victims of inadequately specified systems. To avoid this fate the project team has been encouraged to re-schedule the time-table to ensure sufficient time and resources are available to get it right first time.

This means that at the time of writing (March 2002), progress has so far been confined to a pilot. One lesson has already emerged: the timescale for 'fast track' is too speedy for some people, such as frail older people, and more flexibility will be needed when we go 'live'. This means that clear guidance will be needed for front-line managers, otherwise a 'flexible' system could become as inflexible as the one it is replacing.

Clarifying the implications

The project team had debated at some length the looser controls this system inevitably involves. It is probably more open to some abuse. It relies more on self-certification by the applicant. In some instances – for example, if the size of the household is falsely declared – this may result in termination of the tenancy when discovered. The overall conclusion, however, was that some scope for abuse must be part of the trade-off for the benefit of a faster-moving, more responsive system designed to reconcile broad commitment to meeting housing and social need with the customer's right to choose the home and location in which they wish to live. The Board endorsed these arguments.

Interestingly the main point of debate was not the policy changes – unanimously supported by the Board, strongly by tenant members – but the reliance on an interview. Concern was expressed that this may discriminate against those who might be intimidated by such an approach and the absence of a traditional claimant's form as an attribute of a fair and transparent system. This draws attention to the tensions involved in such public sector reforms when driven by a consumer rights and marketing culture that potentially conflicts with a claims culture.

Social housing is caught in an interesting junction on its map of changes at the moment. On the one hand, the 'choice and rights' emphasis is similar to that being promoted, for example, in the health service. On the other, there is a residual collectivism represented by a still quite traditional approach to tenant involvement, the importance of community and neighbourhood management and the continuation of statutory definitions of housing priority for local authorities – and by extension, housing associations – to adhere to.

This divide is also reflected in the position of the person in housing need. As an applicant they are treated as an isolated consumer in a managed market, with in reality precious few rights and little leverage. Once housed they inherit the full panoply of rights, including the enfranchisement represented by Best Value (described in Chapter 7) and its stated objective of placing customer preference and judgements at the heart of the service quality project.

Perhaps a more fundamental question arises from the circumstances of many of the people we house. In practice, an increasing proportion bring with them serious and challenging needs and vulnerability that go far beyond the narrow confines of a housing landlord service. Our Vulnerability project is intended to help us respond more proactively and intelligently to these circumstances, both on our own, through our care agency and in partnerships with others such as community mental health services. The project does tend to underscore the shallowness of a consumer rights perspective – a necessary but wholly insufficient value base for public service – and the complexity of relationships we ask our front-line staff to manage.

For *fch* there are significant risks and hurdles to overcome in the venture on which we have just set out. The most significant ones will probably prove to be, first, managing future relationships and practical partnerships with local housing authorities, attempting to dovetail our bespoke system and approach into emergent authority-wide access systems. In principle our new system should be flexible enough to accommodate such initiatives, and the fast-track system should be attractive to local authorities, making us a more valuable resource in responding to urgent housing need.

The second major challenge will be to strike the right balance, both in allocating resources between the access channels and in pursuing the under-lying policy objective of sustainable neighbourhoods, defined as places people still want to live in. In taking this bold step, however, we are encouraged by our conviction that the current system has outstayed its welcome with all concerned, a sound basis for change.

14

Making it work in local government: experiences of Tameside MBC

Michael Greenwood

Introduction

Tameside is a Metropolitan Borough Council in the Greater Manchester conurbation serving a population of 221,000. It is a 'most–purpose' (unitary) authority and is responsible for all local government services in the district. It participates in the joint authorities which deliver police, fire, waste disposal and passenger transport services. In the year 2001/02 the total gross expenditure was £365 million. The Council currently employs a workforce of about 8000 people.

In this chapter the experiences of Tameside Council in trying to improve the quality and cost-effectiveness of local services over a ten-year period are discussed. It describes the long-term programme of organizational development used for this purpose, with particular emphasis on changing the culture and encouraging and teaching the workforce to use the tools and techniques of continual process improvement (see also Chapter 4).

What is 'quality'?

The concept of quality can often speak for itself, but managers and management thinkers do try to define it. One of the most unhelpful definitions of quality is 'conformance to specification'. This can lead to inappropriate understanding of what customers think of as 'quality'. All too often, organizations set their own specifications. They then use systems such as

ISO 9000 to ensure that they are delivered – and somehow believe that this is 'quality'. It may be, but very often it most definitely will not be, being reliant only on the internal specification.

It is also important not to forget the ISO 9000 dilemma. It would be theoretically possible for a manufacturer of concrete lifebelts to set specifications, achieve them, gain ISO 9000 and therefore believe it was dealing in a quality product!

This is not to say that ISO 9000 may not be useful. Where there are complex systems in place, and these may be subject to change, either because of change in customer demands or perhaps through continual process improvement, then some method of ensuring that people are working to the most up-to-date version of the system can be necessary. ISO 9000 can provide this, but it needs to be in the right cultural context and does not, of itself, represent 'quality'.

The best definition of quality that I have seen is that of Deming who says, quite simply, that quality is 'delighting the customer'. That tends to accord with one's own personal experience. It is very rare to have a good meal in a restaurant and say 'well, that conformed to specification'! In local government though, unlike restaurants, some services are imposed on people for the common good, and others are rationed and therefore not available to all who want or need them. Nevertheless, the idea – the challenge – of 'delighting' the user or applicant, willing or not, should lead to better treatment and possibly better outcomes than simply conforming to specification. Of course, if the users are actively involved in developing the specification (in Tameside we are beginning to do this through our user groups) the service is even more likely at least to meet expectations, if not actually to bring 'delight'.

This is because the philosophy of continual improvement, and the cultural change which it can bring about, mean that the desire is always to be better than specification and for a service to be and be seen to be better this month than last month, this year than last year, and so on. It is this meaning of 'quality' that is at the heart of the ten-year programme of change we have been putting into place in Tameside.

The context

Since the early 1980s, as Chapter 6 showed, Local Authorities have been subject to huge change from external pressures, including:

- the demographic and socio-economic changes in our society, which have affected direct demand for services (for example more elderly people or the effects of two recessions)
- increasing expectations from citizens whereby most services and products in our society tend to improve and in many cases actually get cheaper.

These expectations will also manifest themselves as society demanding better public services, locally and nationally

- government policy and new legislation has changed the way Local Authorities work. Examples such as compulsory competitive tendering and best value have had a general effect and the way education and social services are operated is radically different from the mid-1980s
- until 1999, resources for local government have continually fallen. There has been a downward pressure on local expenditure over many years.

The challenge therefore to local politicians and managers has been to try to get more from less.

Local Authorities in the past have been very traditional bureaucracies and many have tended to have some or all of the following characteristics:

- Inward-looking: they tended to be concerned with their own processes rather than responding to customers. The world was inside the Town Hall.
- Producer-focus: the provision of services was seen as valuable in its own right. Continuation of existing provision was much more likely than thinking about alternatives.
- Employment: arising from the above, preserving direct council jobs was used as a justification for activity, rather than as a consequence of an informed decision to provide a particular service in a particular way.
- Costs and quality: bureaucratic tendency to stasis meant that many authorities had services that were of high cost and/or low quality.

In bureaucracies like this, the culture is 'the way we do things around here'. It is quite clear that this model cannot deliver the expectations of 'more from less'. The traditional bureaucratic approach assumes, for example, that a new activity automatically requires new resources; conversely, if resources are being reduced, the automatic response has been to reduce services. This cannot be the right way to provide public services into the twenty-first century.

Tameside's approach

In 1990/91, Tameside realized that the traditional approach to service management and delivery in a Local Authority would not provide what its communities and citizens wanted and needed. The Council therefore embarked on a long-term programme of organizational development, initially called Tameside Towards 2000, and, since that date has been passed, now called rather unoriginally Tameside 20/20 Vision.

This has involved:

- *Customer focus.* There has been a series of programmes and actions which have emphasized the importance of the customer – users, citizens and communities – as opposed to the service. This started off with conventional customer-care training and now sees our access to services programme badged as Customer First. This has been underpinned in recent years by a very extensive programme of communication and consultation with the public. As well as bi-annual MORI polls and ad hoc surveys about specific services, we use our own newspaper and website to keep the public informed and provide opportunities for feedback. We also have a panel of 2000 residents who are our sounding board for a wide range of issues, together with service user groups for many services, especially social services, as well as eight District Assemblies attended by community representatives, which are now linked in with political decision making.

- *Clarifying responsibilities, decentralization and delegation.* The organization used to be hide-bound by rules and a lack of clarity of responsibilities. This meant managers could not always take action and also provided an excuse for weaker managers, 'I'll have to ask Personnel about that' or 'that's the Finance Department's responsibility'. The programme involved extensive delegation of financial controls such as virement and responsibility for staffing matters to managers, well beyond what was normal in local government at the time. In addition, the activities for which managers were themselves responsible were made clear. In particular, budget management tasks were clearly allocated.
- *Communications.* Internal communications have been improved enormously. There is a requirement for regular team briefings of staff, with core messages being given to Heads of Service once a month. Service-based newsletters and other communications systems have also been developed.
- *Employee development.* Our aim was to develop an empowered, motivated workforce. Regular staff surveys measure 'staff satisfaction' with working in the organization (coming out consistently at about 80 per cent satisfaction). Workgroups are actively involved in a 'bottom-up' process of service improvement (see below). The Council has received 'Investors in People' accreditation and actively puts the policy into practice. And a uniform system of employee development review requires that, in addition to normal management supervision meetings, each employee has at least one development interview per annum, focusing on the development needs of both the individual and the organization.
- *Focused training and development programme.* The annual training and development programme is a combination of top-down policy, such as the requirements arising from legislation or Best Value, plus an aggregation of the results from the employee development review process. This is coordinated through individual service training plans and a corporate training plan.
- *Management Team development.* The Council's Management Team, as the main management leadership body, has paid considerable attention to its

own development. It has worked over a number of years with a single consultant but has also undertaken other activities.

While considerable progress had been made within the organization, it was clear that something else was needed, particularly if the necessary vision of delivering better services with fewer resources was to be given full effect. This required a programme of change management towards a different culture and way of working, so that staff could begin to consider the culture as responsive and creative – 'the (new) way we *think* around here'.

In 1995, as part of its development, the Management Team was studying the work of Dr W. Edwards Deming, the American management thinker who is credited with much responsibility for the post-war Japanese manufacturing industry management revolution. The philosophy was considered appropriate to the Tameside Council context and has proved immensely important in the way it has taken its change programme forward (see also Chapter 4).

Deming's philosophy and continual improvement

Deming's management philosophy is a complex and internally consistent system, which covers all aspects of management and is applicable in any kind of organization (Deming 1986; Neave 1990). Two themes, central to Deming's philosophy of 'transforming western management', appeared highly relevant to Tameside:

1 Deming sees quality as essential to the survival and growth of any organization.
2 He emphasizes the need for continual improvement and learning in all activities and processes.

These points resonated with the situation in which Tameside and probably most local authorities found themselves. Quality was certainly going to be essential for the success and probably survival of local authorities (and this has been borne out by subsequent events such as inspection regimes and Best Value), while continual improvement can give practical help to the management challenge of achieving more from less.

But it does not seem that the nature of 'continual (or continuous) improvement' is widely understood. In local government the expression is heard all the time: in speeches by Ministers, in government publications about Best Value, in reports from the Audit Commission and so on. Too often though it seems that the words are simply being used in their literal sense, that is, 'getting better all the time'. In reality, continual improvement is a *philosophy* accompanied by specific *tools and techniques*, which can be selected as appropriate, can be learnt and can be applied to the improvement of any process (see Appendix). It is also referred to as 'business process re-engineering' or Kaizen. This discipline is well understood in much of manufacturing industry but this understanding has not spread widely into the public service, although it is now starting to happen.

It is not the purpose of this chapter to provide instructions on how to carry out continual improvement, but a brief resumé will provide a context for subsequent points (see also Chapter 4).

The tools and techniques of continual improvement include flow charts, histograms, cause and effect diagrams, Pareto analysis and run and control charts. Managers and workgroups can be taught the use and interpretation of these devices quite easily.

The methodology of continual improvement involves analysing the pattern of demand for a service or activity, paying particular attention to understanding the causes of successes and failures. An improvement statement is prepared by the relevant staff workgroup, using data such as public consultation results and complaints as well as internal data and information. This identifies variations, and indicates what is to be improved, such as cutting the time to undertake a task or reducing the error rate. Performance measures are required for these factors.

All those involved in production need to understand the *whole* system, including the effects of suppliers on the system ('inputs') and the level and nature of satisfaction of customers with the results ('outputs'). This system is flow charted (each stage in the existing production process is mapped) and then redesigned on the basis of an analysis of which actions are essential and which could be changed or omitted altogether. The effects are monitored by staff and managers, and sometimes users, using the agreed performance measures. The results are plotted on control charts if at all possible. From then on the cycle is repeated so that the improvement is indeed continual.

Continual improvement in Tameside

Tameside first devoted considerable effort (and a budget) to teaching the *tools and techniques* of continual improvement to the workforce. Nearly 2000 of our 8000 staff have experienced such training in the past five or six years. We also introduced the 'continual improvement' approach to senior managers through some initial training in the management *philosophy* of Deming, so as to understand the theoretical context.

Initially, much of the general staff training was a simulation exercise, which the Council had franchised from consultants. This is a very powerful tool and over an intensive period of three days, workgroups are taught the tools and techniques of continual improvement by working on a real task, processing a sales order, and can see the improvements which can be achieved by process redesign.

Latterly, more bespoke training has been undertaken with particular workgroups, helping them to work on improvement of their own processes. Tameside has increasingly been able to resource this through the skills developed by our own organization and by the development training team.

This training is not just for managers. In fact it is at its most effective when whole workgroups are involved. Management leadership is important, but involvement of teams in their own processes is very powerful. It creates ownership of processes and genuine interest in outcomes. Quality improves but, most importantly, so does motivation, responsiveness and creativity, all of which are vital for the culture change we are aiming for.

It is critical, though, that teaching and encouraging the use of continual improvement is not seen in isolation from organization development (OD) generally. The real trick is for improvement to be the natural state of things in an organization. In a bureaucracy, the status quo is seen to have intrinsic merit. This cannot be sensible in organizations which are working in environments of rapid change – and local government is certainly in this position. It is vital that managers in local government and the public service as a whole see improvement, and not trying to retain the status quo, as what they are about. This cultural change needs reinforcement through all aspects of an OD programme and this is something that Tameside has consistently tried to do.

Getting results

The application of continual improvement has produced many real achievements at the service level. A few of these are mentioned below:

- All the Council's revenues and benefits services now tend to be in the upper quartile of government measures of performance and the lower quartile for cost. This has been a direct result of the application of continual improvement over several years and is continuing.
- The Council regularly achieves the required performance for dealing with householder planning applications within eight weeks.
- The time to supply a library request has been halved.
- In social services, the time between receipt of referrals and allocation to social work teams has been significantly reduced.
- About 95 per cent of undisputed invoices are paid within 30 days.
- The Greater Manchester Pension Fund, which is run by Tameside, has seen large increases in the productivity of its administrative processes.
- Time taken to deliver and install smaller information technology systems and equipment has been greatly reduced.
- From being one of the worst authorities in the country at producing statements of special educational need, within two years Tameside is

now amongst the very best, achieving the issue of all statements within the prescribed period.

New systems for service delivery

The continual improvement thinking does not just apply to smaller operational activities, though these are of course very important to the users of those services. Deming explains that managers must have an understanding of systems. In Tameside we are well aware that many of our services operate in large and complex systems, which go beyond the boundaries of the Council itself.

A good example is links between Social Services and Health. Since the early 1990s, Tameside has operated a joint service with health partners for learning disabilities. This is jointly funded and has developed as a single system, where staff from different professional groups and from the two main services involved accept overall management control and common systems as the basis for their work. This has achieved a holistic approach to assessing the needs of individuals, and practical joint assessment procedures to avoid duplication.

In the mental health services, a similar model has begun to be developed, again moving towards joint assessment and a focus on the individual's overall needs.

Recently, agreement has been reached to design and implement a single service for assessment, commissioning and some provision of services for the elderly. The culture and techniques of continual improvement will be highly relevant to the design of all aspects of this new service, and flow charting has already been used to map the current services – which demonstrated graphically to the workers involved how unnecessarily complicated it has all been for the user.

Learning from experience in Tameside

Despite substantial progress and change, it must not be assumed that all activities in Tameside are uniformly and successfully dealing with improvement of the quality of services. That is certainly the general pattern, but there are some exceptions. It is interesting to analyse why there is more success in some areas than in others.

First, continual improvement can be applied more easily to some services, systems and processes than others. In Local Government there are activities which are quite 'soft'. Some do not have quantifiable outputs or outcomes, or those outcomes that can be measured cannot necessarily be linked with particular changes and improvements in the service delivery process. Economic development is a case in point: while the service might aim to reduce local unemployment, it is not solely the activities of the local authority which would bring this about. However, systems thinking (continual improvement) helps even in areas such as this.

Second, it is very important to involve the whole team. As has been implied above, improvement is not just a matter for management. Management must lead, but the whole work team needs to be involved. It has proved to be highly motivating for a workgroup to redesign their own processes. This, refreshingly, goes against the experience of many people in public service where someone else has designed the system and staff are merely told to get on with it. A workgroup which genuinely has a sense of ownership of its own system is going to achieve better productivity, because it has a deep understanding of what is going on and why changes are being made.

Arising from the above point, senior management leadership is also vital. If workgroups see that managers are merely going through the motions or are not clearly exhibiting through their words and actions that improvement is what matters, then it will be much more difficult for real improvements to be made. Very visual and clear commitment from senior management is essential. Furthermore, an initiative like this can never be 'flavour of the month'. Improvement must be for ever and this again must be clearly modelled in the actions and behaviour of senior managers who must show what Deming calls 'constancy of purpose'. The aim is for staff to internalize the idea that improvement is 'the way we think and act round here'. It must never be seen as an extra or an option.

As part of the way staff can be supported and encouraged to take an active part, targeted training in the tools and techniques of continual improvement, and continued access to advice and support as workgroups develop more skills, are vital aspects of success. Nevertheless, staff at all levels have perceived threats in the process. This is because many improvements will (and should) result in fewer staff producing better work. How issues like this are handled in an organization is very important. In Tameside we have faced up to this from the beginning and have made it clear that staff will not lose employment through being part of an improvement process. Through natural turnover in the organization and training and retraining, we have been able to handle staffing consequences without anyone losing employment, although people have moved to new jobs.

However, partly because they feel threatened in this way, staff may generate excuses for not taking part in the improvement programme. One of the commonest excuses is 'lack of time'. This usually happens in workgroups which are spending too much time on fire-fighting, dealing with complaints and 'rework' – having to do things again which should have been done correctly the first time. However, without spending time on improving processes, this will always continue. Management leadership is vital here. The message must be: find the time or you will never have it!

There have also been problems with some professional groups. Perhaps this is inevitable where in some professions people are taught that their autonomous judgement is the essence of their job, for example when lawyers give opinions or engineers design a new structure. But lawyers and engineers have benefited massively from continual improvement. In many authorities, the time taken to sell a Council house could be reduced from weeks to hours by redesigning the conveyancing activity and associated administration. Or – a real example – engineers may design a road junction without applying systems thinking. This means that maintenance staff are not consulted about how designs can be improved to make maintenance easy – and it is the latter who take the flak when the public see a new roundabout full of rubbish and weeds because curbs and barriers prevented access for cleaning.

We have found that professionals, or people perceiving themselves as professionals, need to understand that many of their processes are just as capable of improvement as any others and that the areas which involve purely professional judgement in isolation are in fact a tiny proportion of the whole. They also need to understand the different kinds of 'expertise' that exist, both among colleagues and partners and, most important of all, the 'experiential expertise' of members of the public (see Chapter 3). If professionals learn to value this kind of expertise, they gain a great deal and can design better schemes or make better decisions because they know and understand what is hoped for or expected by local residents, who may contribute their own good ideas.

A further important point is the perceived trade-off between cost and quality. There is too often an assumption that higher cost (financial input) equals higher quality. With some services this may be the case. For example, it is probably necessary to increase resources in the classroom to improve many educational outcomes. Generally speaking though, this type of 'trade-off' is an erroneous concept. For too many services, cost is incurred in the system through re-work. Improving processes, eliminating error, and getting it 'right first time' can reduce costs, sometimes greatly, and naturally leads to higher quality outcomes. This thinking is not in accordance with the bureaucratic mindset and it is very important that it is understood.

Although in Deming's original concept, the 'customer' could be seen as playing an almost purely passive role, for public services, involvement needs to be much more active. We have found in Tameside that the voice of the customer *must* be heard in the process. Improvement must not just make sense to the providers of services. It is far more important that customers, be they external or internal, identify the nature and methods of improvement and that they value and appreciate the organizational response.

Mechanisms and processes to 'empower' users and non-users to be involved have therefore become increasingly important in Tameside, as noted earlier in this chapter. This is not a tokenistic involvement, but a real one. And this has involved educating the staff about how to encourage participation and how to respond. Again, this feels very different from the traditional bureaucratic way of doing things.

Perhaps the most fundamental learning point from continual improvement is that managers now have to understand that their job is about leading improvement. There is no real need to have managers who see their job in terms of keeping things as they are. Once this is understood, then real cultural change starts to happen.

Is 'continual improvement' sufficient?

The short answer to this question is 'no'. There can be occasions when simply improving existing processes will *not* be sufficient. Organizations must also foster innovation, so that new products and services can be developed and entirely new ways of delivering them identified and put into place.

There needs to be a willingness to respond to needs identified from the citizen perspective, not the organization's, and to develop new, 'cross-cutting' services to meet them. These, of course, must be provided by the most effective means (organizationally and financially).

Furthermore, however much improvement is achieved within certain services, economies of scale can mean that another provider could deliver the service for comparable quality at lower cost. Options such as consortium arrangements between local authorities or partnerships with other local agencies in the public, voluntary or private sectors may start to address this problem. Best Value was certainly intended to encourage just this kind of thinking.

Alternatively, services may require significant investment which is beyond the available resources of a local authority. This would also force an organization that is concerned with service quality to look at alternative arrangements, rather than being locked in producer mode.

In local government terms, an area of work crying out for radical thinking is the care of elderly people. More elderly people are living longer. They have a broader range of (recognized) needs, including not just their physical well-being, but their whole quality of life. These needs are not going to be best met by the limited range of services delivered by a traditional local authority. The 'seamless' joint care assessment referred to earlier will be a first step towards a much more integrated service. And then, within these arrangements, the continual improvement process can be used by all the partners to design and deliver the new services.

Conclusion

Tameside Council realized some time ago that it had to work in new ways if it was to provide better services in a period of rising expectations and demand with fewer resources. It has used an approach that involved long-term organization development, focusing on the needs of the individual, the organization, its staff and the public. A particularly important element of that programme has been the use of practical 'continual improvement', which has delivered significant improvements in many services and has fitted well with the government's 'modernization' agenda.

We are now seeing some very strong advantages from our ten-year programme of change, and from the continual improvement programme in particular. Workgroups which have actively been using continual improvement, found the Best Value process much easier and have come through it with better results. This is perhaps not surprising, but it is rewarding to see external recognition for the work that has gone on within Tameside. In addition, the council has been given 'Beacon' status for 'preventing crime and disorder', 'accessible services', 'maintaining a quality environment' and 'community legal services'. It was in the pilot round of Local Public Service Agreements, covering e-government, housing, schools, older people and road safety. An initial £1 million has thus been levered in from central government, and more will be available if agreed targets are achieved. The organization is now well geared up to do this.

Not all our services are in this position. It has to be hoped that none will learn about the necessity for improvement in a much harder manner: being categorized as 'coasting' or 'failing' by the Audit Commission (see Chapter 7).

The management philosophy of Deming has helped Council managers understand what 'quality' and 'improvement' mean in practice. Working on improving *processes* not only benefits service *outcomes* for the public, but is a strong motivating factor for the whole of the workgroups who are involved.

We cannot be complacent. There is still a long way to go, and we still need to involve staff across the board, professionals, partners, and consumers, citizens and communities who live in Tameside. There can be no end to this process. Expectations will rise, circumstances will change, new challenges and needs will require new responses. But an organization that accepts that it is in the business of improving for ever is more likely to thrive and be successful than one which fears change and is constantly looking to justify the status quo.

Part V

Conclusions

15

Conclusions and reflections

Lucy Gaster and Amanda Squires

Optimism and a systematic approach

This is intended to be an optimistic book. Improving quality may be complicated and difficult – far more so than politicians seem to think – but if it is dissected and thought through carefully, using the model presented in Chapters 3–5, it is comprehensible. And if practitioners think through the methods and timescales that suit them and include appropriate stakeholders, it is also practicable, as Chapters 10–14 show.

The kind of quality discussed here is perhaps not familiar to most people. It is a citizen-centred, holistic and carefully rooted quality, taking as its starting point the actual situation in public service agencies, working singly or, increasingly commonly, together with others.

Some pre-conditions are necessary to ensure that 'the garden will grow', as Pat Scrutton puts it in her chapter on working in partnership with older people (Chapter 11). These include the absolute essentials of *starting* from the citizen, and developing an organizational culture where new ideas can take root and flourish. These pre-conditions do not include throwing extra resources at the problem, developing yet more top-down performance indicators and inspection regimes, or indulging in the restructuring game, which has been such a bane for public services since the 1980s. 'Improvement' and 'reform' are fairly meaningless terms in the mouths of national politicians. What is being advocated here is a systematic and sustained approach to transforming public services so that they are designed and delivered in a way that meets real needs of individuals and of society, in a way that engages the enthusiasm and commitment of the local politicians and staff – front-line staff, professionals and managers – who are responsible and accountable for 'success'.

Investment in this process is necessary, of course. But whether this comes from existing or 'extra' resources, it needs to be carefully targeted and it needs to produce identifiable benefits for producers, consumers and beneficiaries of public services. It is worth noting that while short-term gains are important for the credibility of the process, it is only in the long term – five to ten years – that real and lasting change will be visible. As theorists, 'gurus' and practitioners have emphasized again and again, improving service quality is a long-term strategy, requiring long-term vision and long-term commitment.

This book does not imply that instant solutions are either possible or desirable. It is suggested in Chapter 2 that problem-solving and change management techniques are needed for a considerable period of time in order to develop a sustainable 'quality culture'. Equally vital, as Tessa Harding underlines in Chapter 10, is the process of engaging, involving and empowering the main stakeholders, particularly users, citizens and communities. Other crucial stakeholders include front-line staff and senior professionals and managers, politicians, purchasers, providers and partners: they too need to see why quality is important and not an 'extra', and to be enabled and empowered to play an equal part.

All this requires new skills, new cultures and attitudes, as well as new thinking about the meaning of 'public service' and the meaning of 'quality'. Both 'transformational' and 'transactional' leadership is needed, as Carol Hayden points out in her chapter on the Better Government for Older People partnerships (Chapter 9). Quality needs both vision *and* practical, efficient and inclusive development of dynamic and 'modern' organizations. It needs the full hierarchy of implementation set out in Chapter 4, where the levels of policy, principles, approaches, programmes and initiatives are distinguished. Depending on a series of one-off initiatives or on existing, ready-made systems, is simply not enough. These can be useful, but only if they are set within a wider framework of 'what is the business we are in', and 'what is the kind of quality we are trying to achieve'?

This *combination* of approaches explains the success both of the 'macro' work carried out in Tameside since 1990 (Chapter 14) and the detailed, 'micro' work to develop a new housing allocations system in a West Midlands housing association (Chapter 13). It is also at the heart of the South Lanarkshire Better Government for Older People partnership (Chapter 11), which started from the idea of developing a strategy to tackle the needs and issues given priority by older people. At the same time, the partnership worked at ground level to develop new forms of information and new skills for older people, as a vital way of empowering them to become full partners in the enterprise. Similarly, the practical development of a 'stakeholder' approach to contract specification in the National Health Service described

in Chapter 12 was grounded in values of openness, honesty, mutual information and knowledge, and the importance of responding to real needs and
expectations (which change over time).

Tensions and problems in the public sector

Of course, many tensions affect the delivery of public services. In a general
analysis in Chapter 2, we highlighted some of the broad expectations from
both central government and the public – the need to achieve 'results',
the need to work in 'partnership', and the need to 'consult' users and
communities. Chapters 6, 7 and 8 provided overviews of what has actually
happened in central government, local government and the health service.
This review showed how quickly the policy agendas have been changing
and how difficult it is for public service providers to know what is
expected, what will be rewarded, and what will count as 'failure' and be
punished.

Some of the most pervasive tensions experienced by public service
practitioners – with knock-on effects for the public – are:

- The predominating values: are they mainly rooted in 'public service' or
  in 'business'?
- Performance: get things right for the public or get things right for the
  inspectors?
- Innovation: try out new (risky) things or play safe and fulfil targets?
- Users and citizens: a real shift in attitudes and behaviour, actually changing
  policy and practice (at all levels of government); or tokenistic 'consultation
  and participation' and looking good on bids for funds?
- Top-down or bottom-up: how to combine the need to lead from the
  top (and fulfil external requirements) with the equally pressing need to
  encourage 'bottom-up' engagement and development at the front line?
- Joined up services: put the effort into joint working and partnership, or
  stay in the safe 'boxes' and 'silos' and avoid trouble?

In the face of these and many other pressures, there is a real danger that
practitioners will feel that it is all too difficult and, while saying the right
words about user-led services, fail to make much effort in practice.

This is the pessimistic view, which leads not just to government
exhortation which shows little faith in public services, but to a climate of
reward and punishment, where it is assumed that public servants need
external sticks and carrots in order to make them act at all.

The optimistic view is that, while there *is* now a climate for change –
the direction may be unclear, but 'change' is definitely in the air – it is also
true that many public services, some for many years, have already been
rethinking and redesigning their services. The motivation is old-fashioned
altruism and public service values, which are still pervasive and which lead

public service entrepreneurs to take action *in spite of* the kinds of difficulty outlined above. The reward is to produce services that meet real needs in a way that is understood and valued by members of the public and, if possible, by senior managers, politicians and other agencies. This leads to better job satisfaction, itself a motivator for continuing improvement.

The problem in public services, then, is not so much that nothing is happening, but that it is patchy and over-dependent on enthusiastic individuals. Although this is to some extent inevitable – they are the necessary 'change agents' – the danger of isolated improvements is that they die out when the key person moves on. Also, they can mean that service is excellent in one part of an organization, but it is let down by other parts (or other organizations) which do not have the same quality practices and ethos. This is why we stress the importance of developing a new culture, where it becomes the norm to work across organizational boundaries, to involve users and citizens on the whole process of service design, delivery and review, to accept that 'change with a purpose' is normal – and learning from examples of success within departments, organizations, the public sector as a whole and beyond.

Working together

Even within a small organization, it would be extremely rare for one person to be able to deliver a complete service. Some might argue that, for example, a receptionist or telephonist is offering a complete service. This is not true, though: they, as 'front line' workers, cannot give information or direct the public to the right place unless they have both the necessary information and, more important, the cooperation of people in the 'back line' to deliver the required service. This is a lesson currently being learnt in one-stop shops and call centres, but which is well known to anyone who has worked on the front line in any capacity. If the cooperation or the right information is not there – because for example, professionals think that this will lead to 'amateurs' treading on their territory – the result will be complaints and a lot of flak for these front-line workers. Since they are the people who generally feel the least valued – and are the least well paid – in a public service organization, there is little incentive for them to become involved in new ideas about 'quality'.

We argue that a much more complete, integrated and even 'holistic' approach is needed. This is why Tameside Council's approach is so interesting. Here there is both corporate leadership and corporate understanding of the interdependencies within the organization. We find the 'service chain' is a useful and practical concept, closely related to the Deming 'process mapping' idea widely used in Tameside. As explained in Chapter 4, this enables people inside and outside the organization to understand who is responsible for what, to see where links exist (or should exist) between different processes and different parts of the organization, and it provides a basis for either small but vital improvements or for complete redesign.

The 'service chain' needs to be combined with the 'tight-loose' approach to policy and practice. This means that within clear policy frameworks, authority to act is devolved as far down the line as possible (and out into participative structures where they exist). It means that staff need to have a good deal of discretion – which many professionals would claim they now have or need – but that this discretion needs to be exercised for the benefit of the public, not the staff, as can too easily happen (Lipsky 1980). The 'tightness' of the framework is as vital as the discretionary element: action needs to be taken within the organizational and public values that determine what kind of service is being offered – equality, equity, responsiveness and value for money, for example – as well as within the policies and rules affecting the organization. Conversely, these policies and rules should not be used as an excuse for not acting: if necessary, a 'bottom-up' process must be used to change policies where they are no longer appropriate or useful.

These ideas are even more important when considering the tricky issues of 'partnership' and 'participation'. Both these processes are about moving beyond current organizational boundaries, to respond to problems and to involve stakeholders in new and constructive ways. A great deal of this kind of work already goes on, often in a rather informal and unstructured way. It is the only way practitioners on the ground can get things done. However, they often feel they are working 'against the grain' and that they do not have the support of their organizations. This feels risky, and in the current policy climate, where performance indicators reward targets fulfilled rather than problems prevented, there is a temptation to withdraw and concentrate on 'core business'.

Developing a 'good quality' partnership (however that is defined) is as important as delivering good quality services through that partnership. As both Carol Hayden and Pat Scrutton emphasize in their chapters on the Better Government for Older People programme, the concept of partnership is far more complicated than its simplistic use in public discourse might suggest. Time, energy and the skills of leadership, networking and imaginative thinking are needed to develop and embed the partnership, both as a set of relationships and as an organizational process. Once this is done, the spin-offs seem to be endless, particularly when the partnership is confident that it is doing what is needed, because citizens and users – older people in this case – have been drawn in and are now equal partners in the process.

Equally, though, missing links can mean that partnership working is not always successful: if a vital partner refuses to 'play', for whatever reason, a good deal of skill and patience will be needed to bring them on board in a way that is not threatening and which will bring tangible benefits to themselves and/or their clients (more efficient, better used transport, for example, or more specific queries and complaints about financial services).

As Tessa Harding points out, involving citizens is not particularly easy, but a long-haul process means that older people are now involved at the highest levels of policy making. Getting the policies and quality standards right and relevant at this level – based on dialogue with regional and local groups, of course – will have important effects right down the service line as far as the local user.

Where does 'the professional' come in all this new thinking? Sadly, professionals have too often behaved protectively towards their own professions and negatively towards anyone who questions or challenges their practice. Their 'professional autonomy' can seem too precious, with the result that other practitioners, and certainly the public, have been prevented from knowing enough about what is proposed, and have been given too few opportunities to raise their own concerns or to disagree with the professionals. We would argue that good quality public services desperately need high-quality professionals, as part of the 'fitness for purpose', which underpins 'technical quality' (see Chapter 3). However, in the new world of citizen-led, integrated services, professional territorialism and individualism will have to give way to a more collective approach to service delivery, which is equally rewarding once it has been tried.

Leadership, recognition of 'good practice', performance indicators which reward joint working, and preventative and developmental work – all these would play an important part in bringing professionals on board and helping them to see that working together generally produces better results than working separately or in a hierarchical manner.

A model for quality

Before making any final suggestions about what stakeholders can now do to get going on quality improvement, the main features of the citizen/ stakeholder-led 'model for quality' are summarized (see Figure 3.1, reproduced opposite, and Chapters 3, 4 and 5). The different but connected stages are set out below.

Stakeholder involvement

In public services, it is 'voice', not 'choice' or 'exit' that is the key to the relationship between the public and the services provided to meet their needs (that is, the needs both of individuals and of society as a whole). Citizens and users will not be heard (except as protesters) unless particular efforts are made to ensure that they are, and that they are not only heard, but listened to and actively involved in debate and decision making. There is a strong moral case for involving citizens and consumers: they pay for the services and they have rights to services when they need them. It follows

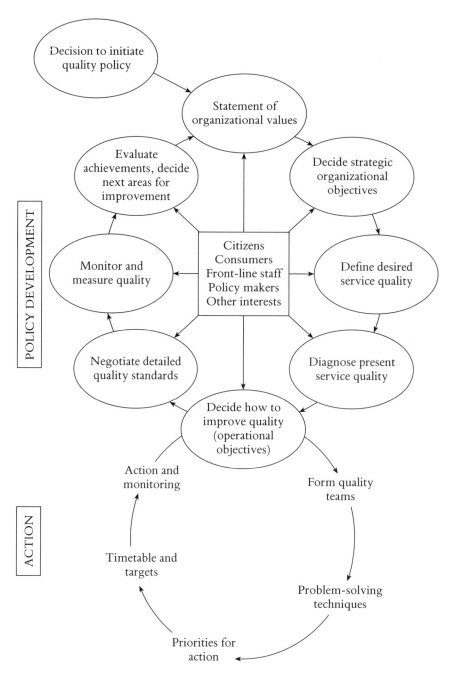

Figure 3.1 A model for service quality.
Source: Gaster 1995a.

that they (we) should also have rights to say what they feel and to make suggestions for how services could be better.

Other stakeholders also have an 'interest' or a stake' in service delivery. Their needs and expectations are diverse and dynamic. Identifying, involving and nurturing all stakeholders right round the whole cycle of quality is important. If this is left too late, the policies and practices developed in the name of 'quality' may be neither credible nor practicable. They could even be undermined, actively or passively, by staff, unions, managers, politicians or partners. So involving stakeholders is not only a moral issue, it is also a highly practical one: the policy will not work without them.

The decision to initiate quality policy

The first step in the cycle is to decide to develop a specific policy to examine and improve the quality of the services for which a public service organization is responsible. As noted above, 'quality' is indisputably on the national and local public sector agenda, but pockets of individual and organizational resistance remain. This resistance may be caused by:

- lack of conviction that quality is a real issue
- lack of clarity about what can be done in the short and long term
- lack of information or lack of a decision about which quality philosophies, systems and tools to use
- absence of a conducive corporate culture for change
- lack of local ownership of the policy: it is imposed from above.

It is at this early stage that leadership and clarity of purpose, backed by a long-term strategy for change, are absolutely essential. Exhortation from outside will not help unless support is also forthcoming. Much more important is the local leadership and involvement of, in local government, politicians as well as senior officers; and in other services, board members and senior professionals as well as managers. If ideas about quality are coming up from the front line and from users and the public, so much the better: but they need to be listened to and acted on if such 'bottom-up' interest is not to fade and become cynical. The key is to capture enthusiasm, commitment and know-how where it exists and to develop it where it does not. Bringing key stakeholders on board at this stage, including very importantly, trades unions and professional associations, is vital for success.

Statement of organizational values

Once the policy has been established, and stakeholders brought on board, agreement on shared values provides an essential starting point. These may differ considerably between stakeholders who are users, providers, from different agencies, from different backgrounds, board appointments and funders. The kind of values that will influence quality include the three 'E's of economy, efficiency and effectiveness together with equity, equality and diversity, democracy and accountability, empowerment and community orientation, variation, and choice, and working together, partnership and cooperation.

Stakeholders, individually or organizationally, may well work to different dominant values. However, mutual understanding is a first step. Adjusting values to achieve consistency across services would be a desirable, though difficult next step. If, for example, health and social services are to work together more successfully than they have done in the past, this stage of mutual understanding and adjustment looks like a necessity.

Decide strategic organizational objectives

From values, strategic objectives can be derived. It is the combination of values and objectives that defines the 'business' that public service organizations are in.

Define desired service quality

No consensus exists on a definition for public sector quality. The 'best fit' seems to be a combination of the four 'dimensions' of quality – technical ('what?'); the non-technical ('how?'); and the environmental ('where'?) and the 'democratic' dimension ('who for and with'?). At a general level, this means that a good quality service needs to:

- do what it is designed to do, meeting the requirements of those for whom it is designed
- be provided in such a way that the relationship between those providing the service and those receiving it makes the experience of the core service better or at least more acceptable
- be provided in surroundings that are efficient and easy to understand (signposting, queuing, seating, etc.) and give the message to the public and to front-line staff that they are valued
- involve consumers and citizens from beginning to end.

Such a service has a good chance of being reliable, providing good and relevant information, timely and acceptably speedy, accessible and helpful. These characteristics, set within the four 'dimensions' listed above, are some of the aspects of public services that have been shown to be highly valued by the public, providing a good starting point for analysing the present state of existing services. It is important to get this right, aiming to meet 'basic' needs, before beginning on some of the more exotic aspects of service improvement – the icing on an insubstantial cake.

Diagnose present service quality

For diagnosis, writers on TQM and continuous improvement stress the use of problem-solving techniques to assess the present state of play and to identify which problems can most profitably and practically be tackled. These techniques have been little used in the public sector but are quite compatible with it. It is not simply a matter of meeting expressed needs, but also of finding out unexpressed needs.

Such diagnosis, by identifying the gap between existing quality and desired quality, will produce information on the aspects of service that need attention. These will probably include issues like bureaucratic structures and procedures, and the problem of barriers between departments and agencies – these are often the weak links in the service chain. The diagnosis could uncover the problem of how to respond to 'demand-led' services within fixed resources, raising questions of (hidden or overt) rationing and eligibility. The diagnostic process should also raise the 'Best Value' question of whether the service is the right one at all, or whether new, different or redesigned services should replace it.

Decide how to improve quality – implementation

An eclectic approach, within an encompassing philosophy, seems the best way forward, probably using multi-stakeholder task groups or 'quality circles'. There are large numbers of 'ready-made' systems and quality tools on the market, and there is a real danger that public service managers could be seduced, as they have been in the past, to think that one or other will provide 'the answer'. So it is particularly important to decide on systems, tools and techniques that are consistent with the overall philosophy *and* can help to put it into practice, within the local context and within manageable and realistic timescales. It is likely that attention will need to be paid to the organizational infrastructure too: the culture, the skills and training that will be needed, the way front-line staff are treated and valued and, above all, the policy and practice of public consultation and participation.

The effects of the contract culture could be particularly evident at this stage. Relationships between clients and contractors, or between commissioners, purchasers and providers, need to be good enough for open discussion about the best way to improve the service. In the climate of 'commercial confidentiality' and competition between potential providers, this trust-based relationship is likely to be particularly difficult to achieve. However, as our chapter on health commissioning shows, it can be done, as long as all the parties (including users and their representatives) are regarded as *equal* participants to the process, which is necessarily separate from the actual process of letting contracts.

Negotiate detailed quality standards

Having undertaken a diagnosis of the problem and agreed the style of approach, the next stage is the setting of challenging but achievable standards. These should be developed and agreed between stakeholders. Standards that cross agencies are both the most important and the most difficult to develop. The results can be presented in terms of both 'ideal' (long-term) and 'achievable' (short-term) standards. They are then available as a written statement available to both staff and the public, both to know the quality of service expected, and as the basis for redress.

If staff are involved in developing standards (along with other stakeholders), there could be a better chance of putting them into practice. If they are imposed from outside or from 'the top', and if they do not reflect the real concerns of users and could only be put into practice by losing other aspects of quality (cutting waiting lists as opposed to giving the most urgent treatment), quality standards are more likely to be perceived as a threat. The likely result is that they will be ignored or even actively resisted and subverted.

The setting and publication of quality standards inevitably raises public expectations (unless, like many of the original Citizen's Charter standards, they are merely set at the achievable minimum). High-quality discussion and debate between stakeholders is therefore essential. This can be used to identify the necessary 'trade-offs' and set timescales for the achievement of aspirational but realistic standards. Otherwise, standard setting may lead to a wave of complaints without acting as a trigger to improve the service.

Monitor and measure quality

Measuring, monitoring and evaluating are, as we say in Chapter 5, complex issues in their own right. Measures need to be relevant and reliable, and the methodology robust enough to stand up to external scrutiny, remembering that those who need to be 'satisfied' are likely to be those most dependent on the service. The results need to give an honest picture of what the public can expect to find when they need services, and they need to measure progress in achieving agreed quality standards. Although 'summative' evaluation is needed in order to be able to see whether objectives have been achieved, and to make comparisons over time and place, we feel that 'formative' evaluation, which is non-judgemental but involves giving feedback and suggesting areas for improvement, is more relevant to the improvement of quality.

Evaluate achievements, decide next areas for improvement

The final stage in the first round of the quality cycle is to evaluate achievements as well as concerns, understand the reasons for such results, feed these back and discuss them with all stakeholders, providing support for staff where necessary.

From the results, further issues will emerge. These will need to be considered alongside other demands, both internal and external, as policies, services and expectations change. Involving all stakeholders in understanding, debating priorities and widely communicating the next series of actions continues to be essential for success. The model then starts over again with reconsideration of organizational values and objectives in the context of the changing policy agenda and (possibly) rising public expectations.

The costs and benefits of quality

One further, but often forgotten, form of evaluation is also needed. Ideas like 'quality is free', or government requirements for the achievement of 'efficiency targets', assume that all this activity is at least cost neutral if not actually producing savings. The conversion of the infrastructure, the processes and the technical changes into real results for citizens needs to be seen in financial terms, just like any other management or policy change (and 'quality' is both of these). Initial savings can be made as services tighten up their processes and eliminate built-in 'failures', but it is difficult to sustain these over the five to ten years needed to embed the new culture. If services are redesigned rather than just tinkered with, it becomes difficult to identify the specific costs and benefits, particularly over long periods of time and particularly when they involve a lot of staff and other time to make them work (which is a particular problem for some partners like small voluntary organizations). This, however, is a weakness of any cost–benefit analysis. The answer is to include qualitative as well as quantitative measures, relying on staff and the public to make their own assessment of the costs and benefits and assigning financial values to these, as is done in other forms of cost–benefit analysis. It is important not to exclude this kind of evaluation on the grounds that it is too difficult, or because early 'results' will almost certainly take the form of new quality processes than tangible outputs and outcomes.

What needs to be done?

In the end, what is needed is a 'quality infrastructure' that can deliver 'quality' services. Five building blocks can be identified to create this infrastructure and its accompanying citizen-oriented culture:

1 Make 'problem-solving approaches' normal at every level, addressing real problems and creating better and more imaginative solutions.
2 Introduce and sustain 'change management' methods and skills to ensure organizational capacity and readiness for change.

3 Develop a clear and honest local strategy for public consultation and participation and ensure organizational capacity to make it work.
4 Engage stakeholders, understand different viewpoints and create clarity of direction and synergy through partnership working. This must be seen as mainstream, not 'add-on', with agreed purposes, processes and levels of involvement.
5 Be oriented to achieving results, but think carefully and consult locally about what the best results would be for local people and communities.

These ideas are not particularly radical, and many organizations are developing them in whole or in part. However, they need to be seen, not as something that will enable managers to 'tick the box', but as a way of enabling the organization to do its job better. This cannot be done in bits and pieces: there are too many knock-on effects when poor services are being delivered somewhere within an organization or partnership and, sadly, not enough knock-on effects when good services are being delivered. Taking into account the complexities of modern services and the complex needs of individuals and communities, a 'whole organization' approach is therefore absolutely essential.

The key to this is to create an organizational culture where quality improvement is embedded in every action, stakeholder involvement is the norm, and the identification of 'service failure' is seen, not as an opportunity to blame someone else, but as a positive stimulus for improvement. For this to be successful in traditional, bureaucratic and publicly denigrated services is probably the biggest challenge these services have *ever* faced. Success can only be achieved by comprehensive and consistent direction and effort, involving a web of stakeholders across linked government departments and local agencies.

If, then, the question, 'What can *I* do to start improving quality?' is asked, the answers might be different for different stakeholders.

- *Politicians* can work on the development of leadership and long-term strategies on the basis of listening to their public and their organizations. They can debate, develop and foster a culture and vision to enable the detailed work to evolve successfully. And they can learn to work co-operatively with others to put their ideas into practice.
- *Senior managers* are also responsible for developing and supporting a new culture and vision of future public services on the basis of listening to the vision of politicians and the views of their staff and public. In particular they need to develop their skills in leadership ('transformational' as well as 'transactional') and in change management. They also need to find out different ways of putting quality into practice, not to proselytize or impose, but to start the debate about the best way forward.
- *Front-line staff* need to be empowered to take decisions, and trained to do their job as well as possible. They need to learn about the public and the communities they serve as well as the vision of their political masters.

They need to learn, through consultation and participation processes and skills, to work on a daily basis with a whole panoply of users, citizens, partners and contractors to develop and achieve acceptable and consistent standards of basic quality and to deliver services that meet needs. They need to feel safe to 'make mistakes' and to know that if they feed their experience into the organization, they will be listened to and respected.

- *Citizens and users* also need to be empowered to take a full part in the cycle of quality, through processes of informed democracy and community development, through accurate, honest and user-friendly information, and through continued dialogue with service providers. They need to learn about public services and the organizations that deliver them. They need to be supported to challenge and ask questions, and not to fear that services will be taken away from them if they do this.

- *All stakeholders* also need to take responsibility for developing the vision and culture, for learning to solve problems, to activate change, to plan and take action, and to learn from each other, continuously and mutually.

All this can be done because it *has* been done. Improving quality is difficult but possible. Much of it is common sense, consistently applied. It is a good idea to work to improve and renew the idea of 'public service' in the public services. This could do wonders for the morale of those who are working in those services. It would also increase the respect they would receive from government, local partners and, above all, from the public who, in the end, vote and pay for them.

Appendix

The language of quality – a glossary of terms

Introduction

This Appendix describes and defines the main current approaches to quality improvement and the quality language (or jargon) that tends to be used. This is not an easy task, since most processes and approaches are defined in different ways, depending on who is championing them and taking them forward. They are all open to local interpretation, and the emphases often change as implementation proceeds. While for one authority (or department), 'TQM' may mean developing a more customer-oriented approach, for another, using exactly the same language, the key element is statistical control and the reduction of variance. The key features picked out here therefore aim to highlight the underlying philosophy and common characteristics, rather than trying to interpret specific words and language.

Most of the systems and techniques were originally developed in the context of private sector manufacturing. Careful consideration of their transferability to the service sector and to democratically based public services is needed. Each technique has its advocates and its opponents. Each has been subject to management fashions. Perceptions and experience of all the models will vary according to the local context. The important thing here is to try to distinguish between the *real* advantages and difficulties attached to each, and those that spring, not from the inherent nature of the technique or approach, but from how and where they are used.

The ideas and approaches are presented in alphabetical order.

Benchmarking

Benchmarking aims to encourage mutual learning. Benchmarking can be used to improve detailed processes, or even parts of processes (reception, making appointments, answering the phone, etc.) by copying 'best practice' from wherever it can be found. It involves a detailed analysis of everything that went to make up the 'good' service, and then transferring it as far as possible into your own setting. It depends on the cooperation of the benchmarked organization to give the necessary information. This is more likely to be forthcoming from non-competitors, so it is important to find the right benchmarking partner. A Global Benchmarking Network exists to do this. Benchmarking was tried in the Welsh National Health Service, follwing these principles (see Bullivant and Naylor 1992). The process of benchmarking goes through five stages: (1) documenting your own process; (2) identifying role models; (3) comparing activities; (4) preparing and implementing an action plan; and (5) following up results.

Advantages: it helps an organization to look outwards and to reinforce organizational learning. It depends on a detailed and systematic analysis of what you are doing and what you are trying to do.

Points to think about: in a competitive world, it could be seen as a 'copy-cat' approach (but is this a bad thing?). It may be difficult to find a suitable partner. It needs to be part of a wider approach to quality improvement, otherwise it could be too piecemeal.

Business Excellence Model of Quality

The nine-part 'Business Excellence' model has been developed by the European Foundation for Quality Management (EFQM, launched 1988) and is often known as the EFQM model. It is closely linked with TQM. It can be used as an evaluation and as a self-evaluation tool and sets the criteria for the UK Quality Award (introduced in 1994 by the British Quality Foundation). Its advocates claim that it is 'a comprehensive and coherent way of showing all the aspects that contribute to an organisation's success' – success being seen in terms of competitiveness and 'excellence'.

The model is based on the components shown in Figure A.1. It identifies four 'results' of a quality policy. The ultimate goal is 'business results' – measured in terms of actual performance, achievement of targets, and comparisons with others (benchmarking). 'Business results' include financial and non-financial results – profits, turnover, market share, ability to introduce new products, numbers of defects, etc. Related but separate are results defined in terms of 'people satisfaction' (i.e. staff), 'customer satisfaction' and 'impact on society'. In order to achieve these results, the model includes five 'enabler' factors: leadership; people management; policy and strategy;

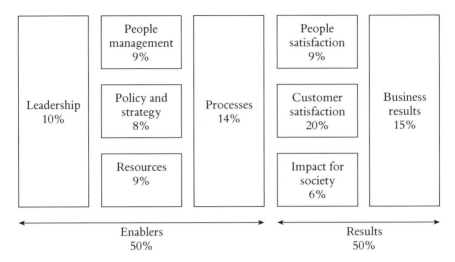

Figure A.1 The European model for TQM.

resources; and processes. All these criteria can be defined according to local circumstances.

Advantages: the model is comprehensive and comprehensible, and is adaptable to an organization's own purposes and functions. It provides a framework for self-assessment, based on 'objective' measurements rather than individual perception and it involves staff.

Points to think about: it could stop at the assessment stage, especially if this is used for award-seeking. It needs to link with action. There are high up-front costs, while benefits of self-assessment may take time to emerge.

Business Process Re-engineering (BPR)

BPR is a concept introduced in 1993. The aim is to bring about radical, rather than incremental or marginal change. It starts from the questions: 'What are we doing?' and 'Why do we do things as we do?' Its main purpose is to reduce costs.

As defined by the original authors Hammer and Champny (1993, quoted in FITLOG 1996) 'Re-engineering is the fundamental re-thinking and radical redesign of business processes to achieve dramatic improvements in critical contemporary measures of performance such as cost, quality, service and speed.' Its main features are: (1) radical change from existing practice – or at least, radical *thinking* about existing practice; (2) the use of a planned process of change, led by a special team; (3) clear objectives and bold targets; (4) tends to be cross-functional – does not work within traditional organizational boundaries; (5) tends to be linked with ICT (Information and Communication Technology).

Advantages: BPR should enable organizations to do imaginative and 'zero-based' thinking about their role, purpose, function and processes, including the services provided and their desired quality. It starts from the future and works back to the present. It encourages lateral and holistic thinking and includes a systematic approach to putting the new ideas into practice – process mapping, service planning, setting 'bold' rather than 'safe' targets. It provides a possible framework for designing new or radically changed services. BPR requires clear definitions of core processes and of what aspects are to be measured and how. It will be supported by staff if they are involved from the beginning, and if they see the process as a way of becoming more competitive or valued by the public, thus keeping services in-house and preserving jobs.

Points to think about: if staff are not involved, BPR, even more than most quality processes, will be seen as a threat to jobs. Continued leadership and practical commitment (including project teams and 'product champions') are vital to success. There is no in-built process for involving the public. The emphasis may be more on reducing costs than on improving quality.

Charter Marks (see under Citizen's Charter)

Charter Marks were introduced in 1992 as an adjunct to the Citizen's Charter programme. All public services, including privatized utilities and Next Steps agencies and, from 2002, services without a direct link to the public (e.g. Defence), are eligible to apply. The award lasts for three years. External assessors evaluate applicants against nine criteria and give feedback to applicants. The original criteria were: (1) standards (setting, publishing and monitoring); (2) information and openness; (3) consultation and choice; (4) courtesy and helpfulness (plain English, community languages, physical access, opening hours, etc.); (5) putting things right (responding to complaints); (6) value for money; (7) user satisfaction; (8) improvement in quality (change in response to identified need); (9) enhancement to services (innovations and improvements) (para 3.34, HMSO 1996) (see also Chapter 6).

Advantages: the award of a Charter Mark gives public recognition to public services. The credibility of this award is enhanced by the fact that it can be taken away.

Points to think about: the process of applying for an award can be experienced as a manager's ego trip, without any clear benefits for staff or the

public, and possibly distorting internal activity and priorities in the meantime. It could be merely documenting existing practice, rather than being
used as a trigger for improvement. It is time-consuming to prepare for and,
hence, expensive in staff time.

Citizen's Charter

The idea of 'Citizens' Charters' was first introduced by *local* government in
the late 1980s. It was picked up later by Central Government. 'The Citizen's
Charter' was a Prime Ministerial initiative in 1991. It was a ten-year programme. The aim was to 'continually improve the quality of public services
for the people of this country and to make them first class' and 'to ensure
that public services respond to the needs and wishes of their users' (John
Major's Foreword, HMSO 1996). By 1996 there were 46 national charters
and an estimated 10,000 local charters.

   The six principles underlying the Charter were: (1) explicit standards
of service; (2) information and openness (publication of performance indicators, league tables); (3) choice (wherever practical) and consultation with
users; (4) courtesy and helpfulness: user rather than staff-oriented services;
(5) putting things right – responding to complaints; (6) value for money –
efficiency and economy through competition. The main addition in 1996
was a new emphasis on 'localization', i.e. the development of local charters, either as an improvement on a national charter, or as a local initiative
(see Chapter 6 for developments since 1997).

Advantages: the philosophy of public accountability, of setting out what the
service intends to do, and providing the basis for redress, are all desirable in
services where people cannot take their 'custom' elsewhere. The public
service values that prompted the early developments in local government
are still relevant.

Points to think about: the Charter needed to be accompanied by implementation plans and processes. It could only include the 'easy', minimum and
most easily measurable aspects of service, which were not necessarily those
that really matter to the public. There was deep public and staff cynicism
about the use of the Charter as part of a purely political and ideological
agenda. It was difficult to separate these elements from the genuine benefits
of developing and writing down service standards.

Conformance to specification

A focus on conformance reflects a concern for consistency and reliability.
Conformance to specification – one definition of quality – means that a
product or service matches the characteristics set out in its 'specification'.

For a manufactured product, such characteristics will include size, colour, materials, etc. It is easy to measure whether the final product has those characteristics and whether and what variation ('variance' in quality language) has occurred during production. Services differ from manufactured products in that they are the product of an interaction *between* the service producer and the consumer. Each interaction is different, less so in some of the more routine services, such as taking the details of a housing repair, more so in more personalized services, such as personal care. For a service, it is far more difficult and problematic to set out detailed specifications by which 'conformance' may be measured. In many cases it is also less desirable, in that the potential to respond to different circumstances, with discretionary decision making at the front line, can be severely constrained.

Advantages: in public services, many services have been delivered on the basis of 'custom and practice' or through definitions learnt during professional training. Codes of practice, etc. tended to focus on process, not on output. Efforts to define outputs or outcomes – a specification to which to 'conform' – helps both staff and consumers clarify the nature of the service. It also provides a potential basis for negotiation, e.g. about service standards, contract specifications and service level agreements.

Points to think about: if the tolerance levels for variation around the specification are too narrow, desirable levels of flexibility and responsiveness will be reduced. Managers obsessed with achieving conformance are unlikely to support experimentation and innovation. The specification itself can easily be drawn up with considerations other than the needs of the public in mind, e.g. to meet managerial agendas, enable performance targets to be fulfilled, to come top in league tables, etc.

Continual improvement

'Continual improvement' derives from the Deming approach to quality. Deming (1986) identified '14 points' essential to quality improvement in manufacturing processes. The aim was to reduce variance and increase profits and market share. Translated into the public service sector, the key features of 'continual improvement' (as practised in Tameside) signals a move away from the inspection approach, and a move to a thought-through process of integrated service improvement. It is based on the underlying Deming framework of a continuing cycle of action: 'Plan, Do, Check, Act'. It uses statistical and mapping techniques to study service processes from the point of view of the public, identifying weak points and looking for underlying and deep-seated causes. This contrasts with traditional 'knee-jerk' reactions when something goes wrong. It encourages a comprehensive approach, crossing traditional service and departmental boundaries in 'service streams'. It is also a tool for encouraging team approaches to service improvement, and an opportunity for rethinking the service design. It has to be implemented in such a way as to encourage innovation, to 'drive out fear' and to develop a sense of ownership among staff. 'Constancy of purpose' is one of the watchwords: it is seen as a long-term programme.

Advantages: analysing and mapping current services from the point of view of the public can stimulate new thinking about what is or is not appropriate. While it focuses on internal processes, it can help identify external factors affecting the service. It is a potentially useful aid to developing a more integrated approach to service production and delivery.

Points to think about: as with BPR (see above), it is essential to provide safeguards for staff who could feel that their jobs are vulnerable if too much new thinking is encouraged. The active involvement of the public is not built in. Service improvement processes need to be linked with service planning. A 'whole organization' approach is probably necessary for the same reason.

Customer care

Customer care programmes are usually focused on the day-to-day dealings by the front-line staff with members of the public with whom they come into contact. They concentrate on the service interaction at the point of delivery, including interpersonal skills, politeness, respect, avoidance of stereotyping and discrimination and other processes symbolizing respect, sensitivity, etc. Some organizations see 'customer care' as extending to internal relationships between departments, teams, levels within the hierarchy, and with external suppliers and contractors. However, such programmes can be highly simplistic, requiring a name-badge, or a 'have a nice day' attitude, which takes little account of the actual needs of the public or of the kinds of service front-line staff are 'fronting'.

Advantages: customer care programmes can symbolize an attempt to develop new relationships with the public. They are a counter-balance to programmes which focus entirely on internal management processes. They can form part of a wider package of quality improvement measures where feedback from the front line is valued and used effectively.

Points to think about: if introduced in isolation, in organizations where traditionally front-line staff have very low status, staff may not see customer care programmes as an opportunity to learn new skills. If they are expected to treat the public better than they are themselves treated, they will be cynical. Possibly more than most quality programmes, customer care can be seen as an implied criticism of past performance, most of which is not under the control of front-line staff. On its own, customer care does not tackle the fundamental organizational back-line problems that have in the past made front-line staff unable to deliver a satisfactory service. It can seem very superficial and tokenistic.

The Deming approach

See under 'Continual improvement' above.

Fitness for purpose

The concept underlying the idea of 'fitness for purpose' is that the service (or product) does what it is supposed to do. There is a clearer notion than in the 'conformance to specification' formula that specifications cannot be drawn up in a vacuum: they need to express in concrete terms what are the underlying values and strategic purposes of the service. In public services, there is more chance of including the public interest if the notion of 'fitness for purpose' is used. Tolerable or desirable variation (e.g. to reflect equalities policies and the need to respond to diversity in the community) can be included within the definition. The underlying principle relates more to reliability and consistency than to standardization and non-conformance.

Advantages: the concept of 'fitness for purpose' should stimulate the questions: why and for whom are we providing this service? What should an appropriate service look like? The process may not only help make explicit what are the current characteristics of a service, but also stimulate analysis about whether it *is* fit for purpose, or whether it needs to be changed. As with service specifications, thinking about this can provide a forum for debate about the service, and the basis for subsequent development of service standards – to what *degree* can we expect the 'purpose' to be fulfilled, over time and in the context of resource constraints?

Points to think about: the main danger is that a narrow or simplistic concept of 'purpose' is taken. For example, a public service may fulfil different purposes for different interests/stakeholders, but the service may be designed with only selected stakeholders in mind (e.g. excluding the views of citizens, minority users or front-line staff).

Investors in People (IIP)

IIP is a UK award developed in 1990 with leading UK businesses. It was initially managed by Training and Enterprise Councils (TECs) and, in Scotland, by Local Enterprise Councils (LECs). The key principles are to set and communicate business objectives, and to develop people (i.e. staff) to meet them. The aim is to ensure that what people can do and are motivated to do matches what the organization needs them to do. The distinctive feature of IIP is its emphasis on staff training and development and on evaluating the effectiveness of that training in relation to the organizational objectives. By 1996, the British Quality Foundation found that 23 per cent of the UK workforce in 20,000 organizations were actively involved in achieving or working towards the IIP standard. External assessors are licensed by the TECs/LECs. The four stage 'Plan/Do/Check/Act' cycle of continuous improvement (Deming) is the foundation for the IIP approach, expressed as 'commitment, planning, action, evaluation'.

Advantages: IIP can be applied to part or the whole of an organization. Recent research (British Quality Foundation 1996: 17) shows improvements in performance (profitability, competitiveness), in the ability to address organizational change, in employee communication and morale, and in improved internal planning processes.

Points to think about: going for the award could displace other, more important agendas relating directly to service improvement. It is a means to an end, not an end in itself. As with all award-based quality programmes, the issue of sustainability after the award has been achieved must be addressed.

ISO 9000

ISO 9000 replaced British Standard (BS) 5750 as the British Standard for quality systems (quality assurance) in July 1994. Its full title is BS EN ISO 9000. It is intended to provide a framework for assessing management systems designed to produce 'conformance to specification' or 'fitness for purpose'. It consists of several parts, applicable to different types of service. These are: ISO 9001 (covering design, production and delivery); ISO 9002 (production and delivery – the most widely used); and ISO 9003 (applicable to services whose quality can only be determined through inspection).

Approximately 44,000 UK organizations had ISO 9000 certificates in 1995. Organizations can seek certification in whole or in part, and will achieve it if they comply with all 20 parts of the standard (as in ISO 9001). These parts spell out all the functions and actions that need to be defined, together with assigned responsibilities within the organization. The system also applies to suppliers of services and goods contributing to the applicant organization's performance.

Advantages: being forced to specify what is to be achieved and the methods of doing this can bring clarity and consistency that were missing before. ISO 9000 is also potentially helpful when competing for contracts, depending on the client's requirements.

Points to think about: the process of going for and sustaining certification can 'take over', at the expense of effort to make real improvements. Consumers are not generally involved. Imposing an ISO 9000 requirement in contract specifications can disadvantage small organizations. Certification is not cheap. Staff could feel that they have lost the opportunity for creativity and the use of professional discretion.

Process mapping, flow charting

Flow charting is one of many problem-solving and analytical tools used to help describe a service and identify areas for improvement or change. Flow charts or process maps are intended to help identify pictorially the stages through which a service goes, the inputs and outputs, and the points of decision, where one decision leads to one set of processes, and another decision leads to a different set.

Advantages: flow charts, etc., help those involved to see where their work contributes to the whole. They identify weak points, duplication, gaps, etc., and explain why the front line never seems to get what it needs from the back line. They can help front-line and reception staff become more knowledgeable and give better quality information about what will happen in particular services.

Points to think about: charting of this kind is only a means to an end, not an end in itself. It is important to avoid charting for the sake of charting. Charting needs to be used regularly in order to become an ingrained method of self-appraisal and analysis.

Quality assurance

The aim of quality assurance is to 'build quality in' through processes aiming to *prevent* faults and *build in* quality. This can be contracted with 'quality control', where faults are 'inspected out' after the event (see below). Its main aim is to achieve consistency of the product by reducing 'variance' in relation to the product specification. Although developed to achieve consistency in manufactured goods, it is a particularly important concept for services, where post-inspection is often impracticable and always too late – the service has already been provided.

Quality assurance can be approached in many different ways and each organization can devise its own methods. It is the underlying philosophy of prevention that differentiates it from other approaches. It is the aspect of quality that is most often subject to external certification, first through BS 5750, now through ISO 9000.

Advantages: QA encourages a close look at processes and should help identify efficient and effective methods of achieving particular objectives. It encourages a systematic approach, requiring all the actions making up a complete service to be spelt out. This should help prevent overlap and duplication and identify areas for improvement.

Points to think about: a long-standing criticism of QA is that you can have a perfect system producing something that nobody wants. However, if QA is clearly linked with other policies to define quality, to involve staff and the public, etc., this danger can be avoided. If QA is too procedure-driven, staff may spend more effort 'doing things right' than 'doing the right things' (Deming). QA may reinforce a 'fear' or 'blame' culture if there is too much emphasis on 'conformance' and too little on change and innovation. Flexibility and responsiveness may be the victims of standardization caused by fear of 'making a mistake'.

Quality circles

Quality circles, invented in the 1960s by Kaoru Ishikawa for the Japanese manufacturing industry, are a special kind of working group, focusing on quality. They represent a shift from an emphasis on *prevention* of non-conformance to an emphasis on ideas for *improvement*. They reflect the idea that it is the workers themselves who may come up with the best ideas, based on their practical knowledge; and that people work more effectively in groups. Quality circles are composed of groups of six to ten people performing much the same work, led by a trained facilitator/supervisor and making formal presentations to management. They are expected to tackle one problem at a time, and are trained in problem-solving techniques, which are at the core of their work.

Advantages: quality circles provide an opportunity for a bottom-up and collective approach to quality improvement and for involving staff at all stages of the process. They help to ingrain the use of problem-solving techniques and embed team approaches as a normal way of working. They can come up with innovative and cost-saving solutions and service improvements.

Points to think about: quality circles need to be introduced in an organizational culture which values the contribution of staff at all levels; they need to be legitimized within the decision-making structure; they need senior management support; and they need an investment of training.

Quality control

Quality control is a process that was developed specifically for manufacturing. Its main component is post-production inspection and where necessary rectification. Like quality assurance, the aim is to produce 'conformance to specification' and the emphasis is on consistency and reliability. As long as the specification is explicit, inspection can be carried out by experts or by lay people. Since quality control is generally carried out through sampling techniques, an underlying assumption may be that a certain proportion of mistakes is acceptable. This is a different philosophy from quality assurance, where the complete prevention of 'mistakes' is the aim. However, if the causes of mistakes/faults discovered through a post-production inspection are analysed and fed back into the production process, the loop can be closed, and organizational learning result. The cost of reworking and of compensation to 'customers' is a powerful incentive to reducing such events as far as possible.

Advantages: quality control is a useful technique for tangible products and routine services. It builds monitoring into the production process. It could reassure a public used to services with high numbers of errors that something is being done. It is organizationally fairly simple to introduce. It could be useful in contract competitions and contains the potential for involving the public in monitoring public services.

Points to think about: QC is not a substitute for other approaches to quality improvement, but a part of them. It is likely to emphasize the importance of standardization at the expense of variation and flexibility. Its actual utility will be closely related to the rewards and punishment systems within the organization using it.

Total Quality Management (TQM)

TQM is generally billed as a complete approach to quality, designed to encourage a holistic, customer-oriented and long-term approach to quality improvement. A common phrase is 'delighting' customers, or 'exceeding customers' expectations'. Like quality assurance, its emphasis is on conformity and non-variance, and the main technique – 'statistical process control' – is explicitly designed to reduce variability. A great deal had been written on TQM, mostly by TQM 'missionaries'. There is no single definition, but it is often described as if there were. It is difficult to find an objective analysis of its strengths and weaknesses based on empirical research in companies and organizations that have put it (however 'it' is defined) into practice. The description here is largely based on the writing of J.S. Oakland (1989), the only British TQM 'guru'. Various requirements are generally listed by writers on TQM. These are: (1) within the organization: leadership, involvement of the workforce, teamwork, staff training; (2) a timescale that allows each stage to be properly developed: awareness, assessment/diagnosis, planning and preparation, implementation, continuous/intensive improvement, review; (3) focus on 'chronic' problems rather than firefighting; (4) use of problem-solving techniques, quality teams; (5) recognition that TQM is a process of organizational change and that it should be managed as such: it is a whole culture that is at stake.

Advantages: TQM is very comprehensive and recognizes many of the complexities of working in large organizations. It provides an opportunity for embedding a service and public-oriented culture over a reasonable period. In addition, it recognizes that quality is not a 'quick fix'.

Points to think about: it is prone to top-down introduction by 'missionaries' as a panacea and does not take into account the different nature of public services. TQM does not appear to involve the public (as users or citizens) or trades unions, even though far-reaching changes affecting roles and working conditions would/should be the result of a TQM policy. In theory, it involves all staff; in practice, staff often feel marginalized because they are not involved early enough.

Bibliography

Note: Websites (URLs) checked in November 2002.

Abel-Smith, B. (1994) How to contain healthcare costs: an international dilemma. Lecture, 15 November, London School of Economics.

Alimo-Metcalfe, B. (1998) '360 degree feedback and leadership development', *International Journal of Selection and Assessment*, 6(1): 35–44.

Allen, I. (1992) 'Older people: their choice and participation', in B. Lively (ed.) *Towards a Social Policy on Ageing: A Consultation Report*. London: The Research for Ageing Trust/Academic Department of Medicine for the Elderly, Chelsea–Westminster Hospital.

Allsop, J. (1984) *Health Policy and the National Health Service*. London: Longman.

Anderson, C.A. and Daigh, R.D. (1991) 'Quality mind-set overcomes barriers to success', *Healthcare Financial Information*, 45(2): 21–32.

Appleby, J., Robinson, R., Ranade, W., Little, V. and Salter, J. (1990) 'The use of markets in the health service: the NHS reforms and managed competition', *Public Money and Management*, Winter: 27–33.

Arnstein, S. (1969) 'A ladder of citizen participation in the USA', *Journal of the American Institute of Planners*, 35(4): 216–24.

Audit Commission (1992) *Citizen's Charter Indicators: Consultation Paper*. London: Audit Commission, Directorate of Management Practice.

Audit Commission (1993) *Putting Quality on the Map: Measuring and Appraising Quality in the Public Service*. London: HMSO.

Audit Commission (1998) *A Fruitful Partnership: Effective Partnership Working*. London: Audit Commission.

Audit Commission (2001) *Changing Gear: Best Value Annual Statement 2001*. London: Audit Commission.

Audit Commission (2001–2) *Best Value website*: http://www.bestvalueinspections.gov.uk

Audit Commission (2002) *Delivering Improvement Together. Audit Commission Strategy 2001–2004*. London: Audit Commission.

Baines, D. (1992) Delighting the customer, in M. Hand and B. Plowman (eds) *Quality Management Handbook*. London: Butterworth-Heinemann.

Barnes, M. (1997) *Care, Community and Citizens*. London: Longman.

Beaumont, D. (1992) 'Consumer relations', *Care of the Elderly*, 4(10): 456–7.

Bendell, T. (1992) *The Quality Gurus: What Can They Do for Your Company*. London: Department of Trade and Industry.

Bendell, T. and Merry, T. (1992) The tools and techniques of total quality management, in M. Hand and B. Plowman (eds) *Quality Management Handbook*. London: Butterworth-Heinemann.

Benington, J. and the Local Government Centre (1998) *Local Strategies and Initiatives for an Ageing Population*. Coventry: Warwick University Local Authorities Research Consortium.

Beresford, P. and Croft, S. (1993) *Citizen Involvement: A Practical Guide for Change*. London: Macmillan.

Beresford, P., Croft, S., Evans, C. and Harding, T. (1997) The developing role of user involvement in the UK in A. Evers, R. Haverinen, K. Leichensring and G. Wistow (eds) *Developing Quality in Personal Social Services*. Aldershot: Ashgate.

BGOP (1999) *Making it Happen. Report of the First Year of the Better Government for Older People Programme 1998–9*. London: Cabinet Office.

BGOP Conference (1999) *It's in our hands*. Report of the Better Government for Older People conference, 'Participation, politics and older people', Ruskin College Oxford, 5–7 July. Internet: http://www.bettergovernmentfor olderpeople.gov.uk

BGOP (2000) *All our Futures: The Reports of the Better Government for Older People Programme*. London: Cabinet Office.

BGOP Scotland (2001) *All our futures*. A report from the Scottish pilots on the implications of the activities, achievements and learning of the Better Government for Older People programme in Scotland, with a response from the Scottish Executive. Published on internet October 2002: http://www.scotland.gov.uk/library3/society/bgop_oo.asp

Bird, J. (1985) *You won't do it*. Report of the Pacific Basin Study Mission. London: DTI.

Blair, T. (2002) *The courage of our convictions: why reform of the public services is the route to social justice*. London: Fabian Society.

Blunden, R. (1998) *Terms of Engagement: Engaging Older People in the Development of Community Services*. London: King's Fund.

Boaz, A., Hayden, C. and Bernard, M. (1999) *Attitudes and Aspirations of Older People*. Research report for Department of Social Security. London: Corporate Document Services.

Boddy, M. (1995) *TECs and Racial Equality: Training, Work Experience and Ethnic Minorities*. Bristol: University of Bristol.

Bouckaert, G. (1990) Productivity measurement: certain diseases and uncertain cures. Paper to Fourth National Public Sector Productivity Conference, Albany, New York (Catholic University of Leuven, Belgium, unpublished).

Bovaird, A.C. (1975) 'Analytical techniques for performance review', *Corporate Planning*, 2(3): 26–39.

British Quality Foundation (1996) *Quality Links*. London: British Quality Foundation.

Brokenshire, P. (1987) *Performance measurement: the case of local government*. Paper presented to research conference of the Institute of Chartered Accountants in Scotland (ICA) and the Chartered Institute of Public Finance and Accountability (CIPFA), December.

Bullivant, J. and Naylor, M. (1992) 'Best of the best', *Health Service Journal*, 27 (August): 24–5.

Burns, D., Hambleton, R. and Hoggett, P. (1994) *The Politics of Decentralisation: Revitalising Local Democracy*. London: Macmillan.

Cabinet Office (1998a) *The Citizen's Charter – A Consultation Exercise: The Government's Response*. London: Cabinet Office.

Cabinet Office (1998b) *Service First: The New Charter Programme*. London: Cabinet Office.

Cabinet Office (1999a) *Modernising Government*. White Paper, Cm 4310. London: Cabinet Office.

Cabinet Office (1999b) *Assessing Excellence. A Guide to Using Self-assessment to Achieve Performance Improvement in the Public Sector*. London: Cabinet Office.

Cabinet Office (1999c) *A Guide to Quality Schemes for the Public Sector*. London: Service First Unit, Cabinet Office.

Cabinet Office (2000a) *Progress Report Against the Executive Summary of the Modernising Government White Paper 1999*.

Cabinet Office (2000b) *Modernising Government News* (November edition), Cabinet Office.

Cabinet Office (2001) *Be the Change: Peer Review Report of the Cabinet Office Role in Modernising Government*. Website publication:http://www.cabinet-office.gov.uk/moderngov/peerreview

Cabinet Office (2002) *An Introduction to the Cabinet Office*. http://www.cabinet-office.gov.uk/organisation/introleaflet.htm (page deleted, November 2002).

Cabinet Office and Department for Environment, Transport and the Regions (2000) *Guide to Quality Schemes and Best Value*. London: DETR and Cabinet Office.

Calman, M. (1987) *Health and Illness: The Lay Perspective*. London: Tavistock.

Carter, N. (1989) 'Performance indicators: "backseat driving" or "hands-off" control?', *Policy and Politics*, 17(2): 131–8.

Carter, N. (1991) 'Learning to measure performance: the use of indicators in organisations', *Public Administration*, 69(Spring): 85–101.

Carter, T. and Beresford, P. (2000) *Age and Change: Models of Involvement for Older People*. York: Joseph Rowntree Foundation.

Centre for the Evaluation of Public Policy and Practice (1992) *Considering Quality: An Analytical Guide to the Literature on Quality Standards in the Public Services*. Uxbridge: Brunel University.

Charities Evaluation Services (1997) *PQASSO: Practical Quality Assurance System for Small Organisations*. London: CES.

Chatham, W. (1998) Clinical effectiveness, what are the choices? Paper presented to the AGILE Conference, Cardiff, 2 April.

Clark, H., Dyer, S. and Horwood, J. (1998) *That Bit of Help: The High Value of Low Level Preventative Services for Older People*. Joseph Rowntree Foundation. Bristol: The Policy Press.

Clarke, J. and Newman, J. (1997) *The Managerial State*. London: Sage.

Clarke, L. (1994) *The Essence of Change*. London: Prentice Hall.

Coch, L. and French, J.P.R. (1952) Overcoming resistance to change, in G. Swanson, T. Newcomb and E. Hartley (eds) *Readings in Social Psychology*. New York: Holt & Co.

Cole, A. (1994) 'A prescription to loosen tongues', *The Guardian*, 22 June: 12.

Commission on Poverty, Participation and Power (2000) *Listen Hear: The Right to be Heard*. Bristol: The Policy Press.

Conner, D.R. and Patterson, R.W. (1982) 'Building commitment to organisational change', *Training and Development Journal*, 36(4): 18–30.

Council of Europe (1985) *European Charter of Local Self-Government*. Strasbourg: European Treaties No. 122.

Craig, A. (1990) *Buying health care for the community: The role of health authorities as purchasers*, Royal Institute of Public Health and Hygiene Symposium, London, 25 July.

Crosby, P.B. (1980) *Quality is Free*. New York: Mentor.

Czepiel, J.A., Solomon, M.R. and Surprenant, C.F. (eds) (1985) *The Service Encounter: Managing Employee/Customer Interaction in Service Businesses*. Lexington, MA: Lexington Books.

Davies, S., Nolan, M., Brown, J. and Wilson, F. (2000) *Dignity on the Ward: Promoting Excellence in Care. Good Practice in Acute Hospital Care of Older People*. London: Help the Aged and Orders of St John Trust.

Davis, H. and Walker, B. (1998) Trust and competition: blue-collar services in local government, in A. Coulson (ed.) *Trust and Contracts*. Bristol: The Policy Press.

Deakin, N. (1994) *The Politics of Welfare: Continuities and Change*. London: Harvester Wheatsheaf.

Deakin, N. and Parry, R. (2000) *The Treasury and Social Policy: The Contest for Control of Welfare Strategy*. Basingstoke: Macmillan Press.

Debrah, Y.A. (1994) 'Evolution and implementation of a quality improvement programme: a case study of two organisations', *Total Quality Management*, 5(3): 11–25.

Deming, W.E. (1986) *Out of the Crisis*. Cambridge, MA: Massachusetts Institute of Technology.

Department of the Environment, Transport and the Regions (DETR) (1998) *Modern Local Government: In Touch with the People*. London: The Stationery Office.

Department of the Environment, Transport and the Regions (DETR) (1999a) *Cross-cutting Issues Affecting Local Government*. London: University of the West of England and the Office of Public Management.

Department of the Environment, Transport and the Regions (DETR) (1999b) *Cross-cutting Issues in Public Policy and Public Service*. Birmingham: University of Birmingham.

Department of the Environment, Transport and the Regions (DETR) (2000a) *Quality and Choice: A Home for All*. Housing Green Paper. London: DETR.

Department of the Environment, Transport and the Regions (DETR) (2000b) *Guide to Quality Schemes and Best Value*. London: DETR and Cabinet Office.

Department of the Environment, Transport and the Regions (DETR) and Ministry of Agriculture, Fisheries and Food (MAFF) (2000) *Our Countryside, Our Future*. Rural White Paper. London: DETR/MAFF.

Department for Transport, Local Government and the Regions (DTLR) (2001a) *Improving Local Services: Final Evaluation of the Best Value Pilot Programme.* London: DTLR.

Department for Transport, Local Government and the Regions (DTLR) (2001b) *Strong Local Leadership – Quality Public Services.* White Paper on local government. London: DTLR.

Department for Transport, Local Government and the Regions (DTLR) (2001c) *Use of Local Performance Indicators in the Best Value Regime: Final Report.* http://www.local-regions.odpm.gov.uk/bestvalue/indicators/regime/summary.htm

Department of Health (1989a) *Working for Patients.* London: HMSO.

Department of Health (1989b) *Caring for People.* London: HMSO.

Department of Health (1991) *The Patient's Charter.* London: HMSO.

Department of Health (1998) *A First Class Service: Quality in the New NHS.* London: HMSO.

Department of Health (1999) *Patient and Public Involvement in the New NHS.* London: Department of Health.

Department of Health (2000) *The NHS Plan.* London: The Stationery Office.

Department of Health (2001a) *The National Service Framework for Older People.* London: The Stationery Office. http://www.doh.gov.uk/nsf/olderpeople.htm

Department of Health (2001b) *Draft Guidance on Governance of Care Trusts.* http://www.doh.gov.uk/caretrusts/governance.htm

Donabedian, A. (1980, 1982, 1985) *Explorations in Quality Assessment and Monitoring: Vol. 1: The Definition of Quality and Approaches to its Assessment; Vol 2: The Criteria and Standards of Quality; Vol 3: The Methods and Findings of Quality Assessment and Monitoring.* Ann Arbor, MI: Health Administration Press.

Donovan, N., Brown, J. and Bellulo, L. (2001) *Satisfaction with Public Services: A Discussion Paper.* Performance and Innovation Unit (published on the internet: http://www.cabinet-office.gov.uk/innovation/papers/satisfaction.html (page no longer available).

Farrell, C., Levenson, R. and Snape, D. (1998) *The Patient's Charter: Past and Future.* London: King's Fund.

Firth-Cozens, J. (1996) 'Looking at effectiveness: ideas from the couch', *Quality in Healthcare*, 5: 55–9.

Foster, A., Ratchford, D. and Taylor, D. (1994) 'Auditing for patients', *Quality in Health Care*, 3(suppl): 16–19.

Foundation for Information Technology in Local Government (FITLOG) (1996) *Starting from the Future.* Bristol: FITLOG.

French, S. (1988) The Delphi technique, *Therapy Weekly*, 20 October: 4.

Gaster, L. (1991a) 'Quality and decentralisation: are they connected?', *Policy and Politics*, 19(4): 257–67.

Gaster, L. (1991b) *Quality at the Front Line.* Bristol: University of Bristol.

Gaster, L. (1992) Quality, devolution and decentralisation, in I. Sanderson (ed.) *Management for Quality in Local Government.* Harlow: Longmans.

Gaster, L. (1995a) *Quality in Public Services: Managers' Choices.* Buckingham: Open University Press.

Gaster, L. (1995b) *Management Skills in Decentralised Environments.* London: Local Government Management Board (now Improvement and Development Agency).

Gaster, L. (1996a) Quality services in local government: a bottom-up approach, *The Journal of Management Development*, 15(2): 78–94.

Gaster, L. (1996b) The citizen question: re-thinking service design, in L. Gaster and S. McIver, *Consumerism and Citizenship: improving the quality of public services*. Birmingham: School of Public Policy, The University of Birmingham.

Gaster, L. (1997) *Quality in Local Government: Next Steps*. London: Local Government Management Board/Improvement and Development Agency.

Gaster, L. (1999a) Participation and local government, in D. Campbell and N.D. Lewis (eds) *Promoting Participation: Law or Politics?* London: Cavendish Publications.

Gaster, L. (1999b) 'Quality management in local government: issues and experience', *Public Policy and Administration*, 14(3): 35–53.

Gaster, L. and Hoggett, P. (1993) Neighbourhood decentralisation and local management, in N. Thomas, N. Deakin and J. Doling (eds) *Learning from innovation: housing and social care in the 1990s*. Birmingham: Birmingham Academic Press.

Gaster, L. and Rutqvist, H. (2000) Changing the 'front line' to meet citizen needs, *Local Government Studies*, 26(2): 53–70.

Gaster, L. and Taylor, M. (1993) *Learning from Consumers and Citizens*. Luton: Local Government Management Board.

Gaster, L., Deakin, N., Riseborough, M., *et al.* (1999) *History, Strategy or Lottery? The Realities of Local Government/Voluntary Sector Relationships*. London: Improvement and Development Agency.

Gladstone, D. and Goldsmith, M. (1995) 'Health care reforms in the UK: working for patients?' in D. Seedhouse (ed.) *Reforming Health Care*. Chichester: Wiley.

Goddard, M., Mannion, R. and Ferguson, B. (1997) *Contracting in the UK NHS: Purpose, Process and Policy. Discussion paper 156*. York: Centre for Health Economics, University of York.

Gregory, S. (1998) *Transforming Local Services: Partnership in Action*. York: Joseph Rowntree Foundation.

Greiner, L.E. (1972) 'Evolution and revolution as organisations grow', *Harvard Business Review*, July/August: 37–46.

Grice, A. (2002) 'Clouds gather over Blair's team of "blue sky" advisers', *Independent*, 10 January: 2.

Hall, J.A., Feldstein, M., Fretwell, M.D., Rowe, J.W. and Epstein, A.M. (1990) 'Older patients health status and satisfaction with medical care in an HMO population', *Medical Care*, 28(3): 261–70.

Ham, C. (1992) *Locality Purchasing*. Birmingham: University of Birmingham.

Handy, C. (1985) *Understanding Organisations*. Harmondsworth: Penguin.

Harding, T. (1997) *A Life Worth Living – The Independence and Inclusion of Older People*. London: Help the Aged.

Harding, T. and Beresford, P. (1996) *The Standards We Expect: What Service Users and Carers want from Social Services Workers*. London: National Institute for Social Work.

Hardy, G. and West, M. (1994) 'Happy talk', *Health Service Journal*, 104(5410): 24–6.

Hart, M. (1996) 'Improving the quality of the NHS out-patient clinics: the application and misapplication of TQM', *International Journal of Health Care Quality*, 9(2): 20–7.

Hartley, J. and Allison, M. (2000) 'The role of leadership in the modernisation and improvement of public services', *Public Money and Management*, 20(2): 35–40.

Hayden, C. and Benington, J. (2000) 'Multi-level networked governance – reflections from the Better Government for Older People Programme', *Public Money and Management*, 20(2): 27–34.

Hayden C., Boaz, A. and Taylor, F. (1999) *Attitudes and Aspirations of Older People: A Qualitative Study.* DSS Research Report No. 102. London: The Stationery Office.

Hayden, C. and Boaz, A. (2000) *Making a Difference: Evaluation Report.* Better Government for Older People. London: Cabinet Office.

Healey, M. (1996) 'Max Weber's comeback, wearing topical hats', *People Management*, 11 (January): 17.

Health Advisory Service (HAS) (1999) *Not Because They are Old: An Independent Inquiry into the Care of Older People on Acute Wards in General Hospitals.* London: Health Advisory Service 2000.

Heller, F. (1986) 'Introduction and overview', in F. Heller (ed.) *The Use and Abuse of Social Science.* London: Sage.

Help the Aged (2002) *The Voice of Older People: An Introduction to Senior Citizens' Forums.* London: Help the Aged.

Henkel, M. (1991) 'The new "evaluative" state', *Public Administration*, 69(Spring): 121–36.

Hennessy, P. (1989) *Whitehall.* London: Martin Secker and Warburg (paperback edition, Fontana).

Henwood, M. (2001) *Future Imperfect? Report of the Care and Support Inquiry.* London: King's Fund.

Henwood, M. and Waddington, E. (1998) *Expecting the Worst: Views on the Future of Long Term Care.* London: Help the Aged.

Herzlinger, R. (1997) *Market Driven Healthcare.* New York: Addison Wesley.

Hirschman, A.O. (1970) *Exit, Voice and Loyalty: Responses to Decline in Firms, Organisations and States.* Cambridge, MA: Harvard University Press.

HMSO (1991) *The Citizen's Charter.* Cm 1599. London: HMSO.

HMSO (1992) *The Citizen's Charter – First Report: 1992.* Cm 2101. London: HMSO.

HMSO (1996) *The Citizen's Charter – Five Years On.* Cm 3370. London: HMSO.

Holman, K. (1999) *New Connections: Joined-up Access to Public Services.* London: Community Development Foundation Publications.

Homa, P. and Bevan, H. (1997) If your hospital did not exist, how would you create it?, in K. Holdaway and H. Kogan (eds) *The Healthcare Management Handbook.* London: Kogan Page.

HOPe (2000) *Our Future Health: Older People's Priorities for Health and Social Care.* London: Help the Aged.

House of Commons (Select Committee on Public Administration) (2001) *Memorandum by the Cabinet Office (NC 1) on the Role of the Deputy Prime Minister Delivering Key Government Priorities*; and *Annex B* (1 November 2001), describing the Prime Minister's Delivery Unit and the Office of Public Sector reform.   http://www.parliament.the-stationery-office.co.uk/pa/cm200102/cmselect/cmpubadm/262/1110101.htm

Hugman, R. (1991) *Power in Caring Professions.* London: Macmillan.

Improvement and Development Agency (IDEA) (2001) *Made to Measure? Best Value and the EFQM Excellence Model.* London: IDEA.

Jackman, R. (1985) Local government finance, in M. Loughlin, M.D. Gelfand and K. Young (eds) *Half a Century of Municipal Decline, 1935–1985*. London: George Allen and Unwin.

James, K. (1989) 'Encounter analysis: front-line conversations and their role in improving customer service', *Local Government Studies*, 15(3): 11–24.

Johnson, T.J. (1977) *Professions and Power*. London: Macmillan.

Jordan, P. (1992) *The Case for Costing Quality*. London: Department of Trade and Enterprise.

Joss, R. and Kogan, M. (1995) *Advancing Quality*. Buckingham: Open University Press.

Kano, N., Seraku, N. and Takahashi, F. (1984) Attractive quality must be equitable, *Quality*, 14(2): 39–44 (in Japanese). (Cited in B. Bergman and B. Klefsjo (1994) *Quality*. New York: McGraw Hill.)

Kennedy, C. (1991) *Guide to the Management Gurus*. London: Century Business.

King, A. (1998) 'Telegraph Gallup', *Daily Telegraph*, 5 June: 14.

Kirkpatrick, I. and Lucio, M.M. (eds) (1995) *The Politics of Quality in the Public Sector*. London: Routledge.

Kirkwood, T. (2001) *The End of Age*. London: Profile Books.

Koch, H. (1991) 'Buying and selling high quality healthcare' in P. Spurgeon (ed.) *The Changing Face of the NHS in the 1990s*. Harlow: Longman.

Lawton, A. (1998) *Ethical Management for the Public Services*. Buckingham: Open University Press.

Levitt, R., Wall, A. and Appleby, J. (1995) *The Reorganised NHS*. London: Chapman & Hall.

Lewin, K. (1952) Group decision and social change, in G.E. Swanson, T.M. Newcomb and E.L. Hartley (eds) *Readings in Social Psychology*. New York: Holt.

Lipsky, M. (1980) *Street-level Bureaucracy: Dilemmas of the Individual in Public Services*. New York: Russell Sage Foundation.

Lisswood, L.A. (1989) 'A new system for rating service quality', *Journal of Business Strategy*, July/August: 42–5.

Local Government Management Board (1993) *Quality Initiatives: 1993 Directory of Local Authority Activity*. London: LGMB.

Local Government Management Board (1996) *Quality Initiatives: Report from the Findings of the 1995 Survey of Local Authority Activity*. London: LGMB.

Locker, D. and Dunt, D. (1978) 'Theoretical and methodological issues in sociological studies of consumer satisfaction with medical care', *Social Science and Medicine*, 12: 283–92.

Lofland, J. and Lofland, L.H. (1984) *Analysing Social Settings*. Belmont, CA: Wadsworth.

Lowndes, V., Stoker, G., Pratchett, L., Leach, S. and Wingfield, M. (1998) *Enhancing Public Participation in Local Government*. London: Department of the Environment, Transport and the Regions.

Maister, D.H. (1985) The psychology of waiting lines, in J.A. Czepiel, M.R. Solomon and C.F. Surprenant (eds) The Service Encounter: Managing Employee/ Customer Interaction in Service Businesses. Lexington, MA: Lexington Books.

Martin, L.L. (1993) *Total Quality Management in Human Service Organisations*. London: Sage.

Martin, L. and Gaster, L. (1993) Community care planning in Wolverhampton: involving the voluntary sector and black and minority ethnic groups, in

R. Smith, L. Gaster, L. Harrison *et al.* (eds) *Working Together for Better Community Care.* Bristol: University of Bristol.

Martin, L., Gaster, L. and Taylor, M. (1995) *Client, Purchaser and Enabler Roles.* Luton: Local Government Management Board.

Martin, S. (1999) Learning to modernise: creating the capacity to improve local services, *Public Policy and Administration*, 14(3): 54–66.

McIver, S. (1991) *Obtaining the Views of Users of Health Services.* London: King's Fund.

McKeown, T. (1986) *The Role of Medicine.* Oxford: Blackwell.

McSweeney, P. (1994) 'Health remedy or sick joke?', *Nursing Standard*, 8(42): 20–1.

Messner, K. (1998) 'Barriers to implementing a quality improvement program', *Nursing Management*, January: 32–5.

Moores, B. (1993) 'Quality management and operational research initiatives in a health service context', *International Journal of Health Care Quality Assurance*, 6(1): 6–13.

Morgan C. and Murgatroyd, S. (1994) *Total Quality Management in the Public Sector: An International Perspective.* Buckingham: Open University Press.

Morgan, J. and Everitt, T. (1990) 'Introducing quality management in the NHS', *International Journal of Health Care Management*, 3(5): 23–36.

Mulcahy, L. and Tritter, J. (1994) 'Hidden depths', *Health Service Journal*, 104(5411): 24–6.

Naumann, E. (1995) *Creating Customer Value.* Ohio: Thomson.

National Consumer Council (1986) *Measuring Up: A Consumer Assessment of Local Authority Services – A Guideline Study.* London: NCC.

National Consumer Council (1991) *Consumer Concerns.* London: NCC.

National Consumer Council and Consumer Congress (1995) *Asking your Users.* London: Cabinet Office.

Neave, H.R. (1990) *The Deming Dimension.* Knoxville, TN: SPC Press.

Newman, K. and Pyne, T. (1995) 'Contracting for quality: a study of purchaser practices', *Journal of the Association for Quality in Healthcare*, 3(1): 16–24.

NHS Executive (1997) *The New NHS: Modern and Dependable.* London: NHS Executive.

NHS Executive (1998) *The New NHS: Modern and Dependable: A National Framework for Assessing Performance.* London: NHS Executive.

Nicholls, V. (1999) *Welcoming Local Voices – The Role of Community Involvement in Health Needs Assessments.* London: GLACHC.

Oakland, J. (1989) *Total Quality Management.* London: Butterworth/Heinemann.

Office of National Statistics (2000) *Population Trends 99 – Spring 2000.* London: Office of National Statistics.

Osborne, D. and Gaebler, T. (1993) *Reinventing Government: How the Entrepreneurial Spirit is Transforming the Public Sector.* New York: Plume.

Ovretveit, J. (1991) 'Costing quality', *Health Services Management*, August: 184–5.

Ovretveit, J. (1992) *Health Service Quality.* London: Blackwell.

Ovretveit, J. (1994) 'Physiotherapy service contracts and "Business Autonomy"', *Physiotherapy Journal*, 80(6): 372–6.

Paddon, M. (1992) 'Quality in an enabling context', in I. Sanderson (ed.) *Management of Quality in Local Government.* Harlow: Longmans.

Page, D. (2000) *Communities in the Balance: The Realities of Social Exclusion.* York: Joseph Rowntree Foundation.

Parasuraman, A., Zeithaml, V.A. and Berry, L.L. (1985) 'A conceptual model of service quality and its implications for future research', *Journal of Marketing*, 49(Fall): 41–50.

Parasuraman, A., Zeithaml, V.A. and Berry, L.L. (1988) 'SERVQUAL: A multiple-item scale for measuring consumer perceptions of service quality', *Journal of Retailing*, 64(1): 12–40.

Patmore, C., Qureshi, H. and Nicholas, E. (1999) 'Tuning in to feedback', *Community Care*, 24–30 June: 28–9.

Performance and Innovation Unit (2000) *Reaching Out: The Role Of Central Government at Regional and Local Level*. London: Cabinet Office.

Peters, T.J. and Waterman, R.H. (1991) *In Search of Excellence: Legends from America's Best Run Companies*. New York: HarperCollins.

Pfeffer, N. and Coote, A. (1991) *Is Quality Good for You? Social Policy Paper No. 5*. London: Institute for Public Policy Research.

Pike, J. and Barnes, R. (1996) *TQM in Action*. London: Chapman & Hall.

Pillinger, J. (2001) *Quality in Social Public Services*. Dublin: European Foundation for the Improvement of Living and Working Conditions.

Pirsig, R.M. (1974) *Zen and the Art of Motorcycle Maintenance: An Enquiry into Values*. London: Vintage.

Platt, D. (2002) Working together in inspection. Paper presented to OFSTED Managers' Conference, January.

Pollitt, C. (1988) 'Bringing consumers into performance measurement: concepts, consequences and constraints', *Policy and Politics*, 16(2): 77–87.

Pratchett, L. and Wingfield, M. (1994) *The Public Service Ethos in Local Government: A Research Report*. London: Commission for Local Democracy, in association with the Institute of Chartered Secretaries and Administrators.

Price, R. and Gaskill, G. (1990) 'TQM in research', *Managing Service Quality*, 1(1): 51–6.

PricewaterhouseCoopers (2000) *Report on the Evaluation of the Public Sector Excellence Programme*. London: PricewaterhouseCoopers.

Prime Minister (2001) *Prime minister's speech on public service reform*, 16 October. http://www.Number-10.gov.uk/news

Prior, D., Stewart, J. and Walsh, K. (1993) *Is the Citizen's Charter a Charter for Citizens?* The Belgrave Papers No. 7. Luton: Local Government Management Board.

Propper, C. and Le Grand, J. (1997) *Central Government and Quasi Markets: The Case of the NHS. Discussion paper 6 LSE Health*. London: London School of Economics and Political Science.

Qureshi, H. and Henwood, M. (2000) *Older People's Definitions of Quality Services*. York: Joseph Rowntree Foundation.

Qureshi, H., Patmore, C., Nicholas, E. and Bamford, C. (1998) *Outcomes of Social Care for Older People and Carers*. Practice guidance series no. 5. York: Social Policy Research Unit.

Ranade, W. (1994) *A Future for the NHS?: Healthcare in the 90's*. London: Longman.

Raynes, N. (1998) Involving residents in quality specification, *Ageing and Society*, 18(1): 65–77.

Raynes, N., Temple, B., Glenister, C. and Coulthard, L. (2001) *Quality at Home for Older People: Involving Service Users in Defining Home Care Specifications*. Bristol: The Policy Press.

Redman, T., Mathews, B., Wilkinson, A. and Snape, E. (1995) 'Quality management in services: is the public sector keeping pace?' *International Journal of Public Sector Management*, 8(7): 21–34.

Reynolds, L. (1994) *Beyond TQM*. London: Sheldon Business Books.

Richardson, A. (1983) *Participation*. London: Routledge and Kegan Paul.

Rivett, G. (1998) *From Cradle to Grave – Fifty Years of the NHS*. London: King's Fund.

Rogers, E. and Shoemaker, F. (1971) *Communication and Innovation*. New York: Free Press.

Salter, B. (1998) *The Politics of Change in the Health Service*. London: Macmillan.

Schein, E. (1987) *Organizational Culture and Leadership*. San Francisco: Jossey-Bass.

Schon, D.A. (1971) *Beyond the Stable State*. London: Temple Smith.

Scottish Executive (2001) *All Our Futures in Scotland: Better Government for Older People report*. Edinburgh: Stationery Office.

Scrivens, E. (1995) 'Measuring up', *Health Service Journal*, 105(5447): 22.

Seedhouse, D. (1994) *Fortress NHS: A Philosophical Review of the NHS*. Chichester: Wiley.

Seneviratne, M. (1999) The case for human and social rights in D. Campbell and N.D. Lewis (eds) *Promoting Participation: Law or Politics?* London: Cavendish Publishing.

Seneviratne, M. and Cracknell, S. (1988) 'Consumer complaints in the public sector', *Public Administration*, 66(2): 181–93.

Service First Unit (2000) *Joined-up Services: Results of Research with the People's Panel*. London: Cabinet Office.

Sheppard, B. (2000) *A Voice for Older Londoners in the Doctor's Surgery*. London: Age Concern.

Shewhart, W.A. (1939) *Statistical Method: From the Viewpoint of Quality Control*. Washington, DC: Lancaster Press.

Skelcher, C. (1992) *Managing for Service Quality*. Harlow: Longman.

Skelcher, C. (1998) *The Appointed State: Quasi-governmental Organisations and Democracy*. Buckingham: Open University Press.

Smith, J. (1992) *Community Development and Tenant Action*. Briefing Paper No. 2. London: Community Development Foundation and National Coalition of Neighbourhoods.

Social Exclusion Unit (1998) *Bringing Britain Together: A National Strategy for Neighbourhood Renewal*. Cm 4045. London: Cabinet Office.

Social Exclusion Unit (2001) *A New Commitment to Neighbourhood Renewal: National Strategy and Action Plan*. London: Cabinet Office.

SOL (2001) *Putting the person first – service users' views on the introduction of codes of conduct and practice for social care workers by the four national care councils*. Shaping Our Lives, National Institute for Social Work Briefing April 2001. London: NISW.

Southon, F.C.G. and McDonald, I.G. (1997) 'Challenges for the quality movement', *Journal of Quality in Clinical Practice*, 17: 137–45.

Speller, S. and Ghobadian, A. (1993) 'Excellence in local government: change for the public sector', *Managing Service Quality*, September: 29–34.

Spray, W. (1992) 'The first estate management board in London', *Local Government Policy Making*, 14(2): 49–53.

Squires, A. (2002) *Stakeholder Quality in Healthcare: Synthesising Expectations for Mutual Satisfaction*. PhD thesis. London: City University (unpublished).

Stebbing, L. and Dixon, N. (1992) 'Meanings of quality in health care', *The Health Summary*, 9(6): 7–10.

Stewart, J. (1996b) Democracy and local government, in P. Hirst and S. Khilnani (eds) *Reinventing Democracy*. Oxford: Blackwells.

Stewart, J. (1998a) 'In support of judgement', *Local Government Studies*, 24(3): 67–79.

Stewart, J. and Walsh, K. (1989) *The Search for Quality*. Luton: Local Government Management Board.

Stewart, M., with Gaster, L. and Smart, G. (1997) *The Local Government Commission: Oversized Cloak or Emperor's Clothes?* York: Joseph Rowntree Foundation/York Publishing Services.

Stoker, G. (1997) Local political participation, in H. Davis (ed.) *New Perspectives in Local Governance*. York: Joseph Rowntree Foundation.

Strong, P. and Robinson, J. (1990) *The NHS Under New Management*. Buckingham: Open University Press.

Sullivan, H. (2001a) 'Modernisation, democratisation and community governance', *Local Government Studies*, 27(3): 1–24.

Sullivan, H. (2001b) 'Maximising the contribution of neighbourhoods – the role of community governance', *Public Policy and Administration*, 16(2): 29–49.

Sullivan, H. and Gaster, L. (2000) *'Professionals' and Decentralisation in Local Government: Challenges and Opportunities*. Occasional Paper 23. Birmingham: University of Birmingham.

Sullivan, H., Root, A., Moran, D. and Smith, M. (2001) *Area Committees and Neighbourhood Management: Increasing Democratic Participation and Social Inclusion*. London: Local Government Information Unit.

Sutherland, K. and Dawson, S. (1998) 'Power and quality improvement in the new NHS: the roles of doctors and managers', *Quality in Health Care*, 7(s): 16–23.

Taylor, M. (2000) *Top Down Meets Bottom Up: Neighbourhood Management*. York: Joseph Rowntree Foundation.

Tester, S., Hubbard, G. and Downs, M. (2001) *Defining Quality of Life Among Frail Older People*, in Newsletter 2, Growing Older Programme. Sheffield: University of Sheffield.

Thornton, P. (2000) *Older People Speaking Out: Developing Opportunities for Influence*. York: Joseph Rowntree Foundation.

Turrill, T. (1986) *Change and Innovation: A Challenge for the NHS*. Management Series 10. London: Institute of Health Services Management.

Vuori, H. and Roger, F. (1989) 'Issues in quality assurance – the European Scene', *Quality Assurance in Health Care*, 1(2/3): 125–35.

Wall, A. (1995) 'Hospital check-ups', *The Guardian*, 22 March.

Walsh, K. (1991a) 'Quality and public services', *Public Administration*, 69(4): 503–14.

Walsh, K. (1991b) *Competitive Tendering for Local Authority Services: Initial Experiences*. London: HMSO.

Walsh, K. and Davis, H. (1993) *Competition and Service: The Impact of the Local Government Act 1988*. London: Department of the Environment.

Walsh, K., Deakin, N., Smith, P., Spurgeon, P. and Thomas, N. (1997) *Contracting for Change: Contracts in Health, Social Care and Other Local Government Services*. Oxford: Oxford University Press.

Watt, P. (1998) 'White-collar services in local government: competition and trust', in A. Coulson (ed.) *Trust and Contracts*. Bristol: The Policy Press.

Wener, R.E. (1985) The environmental quality of service encounters, in J.A. Czepiel, M.R. Solomon and C.F. Surprenant (eds) *The Service Encounter: Managing Employee/Customer Interaction in Service Businesses*. Lexington, MA: Lexington Books.

Wilkes, J. (1993) Introduction: quality improvement in health care, *International Journal of Health Care Quality Assurance*, 6(1): 4–5.

Wilkinson, D. and Applebee, E. (1999) *Implementing Holistic Government: Joined-up Action on the Ground*. Bristol: Policy Press.

Williams, B. (1994) 'Patient satisfaction: A valid concept?' *Social Science and Medicine*, 4: 509–16.

Williamson, C. (1992) *Whose Standards? Consumer and Professional Standards in Health Care*. Buckingham: Open University Press.

Wilson, D. (2002) *Unravelling control freakery: redefining central–local government relations*. Paper presented to ESRC seminar series on local government and local governance, University of Birmingham, 25 February.

Wiltshire and Swindon Users Network (1999) *Annual Report*. Devizes: Wiltshire and Swindon Users' Network.

Womack, J.P., Jones, D.T. and Roos, D. (1990) *The Machine that Changed the World*. New York: Rawson.

Zeithaml, V., Berry, L.L. and Parasuraman, A. (1988) 'Communication and control processes in the delivery of service quality', *Journal of Marketing*, 52(April): 35–48.

Zeithaml, V.A., Parasuraman, A. and Berry, L.L. (1990) *Delivering Quality Service*. New York: The Free Press.

Index

DELIVERING WELFARE
Second Edition

Tony Butcher

Acclaim for the first edition of *Delivering Welfare*:

> . . . well exceeds its brief to provide an authoritative guide and essential work of reference.
>
> *Political Studies*

> The important thing about this book is that it brings together, in a careful and scholarly way, information on the changing delivery system for welfare in Britain.
>
> *Public Administration*

> . . . a very useful introductory text which should win the gratitude of many students.
>
> *Teaching Public Administration*

> . . . a clear and comprehensive description of the new organizational structure of British social welfare, and an even-handed appraisal of its achievements and shortcomings.
>
> *Community Care*

> . . . a useful and timely summary of changing arrangements for the delivery of health, housing, education, social security and the personal social services.
>
> *Health Service Journal*

Since the early 1980s, there has been a series of radical changes in the arrangements for the delivery of the major social services. Under the Thatcher and Major Governments, the traditional role of local authorities as front line delivery agencies of the welfare state was challenged. Privatization, the search for efficiency, and the customer orientation became important features of the system of welfare delivery. The Blair Government has continued many of these initiatives, as well as putting its own stamp on the arrangements for the delivery of welfare.

Delivering Welfare provides an up-to-date and critical survey of the role of central government, local authorities, the NHS and other agencies responsible for delivering the social services, and the directions that welfare delivery has taken since the early 1980s. This new edition has been completely revised and updated to take full account of the impact of the Blair Government. At a time when the issues of welfare delivery and the quality of public services are so high on the political agenda, it provides a timely study of an important subject.

Contents
Preface – Abbreviations – Introduction – Part one: The public face of welfare – Central government and welfare – The government of welfare outside Whitehall – The coordination and planning of welfare – Accountability and the public – Part two: New directions in the delivery of welfare – The rolling back of the local welfare state – The privatization of welfare delivery – The search for efficiency and value for money – The customer orientation – Conclusion: the new governance of welfare – References – Index.

240pp   0 335 21016 3 (Paperback)   0 335 21017 1 (Hardback)

EVALUATING PUBLIC MANAGEMENT REFORMS
Principles and Practice

George Boyne, Catherine Farrell, Jennifer Law, Martin Powell and Richard Walker

Governments across the world are pursuing reform in an effort to improve public services. But have these reforms actually led to improvements in services? *Evaluating Public Management Reforms* develops a framework for a theory-based evaluation of reforms, and then uses this framework to assess the impact of new arrangements for public service delivery in the UK. This book:

- identifies the conceptual and practical problems of finding clear criteria for evaluating reforms
- focuses on the shifts in public management towards markets and competition, towards the publication of performance indicators, and from larger to smaller organizations
- considers what impact these reforms have had on the efficiency, responsiveness and equity of services
- comprehensively reviews the evidence on the effects of reform on health care, housing and education
- discusses the implications for public sector management.

Contents
Introduction – Criteria of evaluation – Methods of evaluation – Health reforms – Housing reforms – Education reforms – Conclusion – References – Index.

192pp   0 335 20246 2 (Paperback)   0 335 20247 0 (Hardback)

DELIVERING EXCELLENCE IN HEALTH AND SOCIAL CARE
Quality, Excellence and Performance Measurement

Max Moullin

. . . this is going to be a very useful book. It provides an authoritative overview of approaches to quality management contextualised to health and social care.

Joe Walsh, Independent Management Consultant, formerly Assistant Director of Social Services at the Royal Borough of Kingston upon Thames

. . . the book will be useful, not only to those who want an academic perspective, but to anyone concerned with improving the service that they provide.

David Fillingham, Director of the NHS Modernisation Agency

Many organizations in health and social care are striving to implement the ideas of organizational excellence, performance measurement and process improvement, in the context of a large number of government initiatives including the NHS Plan, Best Value, Clinical Governance and Quality Protects. This book provides a clear explanation of the whole area and includes a wide variety of case studies and examples within health and social care, including the Voluntary Sector.

The book gives extensive guidance on the use of the Excellence Model, but it does much more than just describe how to use the Model. It provides practical guidance on how to deliver services focused on patients and service users, on how organizations can lead, motivate and involve their staff, on partnerships and user involvement, and the vital area of process improvement. There is also a major section on performance measurement.

Written by a senior lecturer at Sheffield Hallam University, who is also a Director of South Yorkshire Excellence, and a member of Trent Regional Health Authority's Modernisation Board, *Delivering Excellence in Health and Social Care* will be of considerable value to managers at all levels in health and social care.

Contents
Foreword by David Fillingham, Director of the NHS Modernisation Agency – What is quality in health and social care? – Quality management – Quality standards and quality systems – The Excellence Model – Leadership, policy and strategy – People development and involvement – Partnerships and user involvement – Process improvement – Performance measurement – Delivering excellence: A final word – References – Index.

256pp   0 335 20888 6 (Paperback)   0 335 20889 4 (Hardback)